FREE Test Taking Tips DVD Offer

To help us better serve you, we have developed a Test Taking Tips DVD that we would like to give you for FREE. **This DVD covers world-class test taking tips that you can use to be even more successful when you are taking your test.**

All that we ask is that you email us your feedback about your study guide. Please let us know what you thought about it – whether that is good, bad or indifferent.

To get your **FREE Test Taking Tips DVD**, email freedvd@studyguideteam.com with "FREE DVD" in the subject line and the following information in the body of the email:

  a. The title of your study guide.

  b. Your product rating on a scale of 1-5, with 5 being the highest rating.

  c. Your feedback about the study guide. What did you think of it?

  d. Your full name and shipping address to send your free DVD.

If you have any questions or concerns, please don't hesitate to contact us at freedvd@studyguideteam.com.

Thanks again!

PHR Study Guide

PHR Certification Study Guide Prep Team

Table of Contents

Quick Overview

As you draw closer to taking your exam, effective preparation becomes more and more important. Thankfully, you have this study guide to help you get ready. Use this guide to help keep your studying on track and refer to it often.

This study guide contains several key sections that will help you be successful on your exam. The guide contains tips for what you should do the night before and the day of the test. Also included are test-taking tips. Knowing the right information is not always enough. Many well-prepared test takers struggle with exams. These tips will help equip you to accurately read, assess, and answer test questions.

A large part of the guide is devoted to showing you what content to expect on the exam and to helping you better understand that content. Near the end of this guide is a practice test so that you can see how well you have grasped the content. Then, answer explanations are provided so that you can understand why you missed certain questions.

Don't try to cram the night before you take your exam. This is not a wise strategy for a few reasons. First, your retention of the information will be low. Your time would be better used by reviewing information you already know rather than trying to learn a lot of new information. Second, you will likely become stressed as you try to gain a large amount of knowledge in a short amount of time. Third, you will be depriving yourself of sleep. So be sure to go to bed at a reasonable time the night before. Being well-rested helps you focus and remain calm.

Be sure to eat a substantial breakfast the morning of the exam. If you are taking the exam in the afternoon, be sure to have a good lunch as well. Being hungry is distracting and can make it difficult to focus. You have hopefully spent lots of time preparing for the exam. Don't let an empty stomach get in the way of success!

When travelling to the testing center, leave earlier than needed. That way, you have a buffer in case you experience any delays. This will help you remain calm and will keep you from missing your appointment time at the testing center.

Be sure to pace yourself during the exam. Don't try to rush through the exam. There is no need to risk performing poorly on the exam just so you can leave the testing center early. Allow yourself to use all of the allotted time if needed.

Remain positive while taking the exam even if you feel like you are performing poorly. Thinking about the content you should have mastered will not help you perform better on the exam.

Once the exam is complete, take some time to relax. Even if you feel that you need to take the exam again, you will be well served by some down time before you begin studying again. It's often easier to convince yourself to study if you know that it will come with a reward!

Test-Taking Strategies

1. Predicting the Answer

When you feel confident in your preparation for a multiple-choice test, try predicting the answer before reading the answer choices. This is especially useful on questions that test objective factual knowledge or that ask you to fill in a blank. By predicting the answer before reading the available choices, you eliminate the possibility that you will be distracted or led astray by an incorrect answer choice. You will feel more confident in your selection if you read the question, predict the answer, and then find your prediction among the answer choices. After using this strategy, be sure to still read all of the answer choices carefully and completely. If you feel unprepared, you should not attempt to predict the answers. This would be a waste of time and an opportunity for your mind to wander in the wrong direction.

2. Reading the Whole Question

Too often, test takers scan a multiple-choice question, recognize a few familiar words, and immediately jump to the answer choices. Test authors are aware of this common impatience, and they will sometimes prey upon it. For instance, a test author might subtly turn the question into a negative, or he or she might redirect the focus of the question right at the end. The only way to avoid falling into these traps is to read the entirety of the question carefully before reading the answer choices.

3. Looking for Wrong Answers

Long and complicated multiple-choice questions can be intimidating. One way to simplify a difficult multiple-choice question is to eliminate all of the answer choices that are clearly wrong. In most sets of answers, there will be at least one selection that can be dismissed right away. If the test is administered on paper, the test taker could draw a line through it to indicate that it may be ignored; otherwise, the test taker will have to perform this operation mentally or on scratch paper. In either case, once the obviously incorrect answers have been eliminated, the remaining choices may be considered. Sometimes identifying the clearly wrong answers will give the test taker some information about the correct answer. For instance, if one of the remaining answer choices is a direct opposite of one of the eliminated answer choices, it may well be the correct answer. The opposite of obviously wrong is obviously right! Of course, this is not always the case. Some answers are obviously incorrect simply because they are irrelevant to the question being asked. Still, identifying and eliminating some incorrect answer choices is a good way to simplify a multiple-choice question.

4. Don't Overanalyze

Anxious test takers often overanalyze questions. When you are nervous, your brain will often run wild, causing you to make associations and discover clues that don't actually exist. If you feel that this may be a problem for you, do whatever you can to slow down during the test. Try taking a deep breath or counting to ten. As you read and consider the question, restrict yourself to the particular words used by the author. Avoid thought tangents about what the author *really* meant, or what he or she was *trying* to say. The only things that matter on a multiple-choice test are the words that are actually in the question. You must avoid reading too much into a multiple-choice question, or supposing that the writer meant something other than what he or she wrote.

5. No Need for Panic

It is wise to learn as many strategies as possible before taking a multiple-choice test, but it is likely that you will come across a few questions for which you simply don't know the answer. In this situation, avoid panicking. Because most multiple-choice tests include dozens of questions, the relative value of a single wrong answer is small. Moreover, your failure on one question has no effect on your success elsewhere on the test. As much as possible, you should compartmentalize each question on a multiple-choice test. In other words, you should not allow your feelings about one question to affect your success on the others. When you find a question that you either don't understand or don't know how to answer, just take a deep breath and do your best. Read the entire question slowly and carefully. Try rephrasing the question a couple of different ways. Then, read all of the answer choices carefully. After eliminating obviously wrong answers, make a selection and move on to the next question.

6. Confusing Answer Choices

When working on a difficult multiple-choice question, there may be a tendency to focus on the answer choices that are the easiest to understand. Many people, whether consciously or not, gravitate to the answer choices that require the least concentration, knowledge, and memory. This is a mistake. When you come across an answer choice that is confusing, you should give it extra attention. A question might be confusing because you do not know the subject matter to which it refers. If this is the case, don't eliminate the answer before you have affirmatively settled on another. When you come across an answer choice of this type, set it aside as you look at the remaining choices. If you can confidently assert that one of the other choices is correct, you can leave the confusing answer aside. Otherwise, you will need to take a moment to try to better understand the confusing answer choice. Rephrasing is one way to tease out the sense of a confusing answer choice.

7. Your First Instinct

Many people struggle with multiple-choice tests because they overthink the questions. If you have studied sufficiently for the test, you should be prepared to trust your first instinct once you have carefully and completely read the question and all of the answer choices. There is a great deal of research suggesting that the mind can come to the correct conclusion very quickly once it has obtained all of the relevant information. At times, it may seem to you as if your intuition is working faster even than your reasoning mind. This may in fact be true. The knowledge you obtain while studying may be retrieved from your subconscious before you have a chance to work out the associations that support it. Verify your instinct by working out the reasons that it should be trusted.

8. Key Words

Many test takers struggle with multiple-choice questions because they have poor reading comprehension skills. Quickly reading and understanding a multiple-choice question requires a mixture of skill and experience. To help with this, try jotting down a few key words and phrases on a piece of scrap paper. Doing this concentrates the process of reading and forces the mind to weigh the relative importance of the question's parts. In selecting words and phrases to write down, the test taker thinks about the question more deeply and carefully. This is especially true for multiple-choice questions that are preceded by a long prompt.

9. Subtle Negatives

One of the oldest tricks in the multiple-choice test writer's book is to subtly reverse the meaning of a question with a word like *not* or *except*. If you are not paying attention to each word in the question, you can easily be led astray by this trick. For instance, a common question format is, "Which of the following is...?" Obviously, if the question instead is, "Which of the following is not...?," then the answer will be quite different. Even worse, the test makers are aware of the potential for this mistake and will include one answer choice that would be correct if the question were not negated or reversed. A test taker who misses the reversal will find what he or she believes to be a correct answer and will be so confident that he or she will fail to reread the question and discover the original error. The only way to avoid this is to practice a wide variety of multiple-choice questions and to pay close attention to each and every word.

10. Reading Every Answer Choice

It may seem obvious, but you should always read every one of the answer choices! Too many test takers fall into the habit of scanning the question and assuming that they understand the question because they recognize a few key words. From there, they pick the first answer choice that answers the question they believe they have read. Test takers who read all of the answer choices might discover that one of the latter answer choices is actually *more* correct. Moreover, reading all of the answer choices can remind you of facts related to the question that can help you arrive at the correct answer. Sometimes, a misstatement or incorrect detail in one of the latter answer choices will trigger your memory of the subject and will enable you to find the right answer. Failing to read all of the answer choices is like not reading all of the items on a restaurant menu: you might miss out on the perfect choice.

11. Spot the Hedges

One of the keys to success on multiple-choice tests is paying close attention to every word. This is never more true than with words like *almost*, *most*, *some*, and *sometimes*. These words are called "hedges" because they indicate that a statement is not totally true or not true in every place and time. An absolute statement will contain no hedges, but in many subjects, like literature and history, the answers are not always straightforward or absolute. There are always exceptions to the rules in these subjects. For this reason, you should favor those multiple-choice questions that contain hedging language. The presence of qualifying words indicates that the author is taking special care with his or her words, which is certainly important when composing the right answer. After all, there are many ways to be wrong, but there is only one way to be right! For this reason, it is wise to avoid answers that are absolute when taking a multiple-choice test. An absolute answer is one that says things are either all one way or all another. They often include words like *every*, *always*, *best*, and *never*. If you are taking a multiple-choice test in a subject that doesn't lend itself to absolute answers, be on your guard if you see any of these words.

12. Long Answers

In many subject areas, the answers are not simple. As already mentioned, the right answer often requires hedges. Another common feature of the answers to a complex or subjective question are qualifying clauses, which are groups of words that subtly modify the meaning of the sentence. If the question or answer choice describes a rule to which there are exceptions or the subject matter is complicated, ambiguous, or confusing, the correct answer will require many words in order to be expressed clearly and accurately. In essence, you should not be deterred by answer choices that seem excessively long. Oftentimes, the author of the text will not be able to write the correct answer without offering some qualifications and modifications. Your job is to read the answer choices thoroughly and completely and to select the one that most accurately and precisely answers the question.

13. Restating to Understand

Sometimes, a question on a multiple-choice test is difficult not because of what it asks but because of how it is written. If this is the case, restate the question or answer choice in different words. This process serves a couple of important purposes. First, it forces you to concentrate on the core of the question. In order to rephrase the question accurately, you have to understand it well. Rephrasing the question will concentrate your mind on the key words and ideas. Second, it will present the information to your mind in a fresh way. This process may trigger your memory and render some useful scrap of information picked up while studying.

14. True Statements

Sometimes an answer choice will be true in itself, but it does not answer the question. This is one of the main reasons why it is essential to read the question carefully and completely before proceeding to the answer choices. Too often, test takers skip ahead to the answer choices and look for true statements. Having found one of these, they are content to select it without reference to the question above. Obviously, this provides an easy way for test makers to play tricks. The savvy test taker will always read the entire question before turning to the answer choices. Then, having settled on a correct answer choice, he or she will refer to the original question and ensure that the selected answer is relevant. The mistake of choosing a correct-but-irrelevant answer choice is especially common on questions related to specific pieces of objective knowledge, like historical or scientific facts. A prepared test taker will have a wealth of factual knowledge at his or her disposal, and should not be careless in its application.

15. No Patterns

One of the more dangerous ideas that circulates about multiple-choice tests is that the correct answers tend to fall into patterns. These erroneous ideas range from a belief that B and C are the most common right answers, to the idea that an unprepared test-taker should answer "A-B-A-C-A-D-A-B-A." It cannot be emphasized enough that pattern-seeking of this type is exactly the WRONG way to approach a multiple-choice test. To begin with, it is highly unlikely that the test maker will plot the correct answers according to some predetermined pattern. The questions are scrambled and delivered in a random order. Furthermore, even if the test maker was following a pattern in the assignation of correct answers, there is no reason why the test taker would know which pattern he or she was using. Any attempt to discern a pattern in the answer choices is a waste of time and a distraction from the real work of taking the test. A test taker would be much better served by extra preparation before the test than by reliance on a pattern in the answers.

FREE DVD OFFER

Don't forget that doing well on your exam includes both understanding the test content and understanding how to use what you know to do well on the test. We offer a completely FREE Test Taking Tips DVD that covers world class test taking tips that you can use to be even more successful when you are taking your test.

All that we ask is that you email us your feedback about your study guide. To get your **FREE Test Taking Tips DVD**, email freedvd@studyguideteam.com with "FREE DVD" in the subject line and the following information in the body of the email:

- The title of your study guide.
- Your product rating on a scale of 1-5, with 5 being the highest rating.
- Your feedback about the study guide. What did you think of it?
- Your full name and shipping address to send your free DVD.

Introduction to the PHR Certification Exam

Function of the Test

The Professional in Human Resources (PHR) Exam is part of the Human Resources Certification Institute's (HRCI's) certification program for human resources employees and managers. The certification process is intended to provide certified individuals with a credential that shows that they are competent and qualified for employment in the field of human resources. The certification process is only open to individuals who meet a certain minimum level of experience in a professional-level HR position, and is intended for those individuals wishing to build upon their experience to further succeed in the HR field. The test is administered and used nationwide. Exact scores on the PHR exam are not reported for passing students, and thus, the scores have no value other than as part of the certification process.

Test Administration

Candidates wishing to take the PHR will incur an application fee as well as an exam fee. Applications for the exam are open throughout the year, although testing takes place only in certain windows at Prometric testing centers. In order to take the exam, a candidate must meet one of the following combinations of experience and educational requirements:

At least this experience in a professional-level HR position:	At least this educational achievement:
four years	high school diploma
two years	bachelor's degree
one year	master's degree

Candidates may not retake the PHR exam in the same exam period. Instead, they must re-apply for a subsequent period.

HRCI promises to comply with the ADA by making accommodations for test takers who provide documentation of a disability. Documentation should include a description from a licensed or certified professional including the nature of the disability, a description of tests and protocols used in the diagnosis, a description of any accommodations previously provided for the disability, and a description of the specific requested testing accommodations.

Test Format

The test consists of 150 multiple-choice questions and twenty-five pretest questions. Each question has four answer choices and test takers are instructed to pick the best or most correct choice. Questions are written to test knowledge/comprehension, application/problem solving, and synthesis/evaluation. Some questions are presented as hypothetical scenarios that an HR professional might face in the workplace, followed by questions based on those scenarios. Topics covered on the PHR include Business Management and Strategy, Workforce Planning and Employment, Human Resource Development,

Compensation and Benefits, Employee and Labor Relations, and Risk Management. Test takers have three hours to complete the exam.

Scoring

Each PHR exam receives a scaled score between 100 and 700. The passing score is set at 500. Test takers who surpass 500 are told only that they pass, while those who do not pass are told their exact score.

Typically, around 3,000 to 4,000 people take the PHR exam in a given window, and about half pass the exam. In the November 2015 – January 2016 testing window, 3,698 test takers took the PHR exam for the first time. Of these, 54 percent received a passing score. HRCI does not release data on the success rates of students retaking the PHR exam.

Recent/Future Developments

The PHR was most recently updated through a practice analysis study in 2010, and HRCI promises updates every five to seven years, so it is likely that the PHR will be updated in or around 2017. Importantly, the exams are modified and updated for each new testing window to reflect the most current employment laws. PHR exam candidates are strongly encouraged to review and learn the specific HR laws and regulations that were in effect at the time that the exam period in which they are testing began.

Business Management and Strategy

Interpreting and Applying Internal Source Information

In order to understand its performance, evaluate which strategies are effective, and identify where improvement is needed, an organization must regularly analyze internal business information. Data is analyzed using *metrics* (sometimes known as key performance indicators). A metric is simply a method of measuring a particular set of data. Different metrics can be applied to different areas of an organization.

For accounting and finance, metrics are essential for evaluating an organization's financial status.

Cash flow metrics are concerned with analyzing money coming in and going out. One straightforward cash flow metric is net cash flow, which measures the difference between incoming and outgoing cash over a fixed period (e.g. monthly, annually). Net cash flow can provide an immediate answer to the question "Are we gaining or losing money over this period of time?" By reviewing this metric, an organization can determine if any strategic planning changes are necessary, particularly if the organization is losing more money than expected.

Another cash flow metric is *return on investment*, or *ROI*. ROI is generally expressed as a ratio or percentage comparing the gains of a particular investment with its initial investment price. In other words, ROI measures the ratio between an investment's profit and its cost. ROI is particularly useful in helping an organization evaluate the overall value of a given investment. For example, one investment may yield a high return, but perhaps the initial investment is costly as well. Another investment with a much lower yield also has a far lower initial cost—so the cheaper investment might actually have a higher ROI than the high-return investment. This metric can help an organization to devote its financial resources to investments with the highest ROI.

Shareholders might be especially concerned with an organization's *return on equity*, or *ROE*. Like ROI, ROE is also expressed as a ratio or percentage. This ratio can be found by dividing a company's fiscal year net income by the total shareholder equity. The purpose of this metric is to demonstrate how efficiently a company uses investments to generate profit by measuring the company's rate of return on its shareholders' equity. It can give shareholders confidence that their investment is being well-used—or it can tell them to invest their money elsewhere. In order to evaluate its competitiveness, a company can compare its ROE with that of other companies in its field. If the comparison is unfavorable, then it's time to make some strategic planning adjustments.

For marketing and sales, metrics can indicate if a particular marketing strategy is succeeding or if it must be reevaluated. As with financial metrics, there's a wide range of marketing and sales metrics. Let's focus on a few of the most useful categories.

First, many sales and marketing metrics focus on leads. A lead is any person or group who interacts with the organization and might become a customer or client. For example, an online shopping mall might consider anyone who registers an account or joins their mailing list to be a lead. Some helpful metrics consider lead volume (the total number of leads at any given time) or leads generated (the total number of new leads gained during a fixed period, useful for evaluating whether a new marketing strategy is drawing more leads). Sales are like a funnel: the lead volume is wide at the top and then slowly narrows as the sales team nurtures leads into profitable customers. So another leads-related metric includes lead-to-customer percentage (also known as a lead conversion), or the ratio of lead volume to new customers. This allows an organization to gauge the effectiveness of its sales team.

Another important metric is *average transaction value (ATV)*. This metric measures the average amount that one customer spends on one transaction. To return to the example of the online shopping mall, perhaps their ATV is $45—on average, each customer spends $45 when they place an order. This metric allows the online shop to predict its revenue by multiplying the ATV by the anticipated number of customers during a set period. Analyzing this metric also presents different marketing options to increase revenue—the organization can choose to focus on drawing more customers or on increasing the ATV of current customers. Some strategies to increase ATV are to offer rewards programs or special sales to established customers.

Finally, many helpful metrics relate to sales cost. How much money is spent on sales? Is a sales strategy cost-effective? The gross profit margin for a period can be found by subtracting the cost of sales from the total revenue and then dividing that number by the total revenue. This metric shows if a current sales strategy is actually effective and profitable. Another metric is the customer acquisition cost, or the amount spent getting a new customer. Analyzing the ratio between a customer's lifetime value (LTV) and the customer acquisition cost (CAC) can reveal whether current sales strategies are too costly compared to the overall value of a particular customer.

Operations and Business Development

There are also many important metrics related to operations and business development. Three important ones highlighted here are the number of activities, the opportunity success rate, and the innovation rate.

When measuring the *number of activities*, an activity is any task currently undertaken by the organization. This metric can show whether an organization is properly investing its resources in profitable work or if it's overextending its resources into too many tasks. Multi-tasking and diversifying are important in developing a business, but taking on too many activities can hinder an organization's performance.

The *opportunity success rate* overlaps somewhat with the sales and marketing metrics described above. In this sense, an opportunity is a halfway point between a lead and a customer—the lead has been contacted by the sales team but isn't yet a customer. The opportunity success rate measures how many opportunities are closed by sales. This metric can help marketing and sales strategies as well as the overall business development plan. If the opportunity success rate is high, the organization can easily bring in new customers and develop its business. If the opportunity success rate is low, the organization might focus on developing current customers rather than spending resources on new ones.

A third metric to keep in mind is the *innovation rate*. Innovation includes any new or improved products and services. To find the innovation rate, divide the revenue generated by new products and services by the total revenue from all products and services over a given period. This allows the organization to see how much of an impact innovation has on its overall operations, and whether more resources must be devoted to developing innovative ideas that will give the organization an edge over its competition.

Information Technology

Nowadays, organizations rely on information technology to carry out essential business functions. Some conduct the entirety of their business via the internet. These metrics can help organizations get the most out of their IT departments.

One important category analyzes the functionality of an organization's IT resources. That is, how well are IT services working? This can be measured by looking at the number of software bugs over a given period, or the average number of hours required to resolve IT issues. If there's a large volume of IT problems, or if it takes too long to fix critical IT issues, the organization must devote more resources to improving its IT functionality.

IT metrics can also consider online business activities that examine an organization's online sales presence. If a business has a website, one important metric is the number of page views. This measures the organization's reach—how many potential customers is the organization reaching through its online marketing? How many page views lead to actual purchases? How many visitors are registered on the site or subscribed to a newsletter? If the organization isn't satisfied with this number, it's time to try new online marketing strategies. The business can also look at the ratio of online sales to sales from non-internet business (for example, over the phone or in person) in order to determine where it should focus sales and marketing efforts.

Finally, as with any department, organizations must consider the cost of IT. This metric helps the organization see what portion of its financial resources is devoted to IT services, and whether this investment adds value to the organization. For example, an organization may invest on new project management software, but this software increases productivity and helps managers keep project costs low—so the cost of the software is offset by the savings it creates.

Interpreting and Applying External Source Information

We have looked at metrics related to several specific areas within an organization. However, sometimes an organization wants to get a wider view of its field. Next, we're looking at ways that an organization gathers, interprets, and applies outside information in order to analyze the industry at large.

General Business and Economic Environment

An organization can engage in *environmental scanning*, the process of finding and interpreting relevant data to identify opportunities and threats in the field. Three important general business and economic environment metrics are the number of competitors, market share, and customer demographics.

In order to analyze its competition, an organization can look at the number of current competitors—how many similar organizations are currently in the same field?—as well as the number of new competitors—how many competitors have entered the market during a particular period? These numbers give an organization a better idea of the industry environment. If the organization faces more competition than expected, it can focus on finding and developing its competitive advantage. For more on competition analysis, read below about Porter's five forces.

An organization can also get a broad view of its field by analyzing *market share*. An organization's market share can be found by taking the total sales of the organization over a fixed period and dividing it by the total sales of all organizations in that industry. In other words, what percentage of industry sales are being made by this organization? If an organization knows its market share as well as the market share of its competitors, it can easily compare its success in the industry and identify its most powerful competitors.

Finally, *customer demographics* provide essential economic information to an organization. This includes information about customers such as age, education, or income. Some organizations also rely on customer credit information, which can be relayed through a consumer reporting agency (CRA), a third party that collects information related to consumer credit. Knowing more about customers helps an organization find its target customer and market to them effectively. Let's look at one example: average income of customers. This metric lets an organization know the purchasing power of its target market and modifies its sales expectations accordingly. For example, a cosmetic company may have a sales presence in two different areas. The average income of customers in one region is $30,000 and $60,000 in another region. In the high-earning region, the company can market more expensive products that would be difficult to sell in the region with a lower average income.

PEST analysis

This analysis is a macro-environmental analysis that looks at four external factors affecting the organization: Political, Economic, Social, and Technological. Political factors include anything related to government influences in the field like laws, taxes, and trade restrictions. These factors combine to create the organization's legal and regulatory environment and help to define the rules under which the organization must operate. Economic factors include inflation, economic growth, and the exchange rate. The inflation rate can influence the cost of capital, while the exchange rate would have an impact on international operations. Social factors include age distribution and population growth rate, which can be useful in identifying potential markets and targeting customer needs. Technological factors include all aspects of new technology like R&D, automation, and new technological regulations. Technological factors can affect the cost and quality of an organization's products or services.

Industry Practices and Developments

In order to remain competitive with other companies in its industry, an organization must stay up to date on current industry practices and developments. One source of information is publications like magazines, newspapers, and trade journals. Of course, each organization will require different publications that are relevant to its field, but a few big name publications with general business information are *Forbes*, *The Wall Street Journal*, and *Fortune*. These can provide a broad overview of important business news, while trade journals offer more in-depth coverage of important developments in a specific industry.

By researching industry practices, an organization can identify best practices, actions with proven results, effectiveness, and efficiency compared to other industry practices. Best practices are often identified through the process of benchmarking. To benchmark within an industry, an organization finds the top companies in that field, determines their business processes and results, and compares those practices with its own organization: Which practices are producing the best results? How do those practices differ from our organization's current policies? In this way, the organization can benefit from the success of others by adopting best practices from across the field.

Labor Force

The labor force refers to the number of employed and unemployed workers in a given region. The U.S. Bureau of Labor Statistics provides labor force information. In a sense, labor is a business resource and also falls under the rules of supply and demand. By analyzing the current labor force, an organization can get a better picture of the available pool of workers, which is the labor supply. The organization itself provides the demand for labor. Labor supply and demand come together when the organization is in need of new employees and is able to offer competitive wages, working hours, and other job benefits. By analyzing labor force data, HR can determine what level of compensation will attract the necessary workers.

Strategic Planning

Careful planning and goal-setting are essential elements for success in any organization. Strategic planning is an opportunity for an organization to identify the steps and resources needed to get where it wants to go.

First, an organization must start with its objectives. Think back to mission statements and vision statements. The organization should have a clear idea of its day-to-day operations, as well as what it wants to achieve in the future. An organization may have large-scale, primary goals, as well as various secondary goals that must be accomplished in order to reach the primary goals. Having well-defined objectives gives structure and direction to all of the organization's activities. Measurable goals also help the organization to evaluate its strategic plan's progress and effectiveness. (Did this plan help us to reach our goal? If not, what should we change about our strategic plan?)

The next step of strategic planning is analysis. Internal analysis takes a close look at the organization, its strength and weaknesses, assets and liabilities. External environmental analysis takes a wider look at the organization's field or industry in order to identify threats and opportunities. These analyses give strategic planners a better idea of what obstacles they might face when trying to achieve their objectives, as well as what factors are on their side. One type of analysis is a SWOT analysis, which stands for Strengths, Weaknesses, Opportunities, and Threats. Strengths and weaknesses are internal factors. An organization's strength is anything that gives it an advantage over other organizations, while a weakness is anything that puts it at a disadvantage. Examples of strengths include highly skilled personnel, state-of-the art technology, or excellent quality control; weaknesses might be poor management structure or lack of manufacturing capabilities. After identifying internal factors, a SWOT analysis next looks at external factors, such as opportunities and threats. In this sense, an opportunity is anything that an organization can use to its advantage, and a threat is anything that might present an obstacle to its objectives. An example of an external opportunity might be a customer need that isn't currently met by any other organizations. An external threat could be new tariffs or trade regulations.

Next, the strategic plan itself finally begins to form. Keeping in mind the strengths and weaknesses of the organization and potential external threats, strategic planners consider the best steps to maximize their strengths, take advantage of industry opportunities, and reach their established objectives. The strategic plan may go through several forms, growing in complexity and nuance before it's ready to be implemented.

Implementing a strategic plan is an especially important step at mid-size or large organizations, where those making the strategic plan may not be the same people carrying it out. It's important that the strategic plan is clearly communicated to and understood by employees at all levels; even the most well-prepared plan can face failure if it's not properly followed by all members of the organization.

Finally, strategic planning isn't simply a one-time activity, but rather an ongoing, recursive process. The final stage of strategic planning is strategy evaluation. Even after the plan has been implemented, it must be routinely monitored to ensure that it's still the best way to achieve the organization's objectives. If the current plan isn't progressing towards goals as expected, the organization must change the strategic plan. Also, as internal and external factors evolve, so must the strategic plan change to address them. Of course, strategic plans are carefully considered and take time to put into place, but they shouldn't be set in stone. Rather, they should be regularly improving to best serve the organization's mission and vision.

If a strategic plan calls for any changes in employee skills and behaviors, it's up to HR management to facilitate these changes by implementing new training and policies. The strategic plan will be executed by employees, so HR ensures that current employees have the necessary skills to carry out the plan. If necessary, HR also recruits new employees as required if the strategic plan calls for a workforce increase.

Establishing Relationships: Organization and Individuals

In order to best serve its organization, HR must have good relationships with other departments and individuals within the organization. The key to any relationship is communication. HR should maintain open dialogue with other departments and help managers with any employee-related issues. While HR must ensure that departments comply with company policies, it's better to coach and educate managers about following policy rather than complaining about every mistake. When HR is a team player and not just a distant authority figure, it's easier for managers to approach HR and solve problems together.

In this way, HR can also demonstrate its usefulness in aiding organization decisions. Any change in the organization will inevitably affect employees, so HR can help balance the needs of the organization with the needs of workers and advise on decisions that will satisfy everyone. HR also acts as a bridge between executive decisions in the organization and how those decisions will be translated into new policies and procedures.

Establishing Relationships: Outside Organizations

As much as organizations must understand and analyze their internal operations, they must also look outward and engage with the industry as a whole. This is equally true of HR relationships, which should be fostered both within and outside of the organization. By building external relationships, HR professionals can stay abreast of industry developments, develop innovative solutions, and be active (or even proactive) members of their field.

Corporate Social Responsibility (CSR)

Corporate Social Responsibility (CSR) refers to an organization's sense of responsibility for its impact on the environment and community. CSR can be evaluated based on the three Ps of the "triple bottom line": people, planet, and profit. *People* refers to fair employment practices as well as the organization's impact on members of the community; *planet* refers to the organization's environmental impact (such as pollution, consumption of natural resources, etc.); and *profit* refers to the organization's overall contribution to economic growth. Having a CSR program encourages an organization to operate within legal, moral, and ethical boundaries. From an HR perspective, an organization's CSR program can also affect employee recruiting because the program demonstrates the organization's commitment to fair working conditions.

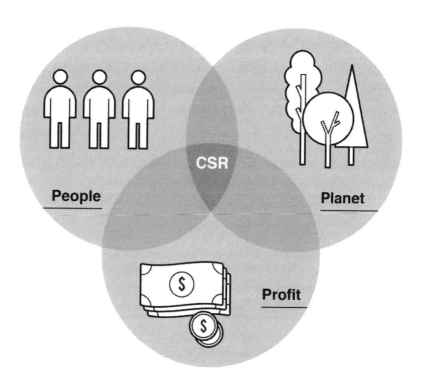

Community Partnership

In addition to financial capital, organizations also rely on *social capital*, the community's relationship with, and attitude toward, the organization. An organization can boost its social capital by engaging community partners from schools to social or volunteer groups to other organizations. These partnerships demonstrate an organization's commitment to the community in which it operates and offer an opportunity for community members to develop a closer relationship with the organization. For example, a computer networking company might partner with the local public school system to offer a free summer camp program for high school students interested in computers.

Managing Organizational Change

In order to remain competitive, adopt industry best practices, and adapt to changing markets, an organization will undergo change at many points. Change might be undertaken to benefit company shareholders and increase the profitability of the company. Change can also occur to reduce costs and increase efficiency. However, especially from an HR perspective, it's important to keep in mind how change affects employees. The truth is that most people don't like change. Also, work force changes in particular (such as outsourcing or downsizing) are certain to be met with employee resistance. Even more minor changes like revised vacation policies may go through an unpopular adjustment period. Change management helps to smooth over these difficulties.

Change Management

Change is inevitable for any organization, especially in fields affected by global markets and technological innovation. Change management seeks to aid organizations through significant transitions in resource allocation, operations, business processes, or any other large-scale changes. Careful change management helps the organization to function effectively even while undergoing a major evolution.

Implementing Change

How should an organization implement change? The classic 1961 text *The Planning of Change* tackles this question. The book outlines three strategies for managing change: the empirical-rational strategy, the normative-reductive strategy, and the power-coercive strategy.

The empirical-rational strategy assumes that people are rational and will naturally follow any course that's in their self-interest. Therefore, they are likelier to accept change when they think it will directly benefit them. To implement change in line with this strategy, an organization must either 1) demonstrate the benefit of the change or 2) demonstrate the harm of the status quo (or both). One way of accomplishing this is to incentivize change. For example, a growing company is gaining new employees, but it doesn't want to expand its available parking. The company decides to limit the number of parking spots and encourage public transportation use. Employees are reluctant to give up the freedom to drive, so the company holds an educational seminar about how to save money by using public transportation and also offers monthly reimbursement for employees who use public transportation.

The next approach proposed in *The Planning of Change* is the normative-reeducative strategy. This strategy assumes that people will closely follow social norms and expectations. In order to implement change, it's necessary to first change people's idea of what is socially acceptable. This is the strategy that harnesses the power of advertising. For example, think of anti-tobacco advertising campaigns over the past few decades. Throughout most of the twentieth century, smoking was socially acceptable just about anywhere. However, especially in the 1990s and 2000s, aggressive anti-smoking advertisements attacked the tobacco industry and started anti-smoking education programs for students. The social norm turned *against* smoking in most public places, and now there are more anti-smoking laws than ever before.

Finally, the power-coercive strategy assumes that people are followers who will listen to authority and do as they are told. This approach to change is basically, "My way or the highway!" Where the empirical-rational strategy seeks to demonstrate how change will benefit employees, the power-coercive strategy says that *not* following change will be *harmful* to employees, who might be punished or even fired for failure to comply. For example, a factory undergoes an intense safety inspection and decides to completely renovate its safety standards. Employees now have new dress code requirements. If they don't follow the dress code, they aren't allowed to work that day; after the third dress code violation, they will be fired.

Deciding which strategy to employ depends on the overall character of the organization (for example, an otherwise friendly and collegial office might respond negatively to usage of the power-coercive strategy) as well as the importance and sensitivity of the change (the power-coercive strategy would be useful for changes with clear legal or financial liabilities, such as when an organization must follow new government regulations).

Reinforcing Value and Expectations

HR is responsible for formulating and enforcing policies about employee behavior. Of course, HR must first educate employees about the organization's expectations. Let's look at some approaches to developing desired behaviors.

Communication

The first step of any business interaction is communication. No matter how carefully an idea is researched and planned, it could all fall apart if it isn't properly communicated to those who must carry it out. For this reason, all HR policies must be clearly communicated to employees, particularly when new policies are enacted or when the same HR issues occur often. Communication can occur in a variety of ways, such as through e-mail, individual interviews, or department meetings.

Modeling

Modeling provides a hands-on approach to teaching new behaviors. Some can learn quickly from reading a book or listening to a presentation. For others, the easiest way to learn is by doing—or by watching other people. Employees can learn new behaviors and skills by watching a manager or trainer perform them first. However, while training situations may involve formal modeling, employees also learn from informal modeling as they observe the behavior of other workers. So it's important to enforce HR policies at all levels of an organization, including upper management. If managers are getting away with unacceptable behaviors like sneaking out of work early or using abusive language in the office, other employees can learn from that modeled undesirable behavior. Both formal and informal modeling should provide positive examples for workers.

Coaching

HR coaching helps employees achieve their potential and continue to develop their skills, matching them with the needs of the organization. Through evaluations and employee self-assessments, HR can nurture strengths while providing training to overcome weaknesses. Coaching can also help employees progress on their career path by identifying areas for advancement within the organization. This gives employees an incentive to stay with the organization and pursue self-improvement goals.

Providing Data to Support Organization's Budget

One essential way that HR participates in its organization's budget is by projecting human capital needs. Particularly when a new strategic plan is implemented, HR must understand how human capital requirements will evolve as a result. HR should be proactive rather than reactive when it comes to human capital needs (that is, anticipate workforce needs *before* they occur). In order to do so, HR professionals must have a clear understanding of the organization's current workforce and its skills and competencies (How many employees do we have? What is their experience level? What tasks are they capable of performing?). Next, they must look at the activities involved in carrying out the strategic plan and determine the activities' workforce requirements (How many employees are needed for this activity? What skills are required to perform this task?). Finally, HR compares the two, identifies any gaps (Do we have enough employees for this task? Do they have the necessary skills?), and works to fill those gaps by providing additional training, reassigning staff, or recruiting new employees.

Of course, training and recruiting cost money, so these human capital projections also aid budgeting for any new plans and projects. In anticipating workforce needs, HR helps managers get a more complete view of a project's budget requirements and avoid any surprise costs later.

Enterprise Risk Management (ERM)

No matter how carefully an organization conducts research, carries out analyses, and develops strategic plans, the organization will always face unknowns. There are risks that activities will fail, outside obstacles will appear, or new threats will emerge. Enterprise risk management (ERM) is a method of managing unknowable risks by anticipating potential risks, focusing on those with the greatest likelihood or potential impact, and planning a response strategy for when risks become realities.

An organization could choose four different responses to a particular risk: reduce the effects of the risk, share it, avoid it, or accept it. In order to reduce the effects of the risk, the organization finds ways to decrease its likelihood or to soften its potential harmful impact. If the organization wants to avoid the risk altogether, it will simply cease all activity associated with that risk. Finally, an organization might decide to go ahead and accept a risk; this might happen when cost-benefit analysis has determined that the benefits greatly outweigh all potential risk to the organization.

Risk management is especially important in human resources, which can account for a significant portion of an organization's financial risk, especially in terms of liability and legal concerns. For example, the organization can be held liable for compliance (or non-compliance) with labor laws, proper management of employee information, and legal concerns of employees like workplace safety and sexual harassment. HR can identify which risks are the most pressing for their organization and plan accordingly, perhaps through an HR audit. Like any audit, an HR audit is an inspection—in this case, of an organization's HR policies and practices. The purpose of an HR audit is to check that policies are in line with all applicable laws and regulations and are properly followed by all employees.

The Organization

Mission, vision, values, and ethics are all concepts that help define different aspects of an organization. Together, they tell why the organization exists, what it plans to accomplish, and what sort of behaviors it will undertake to reach those goals. All of these concepts are closely related to employee behaviors, so HR can be instrumental in their development and implementation. These essential concepts of the organization's identity become actionable employee policies, and HR helps translate those concepts into action.

Mission and Vision
For any organization to be successful, it must have a clear idea of what it's doing and where it's going. Mission statements and vision statements are two ways for an organization to verbalize its objectives. A mission statement focuses on the present work of the organization on a day-to-day basis and might answer the following questions:

- What do we do now?
- Why are we doing it?
- What makes us different from other companies?

A vision statement focuses on the organization's future goals and might answer the following questions:

- What do we want to accomplish?
- Where do we aim to be in the future?

A successful mission statement should be clear and direct and only one or two sentences long. In short, it states *why* the organization exists, and in turn guides its values, standards, and other organizing principles. For example, an organic restaurant might have the following mission statement: "To serve customers healthy meals made from the freshest, locally sourced organic ingredients." With this mission statement, the restaurant could then decide to focus its efforts on building relationships with local farmers or staying up-to-date on health food trends.

A vision statement focuses on specific future goals, and in turn guides the steps that the organization will take to achieve them. The same restaurant might decide on the following vision statement: "To become a top-rated restaurant in the city." The restaurant can then design a plan accordingly, perhaps by focusing on marketing campaigns or inviting influential reviewers to dine at the restaurant.

Values

Just as organizations decide on a mission statement and vision statement, they also must develop a core values statement. This tells what the organization stands for and guides standards of expected employee behavior. For example, a value statement could be: "Our organization is committed to diversity. To this end, we are an equal opportunity employer and serve clients without discriminating based on race, gender, ethnicity, or sexuality." By clarifying its values, the organization communicates its character to both employees and customers.

Ethics

Sound business ethics are essential to establishing an organization's trustworthy reputation. If an organization is ethical, its conduct is fair, moral, and socially acceptable. Of course, some unethical practices are expressly prohibited by law. However, in other cases, the difference between ethical and unethical behaviors must be enforced by the organization itself. If the organization has a strong sense of right and wrong, it will be able to maintain positive relationships with customers and vendors. If the organization has questionable ethical practices, it may face legal charges, loss of business, or harm to its reputation.

HR professionals can help organizations have clear and enforceable ethical standards. Three ways to do so are establishing a values statement, establishing a code of conduct, and conducting HR audits. Similar to a values statement (as explained above), a code of conduct also guides employee behavior, but with greater detail. The code of conduct lays out all policies governing employees' actions, defining acceptable and unacceptable behaviors. HR professionals also must carry out HR audits to ensure that all employees are following organization policies. HR managers can also develop and distribute an Employee Handbook that outlines the company's code of conduct and employee expectations.

Other HR policies to consider with respect to ethics include the process of reporting unethical behavior. How will the organization protect employees who report unethical business practices within the organization? Are employees able to make anonymous or confidential reports about unethical behavior? HR professionals should implement training programs to educate managers and other employees about expected standards of ethical behavior. When it comes to controversial business practices, employees may not be sure what behaviors are acceptable or unacceptable. When an organization's code of conduct changes or when new legal regulations are introduced, it's important to provide appropriate training and education for employees. Finally, HR professionals must have organized review systems in order to evaluate how well the organization is adhering to ethical practices and reporting all business practices appropriately.

<u>Goals and Objectives</u>
While goals and objectives are often used interchangeably, business goals and business objectives differ slightly. A business goal is simply something an organization wants to accomplish, but an objective is a specific, measurable milestone on the way to accomplishing that goal. Just like an organization needs clear mission and vision statements, it also needs goals that are clearly defined. Objectives help to clarify goals, making it easier and more efficient to achieve them. Consider the useful acronym SMART when defining a goal's objectives:

SMART: specific, measurable, achievable, relevant, and time-related

Let's go back to the example of a local organic restaurant. They want to become a top-rated restaurant in the city, so they might come up with a goal like "improve customer satisfaction." This goal is a little vague, so it needs clearly defined objectives that answer important questions. How is customer satisfaction measured? How much must it improve? By when should this goal be accomplished? A specific objective of this goal might be "increase customer feedback card scores by 20 percent over the next year." Because a well-defined objective can be measured and has a deadline, it's easy to track its progress, evaluate its success, and compare it to the organization's past performance. The best goals and objectives are closely related to the organization's overall mission and are achievable according to the resources available.

Legislative and Regulatory Environments and Processes

<u>How Bills Become Laws</u>
Bills become laws only after gaining the approval of Congress and the President through a multi-step process. First, bills begin as ideas from legislators or citizens. If an idea gains support, it's drafted into a bill. A bill must be sponsored by a Representative or Senator and may have co-sponsors from other members of Congress who support it. Once a bill has a sponsor, it's then introduced to the House of Representatives or the Senate. After being introduced, the bill is assigned to an appropriate committee of experts who will research, debate, review, and revise its contents. For example, a bill about the use of chemicals in farming would be assigned to an agricultural committee. After the committee reviews the bill, one of three things can happen.

- They can decide to simply ignore, or *table*, the bill.
- They can assign it to a subcommittee for further research, after which they (the original committee) will consider the bill again.
- They can move forward by reporting the bill to the House or Senate floor.

When the bill is reported to the floor, it's open to debate, discussion, and amendment. After all of the agreed-upon changes have been made, the bill is finally put to a vote and must get a simple majority (more than 50 percent) of approving votes in order to pass. A bill that is passed in the House then moves to the Senate, and a bill that is passed in the Senate then moves to the House. If a bill can gain approval from both the House and Senate, it's finally presented to the President, who has ten days to consider the bill.

The President may choose to:

- Sign the bill into law.

- Refuse to sign, or veto, the bill. However, if Congress strongly believes in passing the bill, they can overrule the President's veto if over two-thirds of Senators and Representatives vote to approve it.

- Do nothing. If the President does nothing for ten days and Congress is in session, the bill automatically becomes a law; however, if the President ignores a bill and Congress isn't in session, the bill cannot become a law. This is known as a "pocket veto."

Influencing Legislation

When businesses want a say in legislation, they can write formal letters to elected officials like Senators, Representatives, and local government officials in order to establish dialogue about new laws. For more in-depth discussion of particular legislative issues, meetings can be scheduled between business representatives and elected officials or authorized members of their staff. Finally, perhaps the most persistent and organized way to influence legislation is through lobbying. Professional lobbyists represent the interests of a particular group or industry (for example, medical association lobbyists may push for anti-tobacco laws). Two businesses in the same field might be in competition and yet could also be united in relying on the same lobbyists to advocate for new laws that serve the best interests of their industry. Lobbying is a highly scrutinized and regulated practice in America, but smart investment in lobbying can also yield high returns for companies.

Management Functions

Generally speaking, there are four basic functions of management: planning, organizing, directing, and controlling. Let's consider all four in greater detail. Before everything, an organization must develop a plan. An organization's plan is its roadmap to success, pinpointing its future goals and recommending the best course of action to reach them. In order to carry out the plan, careful organizing is essential. Organizing involves structuring tasks, locating and acquiring sufficient resources (human resources, financial resources, etc.) to complete tasks, and allocating those resources appropriately. Next is directing, also known as leading or commanding. Directing is people management: giving clear direction, feedback, and motivation to staff so that employees know what is expected of them and can complete their work as effectively as possible. The last function of management is controlling, which is when management evaluates performance by establishing standards, measuring performance based on these standards, and making adjustments as necessary.

Corporate Governance Procedures and Compliance

In business, *governance* refers to how senior executives direct and control an organization. Particularly in large organizations where executives cannot be directly involved in every detail of every department, it's important to have a clear process for communicating the most crucial management information to executives so they can continue to make informed decisions. Governance also includes the processes by which executive decisions are communicated to and implemented throughout all levels of the organization.

Compliance refers to following requirements while carrying out business activities. These requirements could be from industry regulations, corporate policies, contract agreements, or local or federal laws. In order to avoid potential legal problems or fines, organizations should be up-to-date on all relevant laws and regulations and ensure that all departments comply. The Sarbanes-Oxley Act of 2002 (sometimes known as Sarbox or SOX) is an important business law created in reaction to corporate fraud scandals like Enron in 2001. SOX established new regulations for corporate accounting and created the Public Company Accounting Oversight Board (PCAOB). Some of its other major elements include auditor independence (to prevent conflict of interest) and executive responsibility for corporate financial reports (to increase overall corporate responsibility for accurate accounting). Whenever a new law like SOX is created, the organization's policies must be reviewed and, if necessary, revised to ensure compliance.

Governance and compliance are often grouped together with risk management under the term *GRM* (governance, risk management, compliance). By grouping GRM together, an organization can avoid redundancies in procedures and increase the effectiveness of communication between each area.

Mergers and Acquisitions (M&A)

Corporate restructuring that involves mergers and acquisitions require complying with certain laws and regulations and also performing due diligence to evaluate a business contract before making any big decisions. Due diligence is typically performed when a company is buying another company (acquisition) and helps to uncover any potential liabilities or evaluate business and financial risk.

The due diligence process may involve spending time at the business location, reviewing sales numbers, learning about future plans for expansion, and carefully studying documents with vendors such as purchase order and sales agreements. An attorney may be hired to assist with the due diligence process to check for any discrepancies and verify the validity of certain documents and contracts.

In order to cut costs, reduce inefficiencies, or recover financially from a recent downturn, a company may decide to dispose of some or all of its business units by selling the company to another company, closing down permanently, declaring bankruptcy, or relocating overseas (offshoring). This is known as divesting a business. Divestitures can help a company better manage its portfolio of assets by closing some units to focus on others, or by selling off one or more business units to recover from a loss.

Cost-Benefit Analysis (CBA)

A cost-benefit analysis (CBA) is an important factor in many business decisions. A CBA compares the cost of a particular option with the benefits it will bring to the organization. A CBA has two main uses. First, it helps to determine whether a particular option is worthwhile (Do the benefits sufficiently offset the costs?). Secondly, it's a method of comparison when making a decision that has several options.

Of course, any cost-benefit analysis involves a certain level of uncertainty because it's predicting future values under future conditions. For example, a change in the cost of a certain resource or the exchange rate of foreign currency could impact the results of a CBA. For this reason, a CBA usually includes a sensitivity analysis, which determines how much a change in uncertain variables will affect the CBA. This sensitivity analysis takes into account the expected conditions (what will happen if everything proceeds according to the status quo?) as well as worst-case conditions (what will happen if all possible problems arise in this situation?). In this way, a CBA can also reveal the level of risk involved in a decision. An option that appears attractive at first may seem less certain after a sensitivity analysis.

A cost-benefit analysis can also be approached differently depending on the view of the analysis—short-, mid-, or long-term. For many business decisions, the costs are upfront while the benefits may appear immediately or after a longer period of time. For this reason, a short-term and long-term CBA could yield very different results. If an organization needs a quick return on benefits, it might place more emphasis on a short-term CBA. However, if it's willing to wait longer to reap the benefits of a decision, it might compare its options based on long-term CBAs.

Business Concepts

Business professionals must be familiar with a few fundamental business concepts.

Competitive Advantage

A competitive advantage is anything that gives an organization an edge over its competitors. In order to determine its competitive advantage, an organization must have a clear understanding of its direct competitors, its products and services, and its target market. For example, a budget clothing company might be successful based on offering lower prices than other stores. Its competitive advantage is its prices. On the other hand, a luxury designer clothing brand could have the opposite competitive advantage—because its product is high quality and expensive, its name-brand reputation makes it successful with customers in a wealthier target market.

Organizational Branding

An organization communicates a unified message about its identity through organizational branding. Branding weaves together an organization's purpose, values, and strengths to give employees and customers a clear image of the organization's character. Effective branding is an essential part of marketing because it can build an organization's reputation and help it connect with its target market. When customers come to closely associate an organization with its unique character, organizational branding is succeeding.

Business Case Development

A business case is a document that shows the reasoning behind a business change, such as initiating a new project. It makes the case for a change in the business, helping decision-makers inside or outside the organization to justify resources for this activity. In order to develop a business case, it's important to first understand the needs of the organization—how will this new activity benefit its overall goals? How will it fit into the budget and available resources? What makes this activity a better choice than other options? Next, estimate the cost and benefits of the project. These estimates can come from external quotes and bids as well as from internal data from finance and accounting. However, a business case presents more than just financial information. In many cases, costs, benefits, and risks of a new activity include non-financial factors. For example, a non-financial risk might be employee resistance to the business change.

Corporate Responsibility

Corporate responsibility extends beyond an organization's responsibility to adhere to all applicable laws and regulations. It also includes concepts like Corporate Social Responsibility (CSR) and ethics, both explained in greater detail in earlier sections. Corporate responsibility shows that an organization cares about conducting business in a fair and ethical way that adds value to its community and industry.

Business Processes

A business process is a series of activities with the purpose of accomplishing a goal or producing a product or service. An organization depends on many different business processes, and by streamlining them and their interaction with each other, an organization can improve its efficiency.

Operations

Business operations are the core of what an organization actually does on a day-to-day basis to transform its assets into profits. This business process is where the organization's products or services are created and delivered to customers. For example, an online printing service's operations might include taking orders, using their equipment to create high-quality prints, and delivering the finished work to customers.

Sales and Marketing

While operations are responsible for actually creating products or services, sales and marketing help the organization to connect its output with its customers. Even if a company has the highest-quality product on the market, it can't be successful unless it actually reaches customers. Sales and marketing activities include market research, developing leads, and designing and implementing advertisements.

Data Management

We've looked at how organizations evaluate and improve their performance by analyzing data. However, in order for this analysis to occur, an organization needs careful data management. This business process encompasses activities like managing database software, protecting data security, and facilitating data access for employees.

Practice Questions

1. Which best describes corporate social responsibility?
    a. Corporate social responsibility is a policy mandated by the government to coerce corporations to improve their communities.
    b. Corporate social responsibility refers to the responsibility that corporations have toward shareholders.
    c. Corporate social responsibility is an issue of ethics, pursued by corporations that see the health of their business as contingent upon the health of their community.
    d. Corporate social responsibility refers to the social climate of the organization and the policies created to sustain the strength of that climate.

2. CSR can be evaluated on which three P's of the "triple bottom line"?
    a. People, prizes, and proxy
    b. Planet, profit, and projects
    c. People, profit, and prizes
    d. People, planet, and profit

3. What's the purpose of a vision statement?
    a. A vision statement is a memo drafted by management that articulates that if company policy is breached, there will be severe consequences.
    b. A vision statement is a succinct explanation of how an organization plans to deliver quality products/services.
    c. A vision statement is a lengthy and detailed speech given by a CEO to shareholders and other investors.
    d. A vision statement is a short address that low-level employees give to management.

4. In regards to corporate social responsibility, the most common way for a corporation to assimilate into a community includes all of the following EXCEPT?
    a. The most common way for a corporation to pursue social responsibility is to establish alliances with respected members of the community and outside organizations.
    b. The most common way for a corporation to pursue social responsibility is to deliver inexpensive goods and services for the community.
    c. The most common way for a corporation to pursue social responsibility is hiring as many locals as possible.
    d. The most common way for a corporation to pursue social responsibility is by maximizing their profits despite any consequences to the surrounding environment.

5. What's the primary purpose of organizational branding?

I. The intent of organizational branding is letting customers know when they walk into a store.

II. One purpose of organizational branding is to establish a distinctive image for consumers to automatically recognize.

III. Organizational branding allows entities to create a perception of the values and ethics for which it stands.

IV. Organizational branding focuses on promoting the benefits of the company in order to appeal to a target audience.

a. I, II, and IV only
b. I, III, and IV only
c. II and III only
d. I, II and III only

6. What is the main purpose of a cost-benefit analysis?

a. When evaluating a policy or program, a cost-benefit analysis empirically tests its efficacy to ensure that resources aren't squandered.

b. Cost-benefit analyses are rarely conducted because they are expensive and unreliable.

c. When evaluating a policy or program, a cost-benefit analysis is conducted that rationally tests its efficacy to ensure that resources aren't squandered. However, because cost-benefit analyses are antiquated, management typically decides on the policy or program based on its organizational popularity.

d. A cost-benefit analysis is the empirical testing of a policy or program. However, management is typically disdainful of them because of a belief that the testers are inherently biased.

7. What are business metrics?

a. Business metrics are quantifiable measures that describe the productive capacity of a policy, program, or product.

b. Business metrics are informal activities that management occasionally conducts in order to discover the feasibility of a policy, program, or product.

c. Business metrics are typically utilized to weed out underperforming employees.

d. Business metrics are meetings with representatives from each department to voice concerns and establish harmonious, firm-wide standards and practices.

8. All of the following are part of the core meaning of competitive advantage EXCEPT?

a. Competitive advantage is the practice of constantly attempting to increase market share by exploiting advantages.

b. By constantly developing a labor force and technology, competitive advantage is pursued by all corporations in order to edge out competitors in the market.

c. It's mandatory that organizations pursue policies of competitive advantage because they all want to maximize output and increase market share.

d. Competitive advantage is a type of benefit that customers believe they could not get anywhere else.

9. Which of the following statements LEAST describes corporate governance?

    a. Corporate governance is the established policies, rules, and standards that organizations follow in order to fulfill its vision and goal as a for-profit entity and a stakeholder in the broader community.

    b. Public policy influences corporate governance, i.e. the Sarbanes-Oxley Act.

    c. Corporate governance addresses rules, practices and institutions that protects and manages ecosystems in relation to the environment.

    d. Corporate governance is necessary to establish an organization's self-image and can be used to as an instrument to restore institutional trust.

10. Which of the following is true about corporate restructuring?

    a. Corporate restructuring is intended to make a firm more competitive.

    b. Corporate restructuring is a change in operations, legal code, or ownership inside of a firm.

    c. Corporate restructuring is only a euphemism for cutting labor and lowering wages.

    d. The principal purpose of corporate restructuring is to increase profits for senior executives.

11. Which of the following best describes enterprise risk management (ERM)?

    a. Enterprise risk management is when each department crafts its own policies and procedures for handling issues of risk and loss.

    b. Enterprise risk management policies are crafted only by senior executives and then handed down to all departments to follow.

    c. Enterprise risk management is the process of establishing a broad but comprehensive protocol for handling issues of risk and loss.

    d. Enterprise risk management is when a company participates in a high-risk situation in order to maximize profits for the good of the company.

12. All of the following is true about offshoring EXCEPT?

    a. Offshoring is typically done to reduce the costs of business.

    b. Offshoring involves shifting business operations to a country where business can be conducted at lower costs.

    c. The only beneficiary of offshoring is the company itself.

    d. Offshoring is one aspect of corporate restructuring that permits a company to remain competitive.

13. All of the following is necessary for an organization to pay attention to the legislative and regulatory environment EXCEPT?

    a. To anticipate changes and craft corporate governance policies that address new regulations and legislation.

    b. To engage in lobbying efforts in order to fight proposed changes that could be damaging to the corporation.

    c. To modify and make new legislative and regulatory changes more palatable.

    d. To examine competitors and match their own legislation to that of other corporations.

14. Which definition most accurately explains a whistle-blower?

    a. A whistle-blower is a person who reports any unethical information about an organization.

    b. A whistle-blower is a person hired by an organization to cover up illicit or unethical activity.

    c. A whistle-blower is a person who reports or publicizes any illegal or unethical information about the institution. Whistle-blower status is only granted when the organization is private.

    d. A whistle-blower reports or publicizes any illegal or unethical information about the institution. Whistle-blower status is only granted when the organization is public.

15. Which of the following is NOT a key component of a business plan?
    a. Annual goals
    b. Projected growth targets
    c. Net income expectations
    d. Bonuses for executives

16. A stakeholder is any actor that affects or can be affected by a business but doesn't own property of the business. Which of following groups of people are NOT stakeholders?
    a. Employees
    b. Surrounding businesses
    c. Shareholders
    d. The local community

17. Which of the following best describes mergers and acquisitions (M&A)?
    a. Mergers occur temporarily in order to consolidate resources and beat out a competitor; acquisitions occur permanently.
    b. Mergers occur when one company purchases another without a new company being formed. Acquisitions occur when two companies combine to form a new one.
    c. Mergers occur when two companies combine to form a new one. Acquisitions occur when one company purchases another without a new company being formed.
    d. Mergers and acquisitions often occur temporarily in order to consolidate resources and beat out a competitor; then the actions are rescinded and the entities disband.

Answer Explanations

1. C: Corporate social responsibility is an ethical standard pursued by corporations that see the health of their business as contingent upon the health of their community. This ethical issue emphasizes becoming a part of the community and its social fabric. Corporate social responsibility can engender controversy by suggesting that a business has an obligation greater than merely supplying goods and services at a low cost.

2. D: CSR can be evaluated by people, planet, and profit. *People* refers to the organization's treatment of their employees as well as members of the community. *Planet* refers to the impact the organization has on the environment. *Profit* refers to the organization's overall contribution to economic growth. Choices A, B, and C are all incorrect.

3. B: A vision statement is a concise statement that reflects organizational confidence and long-term aspirations about how the firm will achieve more than just economic success. Some questions that may be answered in a vision statement include: How does this firm fit into the marketplace? How would it positively change the world? Institutionally, how does the company plan to deliver their product or service cheaper and more efficiently than competitors? Ultimately, vision statements serve the purpose of boosting trust, confidence, and an image that the firm is engaging in a task larger than itself.

4. D: Maximizing profits despite any consequences to the surrounding environment is not part of social responsibility. When practicing corporate social responsibility, there are several ways an organization can engage the community. First, a firm can establish alliances with influential members of the community or a respected local organization. Secondly, a firm can deliver on its promise of delivering low-cost goods and services to the community. Lastly, as one tenet of corporate responsibility is improving the quality of life in a community, it should hire as many locals as possible.

5. D: Organizational branding can serve multiple purposes. One is creating a distinctive logo that is easily identifiable to consumers. Furthermore, organizational branding represents an opportunity to establish a perception of values and ethics that consumers understand when they see the logo. The famous logo for the Michelin Corporation is a jovial tire man, which articulates friendly service and exactly what the firm sells. The numeral IV is not part of branding, but more of a characteristic of marketing.

6. A: A cost-benefit analysis is an objective empirical study of the precise effects of a specific policy or plan. Cost-benefit analyses are critically important because they indicate if a policy or plan will save resources or squander them. If the costs outweigh the benefits, then an action isn't financially sensible. But if the analysis indicates that benefits will outweigh costs, then the policy can be pursued with confidence.

7. A: Business metrics are quantifiable ways to assess and measure the efficacy of specific policies, programs, or products. Similar to cost-benefit analysis, these metrics are objective and inform the firm whether an action should proceed. Metrics should be used when speaking to consumers and investors in order to establish trust and confidence.

8. D: A type of benefit that customers believe they could not obtain anywhere else is an example of differential advantage, not competitive advantage. Competitive advantage is the strategy of maintaining maximum competitiveness by pursuing policies and programs that increase one's advantage. Examples of competitive advantage are implementing new technology, offshoring to lower business costs, and shedding underperforming or unnecessary laborers.

9. C: Rules, practices, and institutions that address ecosystems in relation to the environment is known as environmental governance. Corporate governance refers to the policies and institutional code that a firm establishes in order to fulfill its role as a for-profit entity and an integral stakeholder in the community. Of course, firms are not the only actors that shape its governance laws—public policy has a salient role. The Sarbanes-Oxley Act mandated new protocol that senior executives must follow in order to increase transparency and accountability. Moreover, corporate governance can serve as a valuable tool for cultivating a firm's self-image.

10. B: Corporate restructuring is a broad term to describe a change in a firm's operations, legal code, or ownership to make it more competitive by increasing productive potential and lowering costs. One aspect of corporate restructuring is offshoring. Offshoring—moving the physical operations of a firm to a different country—is done in order to lower business costs while maintaining maximum competitiveness.

11. C: Enterprise risk management (ERM) are comprehensive policies and procedures that dictate how an organization handles risk and loss. The purpose of ERM is to coordinate and create a harmony of responses to problems facing an organization. ERMs lead to greater levels of stability and structure.

12. C: Offshoring can have many positive effects that transcend the corporation. Offshoring reduces the costs of business, which leads to lower prices for consumers. Lowering business costs doesn't just lead to lower prices—it also frees up revenue to participate in philanthropic activity.

13. D: Choice *D* mimics the wording of the question, but the explanation is irrelevant. It's imperative that firms anticipate potential changes in public policy because they must adjust. The success of this adjustment will depend upon institutional preparedness. Furthermore, if anticipated changes are expected to be damaging, a firm will want to engage in lobbying efforts to modify and amend the policies.

14. A: A whistle-blower reports or publicizes any illegal or unethical information about an organization or industry. An example of a whistle-blower is former tobacco industry official Jeffrey Wigand, who confessed in a televised interview that the tobacco industry was intentionally packing cigarettes with addictive levels of nicotine. Whistle-blowers are generally perceived as villains to institutions, while others believe they risk their livelihood for a just cause. Whistleblowers can operate in public or private institutions.

15. D: A business plan has a variety of different projections. Some of these projections are annual goals, projected growth targets, and net income expectations. However, bonuses for executives aren't calculated in a business plan, which are intended to increase the firm's profitability and productivity.

16. C: Although shareholders can be affected by a business, they are not stakeholders because they have stock ownership. Stakeholders have other interests in a business besides profitability. Employees, surrounding businesses, and the local community all have a stake in the financial state of a business, but their concerns transcend the appreciation of its stock.

17. C: Mergers occur when two companies combine to form a new one. Acquisitions occur when one company purchases another without forming a new company. One notable merger occurred in 1999, when Exxon and Mobile merged to form ExxonMobil. It can be helpful to think of mergers as consolidations.

Workforce Planning and Employment

Workforce Requirements for Short- and Long-Term Goals

Corporate Restructuring

Corporate restructuring involves the act of reorganizing a company in order to make it more profitable for its present-day situation. Corporate restructuring can take on one of two forms: financial or organizational restructuring.

Financial restructuring may be necessary due to a significant decrease in sales as a result of a poor economy. In this case, a company might make changes to its equity holdings, debt-servicing schedule, and cross-holding pattern based on the recommendations of financial and legal advisors to sustain its profitability.

Organizational restructuring may be necessary as a cost cutting measure, in an attempt by a company to pay off debt and continue with its business operations. In this case, the structure of the organization is changed in some manner, such as through redesigning jobs and changing reporting relationships, reducing the number of hierarchical levels (creating a flatter organization), or a workforce reduction (also known as downsizing).

Workforce Reduction (Downsizing)

Workforce reductions are the planned elimination of a number of personnel in order to make an organization more competitive through reducing costs, using technology to replace labor, mergers and acquisitions, or by moving a company to a more economical location.

Once a company realizes it has a talent surplus, Human Resources can take the following steps to avoid a workforce reduction:

- Reduce employees' hours or compensation to retain qualified staff
- Implement a hiring freeze
- Institute a *voluntary separation program*, also known as an *early retirement buyout program*

Although workforce reductions help companies cut costs in the short term, they often hurt productivity. For an organization to successfully implement a workforce reduction, it should communicate with employees throughout the entire process, and provide downsized employees with outplacement services to assist with resume writing, career counseling, and interview preparation. It can also provide referral assistance to exiting employees. Companies should strive to build the trust and commitment of the remaining employees so as to boost employee morale, especially during a downsizing situation.

Employees who are laid off are typically asked to sign a document known as a *separation agreement and general release*. This document, when signed, is a legally binding agreement that states the employee cannot sue or make any claims against the company in exchange for agreed upon severance benefits. Severance pay is not required by law, but most companies will pay employees who are laid off a set number of weeks of salary continuation, based upon their years of service (typically one or two weeks' pay per year of service), to ease their financial burden and to preserve the organization's image. Some companies also include a continuation of healthcare benefits for a set period of time.

An employee is given the agreement during their exit meeting and is allowed to take it home and review it with a lawyer. They have twenty-one days to sign and return the agreement for an individual separation and forty-five days to sign and return the agreement in cases of a group reduction in force. Once the agreement is signed, an employee still has seven days to revoke their signature.

<u>Workforce Expansion</u>
Some companies have a talent shortage. Instead of hiring full-time employees, Human Resources can utilize the following tactics to manage the workforce:

- Allow existing staff to work overtime hours
- Outsource work to an external service provider
- Institute alternate work arrangements (i.e., telecommuting, job sharing, and nontraditional work schedules)
- Reemploy recent retirees on a temporary or part-time basis
- Utilize contingent workers to fill available positions and manage the extra workload (i.e., independent contractors)

Turning to alternative sources for workers can help the company save money on the hiring and interviewing process—a significant cost for many companies. Because many of the above candidates have already been screened for the job and proven themselves on the job, they may be a better match for filling short-term and even long-term staffing needs.

Conducting Job Analysis

A job analysis is a way of systematically gathering and analyzing information about the context, content, and human requirements of jobs within an organization. Typically, a member of Human Resources, an external consultant, or a manager conducts a job analysis. The following methods can be used to gather data during a job analysis to identify the knowledge, skills, and abilities that are needed to qualify an individual to perform a job effectively:

- Observations
- Interviews
- Highly structured questionnaires
- Open-ended questionnaires
- Work logs or work diaries

A job analysis is used to develop or create the following three items:

- Job descriptions: A detailed breakdown of specific tasks, skills, and knowledge required for a position. Job descriptions summarize the most important features of a job, include any duties that support exempt status, and also include the physical requirements of the job for consideration under the Americans with Disabilities Act (ADA).

- Job competencies: A detailed list of broad skills or traits needed for a position, such as leadership skills or attention to detail. Core competencies are those competencies that are aligned with key business objectives believed to contribute to organizational success.

- Job specifications: A detailed description of specific qualifications (i.e., professional licenses or certifications), experience, or education needed to perform the tasks. Job specifications can be included in a separate document or in a separate section of the job description, and they should reflect what is necessary for satisfactory performance in the role, instead of what specific skills the ideal candidate should possess.

Reviewing Essential Job Functions

While updating job descriptions, an employer must also be able to identify and update the essential functions for all positions.

Essential job functions are those tasks and responsibilities that are fundamental to a specific position. Each position is made up of both essential job functions and marginal job functions (duties that are ancillary or incidental to the nature or purpose of the job). For example, essential job functions for a hairstylist are coloring and cutting hair. A marginal job function for a hairstylist may involve answering the telephone to schedule appointments for clients.

There are three main considerations to take into account when determining if a job function is essential or marginal:

- How frequently the task is performed
- The percentage of time spent working on the task
- The importance of the task being completed

Under the Americans with Disabilities Act, for a disabled individual who is qualified, an employer may be asked to make reasonable accommodations to enable them to perform the essential (or core) job functions. That is why it is so important for organizations to properly identify essential job functions in advance.

Establishing Criteria for Hiring, Retaining, and Promoting

Job descriptions should communicate the type of work involved, the difficulty of the work, any unusual elements that may be required, and the frequency with which various tasks need to be performed. Job descriptions should be up to date and reflect current expectations, not past or future expectations, when used as part of the hiring process.

Criteria for job promotions (which can lead to higher retention) involve a number of different factors, such as:

- Seniority: An employee's tenure can be a common element and a prerequisite in determining a promotion. For example, a job description may state that, "An employee must have a minimum of two years' experience with the company in order to be eligible for a promotion."

- Performance: An employee's results from their performance reviews can also be a factor. This can be based on a recent assessment or from a longer period. For example, a job description can state "Must have attained 'Expected Level' in annual review for the past three years."

- Fit: This is usually determined before the decision to promote and is based on the company's framework of competencies. "Good fit" is determined by comparing an employee's current abilities with those required to perform in the new position.

- Workforce planning: If an employee is promoted without an open position created by a vacancy, then it's a general indicator of job progression with increased responsibilities, competencies, etc. Any promotion that requires the old vacancy to be filled requires a manpower and reorganization plan. This is useful for determining promotion eligibility.

Analyzing Labor Market Trends

The supply pool from which employers attract new hires is called the labor market. Employers must identify the labor markets (i.e., geographic, global, industry-specific, educational, and technical) from which they can recruit candidates based on the jobs that need to be filled, especially for key positions.

An analysis of labor markets during workforce planning has a number of benefits, including:

- Gaining an understanding of the unemployment rate
- Identifying where employers are competing for labor
- Researching salaries paid for certain positions
- Identifying employment trends in a particular industry

The main federal institution that measures and collates nationwide employment data is the Bureau of Labor Statistics within the US Department of Labor. This department has separate state departments that also report state-specific data. Among the data collected are market activity, average salaries, basic job duties, and working conditions.

Implementing Selection Procedures

Applicant Tracking

An applicant tracking system is a method used to make the selection process more effective by utilizing a software application to electronically process a company's recruitment needs. An applicant tracking system allows an organization to do this by sorting through large numbers of resumes that are submitted in order to find the candidates who are the best possible fit for a specific open position, based on a search for certain keywords. This allows employers to stay better organized, save time, and stay on top of the hiring process.

All institutions that receive federal contracts are required to track what is known as applicant flow data. This is information collected on the gender and race of all applicants who apply for open positions within an organization. The goal of collecting such data is to be able to perform an analysis of differences in selection rates among various groups for a specific position, to ensure a proper demographic pool is being sourced for the role. This data can be collected by the use of an Equal Employment Opportunity (EEO) information form. Employers must make a reasonable effort to obtain this information. It is important to note that any such type of information obtained is not to be used in hiring decisions. It is for Human Resources' eyes only and cannot be kept with an employee's application or personnel file. This is clearly disclosed in the application, so that the applicant is aware that the company is not basing their hiring decision on demographic information the applicant shares.

Interviewing

An interview allows an employer to further evaluate a candidate's skills and knowledge while giving the candidate a chance to demonstrate their abilities.

The four most commonly used styles of interviewing are:

- Structured
- Semi-structured
- Unstructured
- Non-directive

A *structured interview* is controlled by the interviewer, who has a list of specific, job-related questions prepared prior to the start of the interview. The same questions are asked of all applicants in an effort to make comparisons between them easier. This can result in a better selection decision. A structured interview tends to be much more valid and reliable than other interview approaches.

Semi-structured interviews occur when interviewers have guided conversations with applicants that involve both broad questions and new questions that come about from the discussions that take place.

Unstructured interviews occur when interviewers improvise and ask applicants questions that were not prepared prior to the start of the interview. This can give the interviewer a chance to see how well the applicant thinks on their feet, and whether they can handle a lack of formalities or structure within a professional setting.

A *non-directive interview* utilizes open-ended questions that may be developed from an applicant's answers to previous questions. The interviewer must strive to keep the conversations job-related and to obtain comparable data from each applicant interviewing for the same position. This type of interviewing style is best used sparingly, because comparing applicants is much more subjective than with the other styles.

Reference and Background Checking

Reference checks are very important for companies during the hiring process. They can verify if an individual has the necessary skills, knowledge, and experience, based on prior job performance, while also validating an individual's application for employment.

Reference checks are also an important way for companies to protect themselves from lawsuits or damage to their reputation. For example, negligent hiring takes place when an employer hires an employee, and the employer either knew or should have known that the employee posed a risk to other employees or to customers. An example of negligent hiring is when an employee who is hired as a controller at a financial institution is later charged with embezzlement. The employer (financial institution) can ultimately be found liable for failing to conduct a proper background check on the employee if this employee did have a past history of criminal activity at a previous employer.

Employers can prevent negligent hiring claims by conducting criminal background checks, verifying employment histories and college degrees, checking on past employment gaps, and reaching out to the references of potential employees. In some industries, employers can also perform drug screenings, require physicals, perform credit checks, and check driving records for specific jobs.

A reference list is usually provided upon request, meaning the individual provides the references after a prospective employer asks for them. There are two main types of reference checks a company would need to complete: education and employment.

Education references refer to any certifications, degrees, diplomas, licenses, or any professional documents that can validate an applicant's knowledge and education. Sometimes these reference checks provide employers with specific grades or indicators of performance, but they're mostly made to verify that education was completed.

Employment references refer to feedback from past employers, co-workers, customers, or clients who can verify the individual's professional experience. The main information sought from these reference checks are on-the-job performance feedback from previous employers, as well as the individual's position(s), wages, and duration with past companies.

Two less common reference checks are financial and driving history.

Financial reference checks relate to credit history and how an individual handles money. These are usually for positions where this would be important, such as in the banking industry, but also in the public services industry (positions in schools, hospitals, or government).

Driving history checks relate to an individual's driving record, and verify that they are able to drive safely. This is necessary for positions where driving is required, including an employee's need to use rental vehicles while conducting company business.

Administering Post-Offer Employment Activities

Once a new employee is hired, a number of activities need to be completed for that individual to have a smooth transition into the organization. Some of the typical post-offer activities include:

- Perform any other necessary background checks
- Make copies of the offer letter
- Work with IT and other internal departments to prepare for the new employee's arrival (establish the workstation, create an email account, etc.)
- Prepare the new hire's packet of paperwork that they will need to complete on the first day
- Work to develop an on-boarding plan that includes a list of important people in the company that the new hire should meet
- Inform any internal applicants who were not selected for the position and provide them with feedback
- Notify any external applicants who were not selected for the role

Executing Employment Agreements

Employment-at-will is always presumed when a written employment agreement does not exist; it is a common-law doctrine that states employers have the right to hire, promote, demote, or fire whomever they choose, provided there is not a law or contract in place to the contrary. Under this doctrine, employees are also free to leave an employer whenever they choose to seek other employment.

There are two types of employment contracts (agreements): implied and express. *Implied contracts* are inferred from an employer's conduct or actions. An example of an implied contract is when an employer promises an employee job security or hires an employee for an indefinite timeframe. An employee expectation is established, especially when the employer and the employee have enjoyed a long-term business relationship.

An *express contract* is based on an employer's written or oral words, and is a formal agreement that outlines the details of the employment arrangement. In the past, these types of contracts were reserved for executive and senior management positions. Now they are also being used for technical and highly specialized employees who possess skills that are harder to come by.

Completing I-9/E-Verify Process

Companies must be vigilant in their verification of new hires' right to work in the United States and their identities via the I-9 process within the first three days of employment. Because timeliness is of the essence, the Department of Homeland Security runs a government program to assist with this process; it is called E-Verify. At the current time, use of E-Verify is only mandatory for government contractors and subcontractors. For more information about I-9, please see the content under *Immigration Reform and Control Act (IRCA)* content of the *Federal Laws and Regulations* portion of this section.

Coordinate Relocations

Many companies offer relocation benefits to assist new hires during a very stressful time in their lives. Such benefits can include any or all of the following:

- Paying for temporary living expenses
- Reimbursing for moving fees
- Assisting a "trailing spouse" with their job search
- Allowing for the use of a company car
- Providing financial assistance with selling a home (or buying a new home)

Immigration

Organizations are held responsible for the verification of their new hires' credentials and identities. They must ensure that the documents presented to them (i.e., visas, passports, Social Security cards, etc.) are indeed official and are not fabricated in any way. At any time, the U.S. Immigration and Customs Enforcement (ICE) can audit a company's records to guarantee compliance with employment eligibility laws. If a company's Human Resources department is found with fraudulent documents, the company can be held liable. For more information about immigration, please see the *Immigration Reform and Control Act (IRCA)* content of the *Federal Laws and Regulations* portion of this section.

Implementing an Affirmative Action Plan (AAP) as Required

Affirmative action aids employers with identifying imbalances in the workforce and assists them with placing a focus on hiring, training, and promoting groups of workers who are underrepresented. The following employers are required to have affirmative action plans (AAPs) in place (otherwise, having an AAP is voluntary):

- Employers with fifty or more employees and $50,000 in federal contracts
- Employers who are a member of the federal banking system
- Employers who issue, sell, or redeem U.S. Savings Bonds

The following is a listing of the major elements that make up an AAP:

Introductory Statement

This is essentially a company overview that includes information concerning headcount, along with any significant employment changes that have taken place in the past calendar year. In addition, the company's policy on affirmative action and equal opportunity employment is also mentioned.

Organizational Profile

This depicts the organization's staffing patterns, to determine if any barriers exist to equal opportunity employment. The organizational structure is presented in some format (i.e., graphical chart, spreadsheet, etc.) to show the following information:

- Unit names
- Employees job titles, gender, and minority status
- Total number of males and females
- Total number of males and females who are also minorities

Job Group Analysis

This is a list of all titles that comprise each job group. Jobs are grouped according to whether they have similar content, responsibilities, salaries, and opportunities for advancement. This analysis represents jobs by functional alignment versus departmental alignment.

Job Group Analysis

Title	Salary	Total	Male Female	White	Black	Hispanic	Asian	Native Hawaiian	Indian	Two or More	Minority
Vice President Operations	28	1	1	1	0	0	0	0	0	0	0
			0	0	0	0	0	0	0	0	
Vice President Sales	28	1	1	0	0	1	0	0	0	0	1
			0	0	0	0	0	0	0	0	
Chief Financial Officer	29	1	0	0	0	0	0	0	0	0	1
			1	0	1	0	0	0	0	0	
Chief Operating Officer	30	1	1	1	0	0	0	0	0	0	0
			0	0	0	0	0	0	0	0	
Chairman	32	1	1	1	0	0	0	0	0	0	0
			0	0	0	0	0	0	0	0	
Summary of 1A – Executive		5	4	3	0	1	0	0	0	0	2
			1	0	1	0	0	0	0	0	

Availability Analysis

Organizations examine the internal (employees who are trainable, promotable, and transferable) and external (candidates in the reasonable geographical recruitment area) availability of women and minorities to determine their theoretical availability. External availability statistics can be obtained through state and local governments, which provide statistical data and may even publish it on their websites.

Utilization Analysis

The availability of women and minorities is compared with their current representation in each job group at the company. Companies typically define underutilization as the "80 percent rule." This rule is used to determine adverse impact in the employee selection process by comparing the rates at which different groups of people are hired for a job. Eighty percent was arbitrarily selected as an indication of underutilization. Then, for job groups where underutilization is found, reasonable placement goals are set (expressed as placement rates). It is also important to note that a company can have underutilization without experiencing adverse impact.

Other Required Elements

- Identify the individual who is ultimately accountable for the affirmative action plan

- List all of the problem areas

- Detail the action-oriented affirmative action programs that will aid in reaching set goals

- Discuss how the affirmative action program will be monitored and reported on to management

- Provide executive approval and signature on the affirmative action plan

- Create separate affirmative action plans for qualified, covered veterans and individuals with disabilities

- Ensure proper notices are posted on company bulletin boards about affirmative action and equal opportunity employment

Equal Opportunity Employment (EEO) Reporting

Annual workforce data reporting is required by the Equal Opportunity Employment Commission (EEOC) for all employers with one hundred or more employees and federal contractors with at least fifty employees and contracts of $50,000. The reports are due each year by September 30. In addition, these employers must place EEO posters and notices in prominent locations within their workplaces. EEO reporting aids employers in determining their workforce composition, to ensure they are not discriminating against protected classes.

The various EEO reports collect data by some type of job grouping about race/ethnicity and gender. There are nine EEO job reporting categories:

- Officials and managers
- Professionals
- Technicians
- Sales
- Office and clerical
- Craft workers (skilled)
- Operatives (semiskilled)
- Laborers (unskilled)
- Service workers

As an example, the EEO-1 Report, which is also known as the Employer Information Report, categorizes data by race/ethnicity, gender, and job category. This report applies to employers who are required to file an annual report of employee sex and race/ethnic categories under Title VII of the 1964 Civil Rights Act. Government guidelines for the reporting of race are detailed in the EEO1 report form, which is jointly produced by the EEOC and the Office of Federal Contract Compliance.

Implementing a Record Retention Process

Internet Applicants

The Office of Federal Contract Compliance Programs (OFCCP) created a recordkeeping rule, known as the Internet Applicant Rule, to determine what records need to be kept by federal contractors who have Internet applicants applying for their open positions. Under this rule, a job seeker is classified as an Internet applicant by a contractor if they meet four criteria:

- They have expressed an interest in employment over the Internet or through another related electronic data technology

- The employer considers the individual for employment in a particular position

- The individual's expression of interest indicates that they possess the basic qualifications for the open position

- The individual does not remove themselves from consideration at any point during the contractor's selection process

The following record retention requirements are based on federal guidelines. However, individual states may also have record retention requirements that need to be followed.

Pre-Employment Files
Selection, hiring, and employment records are to be kept for either one year after their creation or following the hire/no hire decision (whichever date is later). Federal contractors must keep these same types of records for three years. The following items are examples of what are included in these types of records:

- Employment applications
- Resumes
- Interview notes
- Records related to promotions, transfers, and terminations
- Requests for reasonable accommodations
- AAP records related to hiring benchmarks

I-9 forms are to be kept for three years after the date of hire or one year after the date of termination (whichever date is later).

Credit reports have no record retention requirement. However, the law requires an employer to shred all documents containing information from such a report.

Drug test records are to be kept for one year from the date the test was administered, or up to five years for any job positions related to the Department of Transportation.

Medical Files
Records associated with family medical leave (for a company with fifty or more employees) are to be kept for three years. The following items are examples of what is included in these types of records:

- Basic employee data
- Dates of leave taken
- Hours of leave taken for intermittent Family and Medical Leave Act of 1993 (FMLA) leave
- Copies of employee notices
- Records of premium payments of employee benefits
- Records of any disputes regarding designation of leave

Benefits Files
Records associated with employment benefits are to be kept for six years. The following items are examples of what are included in these types of records:

- Summary plan descriptions
- Annual reports
- Plan amendments
- Plan terminations

There are no record retention requirements for documentation associated with employees and their dependents who wish to continue group healthcare coverage under the Consolidated Omnibus Budget Reconciliation Act (COBRA) after a qualifying event. However, it is recommended that companies maintain these records for six years to be consistent with the requirements of the Employment Retirement Income Security Act (ERISA).

Federal Laws and Regulations

Title VII of the Civil Rights Act of 1964

Title VII was originally passed as part of the Civil Rights Act of 1964. This portion of the act protects employees from management decisions regarding their employment (i.e., recruiting, hiring, advancement, compensation, work environment, etc.) based on race, color, nationality, or sex. State and local acts may expand this to include sexual orientation. Title VII applies to most employers with fifteen or more employees.

There are a few exceptions to Title VII. Legitimate work-related requirements may prevent an employer from hiring a specific individual, as they may be physically unable to perform the essential job functions associated with a certain position. For example, a work-related requirement for a firefighter may be that they must be able to carry two hundred pounds up eight flights of stairs. Additionally, seniority systems that are already in effect at a workplace are allowed. Finally, Bona Fide Occupational Qualifications (BFOQs) are exceptions to the discrimination rules that allow employers to take into account an individual's age, origin, sex, or religion when considering them for a job (note that race and color are not included). For example, an employer would not want to hire a sixty-five-year-old woman to model children's clothing.

Rehabilitation Act

The Rehabilitation Act was passed in 1973 to prohibit employment discrimination based on physical or mental disabilities. This legislation charges employers with taking affirmative action to hire qualified disabled persons. The act further requires that reasonable accommodation(s) be made for the disabled unless the employer can show an undue hardship based on business necessity or financial cost (spending in excess of $1,000 per employee). The Civil Service Commission, Department of Labor, Department of Veterans Affairs, and the Department of Health and Human Services administer this law, which applies to the federal government, federal contractors with contracts over $10,000, and companies who are in receipt of funds in excess of $10,000 by a company that receives federal monies.

Under this law, disability is defined as a physical or mental impairment that substantially limits one or more major life activities. Examples of reasonable accommodations that can be made under the Rehabilitation Act consist of the following:

- A change in job design: eliminating tasks that are not really necessary to perform the job
- Qualifications: getting rid of unnecessary job specs for everyone, such as requiring a medical exam prior to employment (which will allow the disabled to be hired)
- Job accessibility: adding wheelchair ramps, brail in elevators, etc.
- Nondiscriminatory treatment: eliminating hiring decisions based on people's fear of, or uneasiness with, disabilities

Americans with Disabilities Act (ADA)

The Americans with Disabilities Act (ADA) was passed in 1990 to protect individuals with disabilities against discrimination in relation to aspects such as employment, pay, and benefits. The EEOC defines such disabled individuals as having a physical or mental impairment that limits one or more major life activities.

The ADA applies to companies and organizations with fifteen or more employees. The act specifically dictates that as long as a company or organization does not undergo "undue hardship," they are required to make reasonable accommodations for any disabled employees, such as modifying existing facilities to make them more accessible or adjusting the circumstances under which a job is performed. It is important to know that disabled employees must still be able to perform the essential functions of their job positions, with or without accommodations, when hired.

Identifying reasonable accommodations is an interactive four-step process. First, barriers to the performance of the essential job functions must be identified for a disabled employee. Then possible accommodations that may be helpful in overcoming the barriers are discussed. The feasibility of each of the accommodations is assessed, including whether or not the accommodations are the employer's responsibility and if they will impose an undue hardship to the employer. Finally, the appropriate accommodations are chosen for the disabled employee. An employer is allowed to ask for proof of a disability if it is not obvious, along with information about the accommodation before deciding to make it. An employer cannot ask if an individual has a disability during a job interview. If an interview candidate comes to an interview in a wheelchair, the employer can ask the individual what type(s) of accommodations would be needed. Examples of reasonable accommodations include the following:

- Modifying work sites
- Accessible facilities
- Flexi-time
- Flexi-place
- Providing readers and interpreters
- Modifying work schedules
- Assistive devices
- Reassignment (only available as a last resort)

Pregnancy Discrimination Act
The Pregnancy Discrimination Act, passed in 1978, was an amendment to Title VII of 1964. The act applies to all employers with fifteen or more employees and states that while pregnant women are working, they are to be treated in the same way as other employees who are performing their jobs. Therefore, pregnancy must be treated in the same manner as any other type of temporary disability.

Under this legislation, an employer:

- Cannot refuse to hire a pregnant woman
- Cannot force a woman to take leave or terminate her employment because she is pregnant
- Must give a woman a comparable position to the one that she held prior to her maternity leave (if the company already does so with employees taking short-term disability) upon her return to work
- Must provide a pregnant woman with reasonable accommodation(s) if she is unable to do her job and approaches her manager to that effect
- Cannot discriminate against a woman who has undergone an abortion

When a pregnant woman is interviewing for a job position, she is not required by law to disclose the fact that she is pregnant. If it is obvious that a female interview candidate is pregnant, a prospective employer can only state the job requirements for the position (ignoring the pregnancy) and ask the candidate when she is available to start work.

Uniform Guidelines on Employee Selection Procedures

The Uniform Guidelines on Employee Selection Procedures, passed in 1978, were designed to prohibit selection procedures that have an adverse impact on protected groups. Adverse impact occurs when the rate for a protected group is less than 80 percent of the rate for the group with the highest selection rate. This is also known as the 80 percent rule, or the four-fifths rule. Below is an example:

- Four hundred white candidates applied and two hundred were hired – 50 percent
- One hundred Hispanic candidates applied and forty-five were hired – 45 percent
- 80% of 50 = 40
- NO adverse impact here. If the number was lower than forty, there would be adverse impact.
- Sixty male candidates interviewed and thirty were hired – 50 percent
- Forty female candidates applied and ten were hired – 25 percent
- 80% of 50 = 40
- YES adverse impact here. Females must be hired at a selection rate of 40 percent.

Under these guidelines, procedures that have an adverse impact on women and minorities must be proven to be valid in predicting and/or measuring performance, so as not to be viewed as discriminatory. The *bottom line concept* was an outcome of these guidelines, and it means that an employer is not required to evaluate each component of the selection process individually if the end result is shown to be predictive of future job performance.

If adverse impact is found (which is not always intentional), the employer has four alternatives:

- Abandon the procedure
- Modify the procedure to eliminate adverse impact
- Demonstrate job relatedness:
  - Conduct validation studies
  - Keep detailed records
  - Investigate alternatives with less adverse impact
- Show the business necessity associated with the need to keep the procedure (which is difficult to do)

Immigration Reform and Control Act (IRCA)

The Immigration Reform and Control Act (IRCA) was passed in 1986 and amended in 1990. This act was created to prevent discrimination against individuals based on national origin or citizenship on elements such as employment, pay, or benefits, so long as they are legally able to work in the United States. Employers are also required to verify new employees by making them complete an employment eligibility verification form (I-9) and receiving proof of lawful status within their first three working days. The back of the I-9 form lists all of the documents that are used to show legality to work in the United States, verifying an individual's right to work and identity. Employers must retain I-9 forms for three years, or for one year after an employee's termination, whichever comes later. In addition, this act established civil and criminal penalties for hiring illegal aliens.

Furthermore, this act instituted categories for visas. Immigrant visas are known as green cards. They are permanent or indefinite visas and are obtained through family relationships or employment. Nonimmigrant visas are temporary. An example is the H1-B visa, for which there is a yearly cap. This type of visa is set aside for certain kinds of working professionals who travel to the United States for a specified period of time.

Sexual Harassment in the Workplace

There are two types of sexual harassment that occur in the workplace: quid pro quo and hostile work environment. The translation of quid pro quo is "this for that." Quid pro quo sexual harassment takes place when a superior conditions employment (i.e., promotional opportunity, raise, etc.) on sexual favors.

The type of sexual harassment known as hostile work environment takes place when sexual or discriminatory conduct creates a work environment that a "reasonable person" would find threatening or abusive (i.e., unwelcome advances, offensive gender-related language, and sexual innuendos). It is important to remember that male employees can also be victims of sexual harassment.

There are four well-known court cases that dealt with sexual harassment in the workplace:

- Meritor Savings Bank vs. Vinson: The court held that sexual harassment violates Title VII. This case dealt with an employee who was plagued with unwanted sexual innuendos. The court said that the plaintiff need not prove concrete psychological harm, just an abusive or intimidating environment.

- Harris vs. Forklift Systems, Inc.: This case established the "reasonable person" standard for hostile environment sexual harassment.

- Oncale vs. Sundowner Offshore Service, Inc.: The court ruled that same-gender sexual harassment is actionable. This case dealt with all males working on an offshore oilrig, where a heterosexual male was threatened with rape.

- Faragher vs. City of Boca Raton: The court stated that employers can be held liable for supervisory harassment that results in an adverse employment action. This case dealt with female lifeguards who were sexually harassed. The city was held liable because the lifeguards' supervisors were not informed of the policy (it was not communicated effectively).

The following items are key elements to put in place in order to prevent sexual harassment from occurring in the workplace:

- Provide staff with a written, zero tolerance policy on sexual harassment that contains clear definitions and examples
- Provide a complaint procedure for staff to utilize
- Hold training sessions for employees and document attendees
- Investigate all sexual harassment complaints
- Follow through with corrective action (up through and including termination), if necessary
- Communicate the policy on sexual harassment using multiple methods to everyone in the company

Methods to Assess Past and Future Staffing Effectiveness

Cost per Hire

The cost per hire is calculated by adding together the external and internal recruiting costs and dividing that amount by the total number of new hires during a specific time period. Examples of external recruiting costs include items such as: advertising the position on job boards, recruitment outsourcing, recruitment technology, background checks and drug testing, and pre-hire assessments. Examples of internal recruiting costs include such items as: in-house recruiting staff, payment of referral rewards, and internal recruiting systems.

Selection Ratios

There are a number of different selection ratios used to evaluate recruitment sources. For example, to find the percentage of qualified applicants, the number of qualified applicants is divided by the number of total applicants for a particular position. The percentage of minority applicants is calculated by taking the number of minority applicants divided by the total number of applicants for a position. Additionally, the percentage of offers accepted is the number of offers accepted divided by the number of offers that were extended.

Adverse Impact

There are two types of discrimination: disparate treatment and disparate or adverse impact. Disparate treatment occurs when an employer treats protected classes differently than other employees. Examples of disparate treatment include holding genders to different standards, sexual harassment, and blatantly rejecting a member of a protected class due to stereotypes.

A famous disparate treatment case was McDonnell Douglas Corporation vs. Green. Green was a black employee who was laid off during a regular reduction in force. He protested at the company (as part of a group), chained and locked company doors, and blocked an entrance to company property. His activities did not please the company. When the company began hiring again, they advertised, and Green reapplied. He was denied, and the company continued looking for candidates. Green claimed the rejection was due to his race and his involvement in civil rights activities. This was a precedent-setting EEO case that established criteria for disparate treatment and ruled that a *prima facie* (at first glance) case can be shown if an employee:

- Belongs to a protected class
- Applied for a job when the employer sought applicants
- Was qualified and yet rejected
- Was rejected but the employer kept looking

In disparate treatment cases, an individual must prove:

- They are a member of a protected class
- They applied for a job for which they were qualified and for which the employer was seeking applicants
- They were not hired even though they were qualified
- After they did not get the job, the position remained open and the employer continued to receive applications

Disparate or *adverse impact* refers to a form of discrimination where an employer's policy seems neutral but in fact has an adverse impact on a certain group or a certain characteristic such as race, sex, or disability. This was identified by the Supreme Court in 1971 in the case of Griggs v. Duke Power Co., where it was proven that the requirement of a high school diploma for higher-paid positions was unfairly affecting African-American employees in lower-paid labor positions who had a history of receiving inferior education.

As another example, if an employer requires a potential employee for a position to be at least 5'10'', it may exclude an entire group, such as women. Because statistically, men are taller, this requirement is based solely on biological reasons rather than if the candidate can adequately perform the required role.

An employer discriminating based on certain physical elements, however, can be justified if it is in correlation with job requirements. For example, it is necessary for a fire department to discriminate based on height, facial hair, or grooming to ensure the safety of its employees.

Turnover Statistics
Turnover is typically calculated on either a monthly or an annual basis. Analyzing turnover is necessary to accurately forecast the number of new employees that are needed to replace individuals who have recently moved out of job positions. To calculate turnover, the number of separations per year is divided by the average number of individuals employed per month, multiplied by 100. For example, if fifty individuals separated during the year and there is an average of two hundred individuals employed per month, the turnover rate is $\frac{50}{200} \times 10 = 25\%$.

Recruitment Sources for Targeting Candidates

Recruiting refers to procedures and strategies designed to encourage and find potential, qualified candidates who seek employment. If the labor pool is unsuitable, then reaching these staffing goals is impossible, and so recruiting is essential for any organization's staffing plan.

An organization usually uses three types of recruiting: external, internal, and alternative. External recruiting seeks individuals from outside the organization for employment and usually emphasizes the advantages of employment with the organization, advertising benefits such as pay, insurance, leave, or employee discounts. Internal recruiting encourages individuals from within the organization to seek transfers or promotions to fill vacant positions. Alternative recruiting seeks candidates from internships or temps to perform specific tasks for a limited period of time.

When a company seeks to recruit from within, some of the most common strategies to find potential candidates include internal announcements, which are made to employees before the general public; job bidding, which involves an employee expressing an interested in a position, whether or not it is available; and promotion plans, which detail an employee's skills and training and future positions for which they're qualified.

While the majority of companies will recruit in the ways that are mentioned above, some may look elsewhere to find the required number of candidates. Some of these methods include:

- Passing out fliers
- Recruiting in professional organizations
- Finding employees through prison work programs
- Recruiting outgoing employees from a company's clients, vendors, or suppliers
- Offering sign-on bonuses to prospective employees

The labor pool of available candidates can further be classified into three categories: active, semi-active, and passive.

Active candidates are those engaging in a search for new employment, whether they're already employed or unemployed. Most often these individuals are looking for new opportunities, concerned about their current employer's stability due to their employer's outsourcing, bankruptcy, etc. The most common method employers use to reach active candidates is through job postings. Using social media can aid in reaching the highest audience possible, but can sometimes also attract a large number of unqualified candidates. Another recruiting method involves active sourcing, which is made easier as these candidates are looking to be noticed. Again, using social media such as LinkedIn is an effective way in finding these jobseekers.

Semi-active candidates are not actively looking for work but are preparing themselves for new opportunities. These individuals most often do not have a resume prepared and businesses looking to recruit them often allow submissions of alternatives, such as an online social media profile.

Passive candidates are employed but not looking for work. These individuals are sometimes still worth pursuing by employers, if candidates are willing to listen to a recruiter about a better career opportunity. Proactive searching is the most effective way of reaching this group, again, through avenues like social media.

Employee Referral
Employee referrals can serve as a great tool when recruiting for positions requiring specialized skills that are difficult to fill via regular recruiting methods. Individuals who interview via employee referrals typically know what to expect regarding the work environment from their interactions with the employees who already work there, so there are fewer surprises. Employees who refer candidates usually benefit from a monetary incentive and can experience increased loyalty because they are having a "say" in the building of the workplace culture. It is important for a company not to rely solely on employee referrals to fill all open positions, so as to avoid creating cliques throughout the workplace. Such groups typically include individuals who are very similar to one another, which limits innovation.

Social Networking/Social Media
Social networking/media is a great tool for locating both passive and active candidates. LinkedIn, Facebook, and Twitter are the three most popular social media sites. However, other social media sites, such as Instagram, are quickly gaining more attention. A company's social media recruiting strategy allows candidates to view job openings and gain a better understanding of the company's personality and culture. It is important for companies to designate an individual who will respond to candidates' questions and concerns in a timely manner. In addition, a company's social media efforts can be easily monitored (i.e., page likes, number of followers, etc.) to analyze what is truly working, and then adjust strategy accordingly.

Diversity Groups
Organizations are also working to recruit potential employees via various diversity groups, which also help to further promote their inclusion efforts. Examples include groups for African Americans, Asian Americans, Latino Americans, disability awareness, LGBTQIA (lesbian, gay, bisexual, transgender, questioning, intersex, and allies), former members of the military, multicultural, emerging professionals, and women.

Recruitment Strategies

While businesses may usually use job listings and advertisements to seek out potential labor, they may also use third-party vendors for this purpose.

Career or job fairs allow applicants to contact various employers at once, and are usually held by the employers themselves, recruiters, or universities.

Other recruitment sources that a business may use include labor unions, open houses, unemployment offices, employment agencies, trade and professional associations, school-to-work programs, and nontraditional labor pools.

Staffing Alternatives

Outsourcing
Outsourcing is the practice of delegating work responsibilities in a business to a separate third-party individual or organization not associated with the company.

There are three different types of outsourcing:

- Onshore: The vendor is located within the same country as the business
- Nearshore: The vendor is in a country adjacent to the business
- Offshore: The vendor is in a country far from the business

Frequently, a company will outsource when:

- The expertise needed for a specific task cannot be found within the business
- Cost-cutting is needed
- A greater focus on in-business operations is needed

Outsourcing work does have a disadvantage in that the company may find it difficult to monitor the third-party business's operations as opposed to its own employees. Additionally, there is a risk in entrusting business confidentiality to a third party not near the business at all—especially with elements such as financial information. It is also worth noting that the idea of outsourcing can decrease morale for onsite employees. They may become worried about their own job security, so it's important for employers to introduce the concept carefully.

Job Sharing
Job sharing involves two or more employees performing the tasks of a role normally performed by one person. Usually the individuals are employed on a part-time basis. Job sharing has become more prevalent in recent times due to an evolving work culture and the development of alternative work arrangements.

Candidates looking for a work/life balance may see benefits in job sharing, even though the pay is lower and benefits are fewer, and consequently, overall productivity can increase for the business. However, it is essential for the individuals involved to have excellent communication with each other in order to succeed in a role normally designated for one person.

Phased Retirement

Phased retirement for older employees involves both the cutting back of working hours (or days of work) and the phasing in of retirement benefits such as Social Security funds. Phased retirement arrangements can take the form of part-time work, temporary or seasonal work, or job sharing.

Most commonly, these are informal agreements between an employer and an employee. A possible reason for the lack of formalized programs is the lack of legislation regarding regulations of benefits and salary coverage for potential retirees.

Phased retirement benefits employers by allowing more senior employees with years of workplace knowledge and experience to train their replacements over time.

Planning Techniques

Succession Planning

Succession planning involves preparing current employees for future advancements or promotions by developing their knowledge, skills, and abilities. Ongoing training for any potential open position in the company ensures no loss of productivity or operational efficiency, should key employees leave.

Some common succession planning techniques employers use include special assignments, creating team leadership roles, and sending staff to internal and external training for their continued development. This can also be used as a retention tactic, as employees may recognize the benefit of staying with a company when they can see a clear path toward promotion.

Forecasting

The two main forecasting methods used by companies to determine staffing needs are known as qualitative and quantitative forecasting.

Qualitative forecasting is based on the opinions and estimations of industry experts or managers. *Management forecasting* involves determining staffing needs from the managers of each department and making decisions by using their reports. *Expert forecasting* utilizes industry experts who are able to make decisions based on wider changes in the industry.

A specific example of expert forecasting is the Delphi method, where questionnaires are sent to a variety of experts, the results are shared, and then choices are updated. The objective of this method is to reach the most correct decision via consensus.

Quantitative forecasting is based on raw mathematical data and previous trends, such as employee productivity and output. Some common quantitative forecasting methods include ratio analyses, trend analyses, turnover analyses, and probability models. *Ratio analyses* compare current with past employment ratios to determine where staffing needs may change, such as the number of employees to the number of products made. *Trend analyses* compare single amounts instead of ratios, such as the number of employees. *Turnover analyses* compare the number of employees who leave the company over a certain period of time with past data. Using this data, a company can utilize a *probability model* to predict future changes.

Companies need to determine whether their needs are short- or long-term when deciding which kind of method to use. Qualitative methods are usually more effective in the short term because they can manage changing staffing needs. Quantitative methods are usually more effective in the long term because staffing needs change at a steadier rate. Companies typically require both of these forecasting methods.

Reliability and Validity of Selection Tests/Tools/Methods

Selection tests, tools, and methods must be both reliable and valid. They are said to be reliable if they are free from random errors and are able to predict or measure behavior consistently. For example, an intelligence test is said to be reliable if an individual takes the test on two different occasions and receives similar scores, because intelligence tends to be stable over time.

The following is a list of known errors that can create inconsistent results when evaluating the reliability of selection tests, tools, and methods:

- An interviewer who asks a candidate irrelevant questions during an interview
- An employer who allows candidates different amounts of time when completing a test
- A test that fails to measure an important attribute
- An interviewer who is biased when evaluating candidates

Although selection tests, tools, and methods may be deemed reliable, this does not necessarily mean they are also valid.

To be valid, a screening process should collect information on the candidate relevant to the position. If the process does not test qualifications, or tests irrelevant material, it can be deemed unfair or inaccurate. Information collected should be well defined, relevant, and job related.

A Human Resources professional usually evaluates three elements to determine the validity of a selection tool:

- Content validity
- Construct validity
- Criterion-related validity, which is further categorized into:
  - Concurrent validity
  - Predictive validity

Content validity measures how well the tool's subject matter covers the knowledge, skills, and abilities required for a specific job. The Uniform Guidelines on Employee Selection Procedures and the Equal Employment Opportunity Commission regulate that any pre-employment test or tool must be related to the job position for which it is intended. For example, if a candidate who is interviewing for a bank teller position is asked to take a test that measures mechanical ability, this can be deemed an invalid test. Again, this is important to ensure there are no legal repercussions against the recruiting organization.

Construct validity determines if a screening tool effectively tests and measures the characteristic it claims to measure, such as intelligence, and that the characteristic in question is indeed important for successful performance of the job.

Evaluations with demonstrated *criterion-related validity* can predict how an individual will behave in the workplace based on their test scores. This is done by comparing test result data to specific metrics or criteria required by the job, or to wider company goals, such as the total number of sales or the overall employee retention rate. After testing is completed, a measurement comparing test scores with job performance is taken and expressed as a correlation coefficient ranging from -1.0 to +1.0. Because testing this validity requires a large sample size, it is often the most difficult type of validity to measure.

Human Resources professionals can measure two types of criterion-related validity: predictive and concurrent.

Predictive validity is a measure of whether an individual will possess the required skills, knowledge, or behavioral traits in the future. To be valid, the test results should correlate and accurately predict job performance in the future; in other words, the test should yield a positive correlation coefficient.

Concurrent validity determines if an individual currently possesses the required skills, knowledge, or behavioral traits. To assess this type of criterion validity, a company administers a test to current employees to determine and compare their results to existing measures of job performance. The test is deemed to be valid if the individuals who receive the highest scores also perform best on the job.

Use and Interpretation of Selection Tests

Psychological and Personality Tests
Employers may want to explore candidates' personalities to determine if they are the right fit for open positions in certain situations. In these instances, personality tests (or inventories) are often distributed to candidates to see where they stand in regard to the top five personality traits: extroversion, adjustment, agreeableness, conscientiousness, and inquisitiveness. A company that is hiring new salespeople may be interested in how candidates score in agreeableness and extroversion, because high scores in those personality traits seem to correlate with success in the sales field. Organizations pay for candidates to take a personality test, and the company that owns the test then scores it and provides a corresponding report with details about the candidate's personality. These tests are easy to administer and do not violate any equal opportunity employment requirements.

Cognitive Ability Tests
Cognitive ability tests, which are also referred to as *intelligence tests*, are designed to measure candidates' mental abilities, such as verbal and mathematical ability, along with thinking, memory, and reasoning. The questions on this type of test are used to estimate an applicant's potential to utilize their mental processes to either acquire new knowledge on the job or to solve work-related problems.

Motor and Physical Assessments
Motor and physical assessments can test the muscular movement, strength, endurance, range of motion, posture, and cardiovascular fitness of candidates for roles that require a high level of physical activity, such as warehouse positions. When a company utilizes these types of tests, it is important to ensure that they are indeed job-related and that the tests are not administered to candidates until a conditional offer of employment is made, to avoid any violation of the Americans with Disabilities Act.

Performance Tests
Performance (or *work sample*) tests are designed to have a candidate complete a simulated task that is part of the target job for which they are applying. An example of a performance test is requiring candidates applying for an executive administrative assistant position to quickly type a business letter with no spelling or grammatical errors. Another example is asking an individual who is interviewing for a customer service representative position to read an email from a disgruntled customer and draft an email response that addresses the issue, while also trying to retain the customer's business. In order to be valid, work sample tests must truly address criteria in the open job position.

Assessment Center Tests
Assessment centers can test a number of different skills and abilities, including interpersonal and communication skills, as well as problem-solving and analytical skills. The tests are most often based on the content of the job position for which the candidates are interviewing and include scenarios that the candidates will face on the job. For example, they may test the desired skills needed to give a sales presentation. Oftentimes, the tests are evaluated by several trained raters. Assessment centers are most often utilized when filling managerial positions. This type of selection test can be expensive, but it rarely results in any type of disparate impact and typically results in companies hiring employees that are a good fit for the position.

The main advantages of selection tests are that they allow companies more control over the information gathered, and when given under the same conditions, they can yield consistent results. This is unlike candidate interviews, which may be biased based on the interviewer. Selection tests also incorporate specific questions related to the job requirements at hand and offer more concrete skills results, which may not be apparent in an interview or on a resume.

There can, however, be disadvantages with selection tests. For example, there can be legal issues of discrimination or disparate impact if a test examines skills unrelated to the task at hand, such as testing mathematic skills for a typist position. Irrelevant or poorly-worded questions can also inadvertently make it difficult for certain people to pass an exam.

Interviewing Techniques

Behavioral Interviews
The behavioral interview technique involves interviewers asking candidates to use specific examples to describe how they have handled a problem or performed a task in a past work situation. The thought behind this method is that past behavior is the best predictor of future job performance. Examples of behavioral-based interview questions are: "Can you tell me about a time when you had to go above and beyond the call of duty to get a job done?" and "Tell me about the last time you tackled a project that demanded a lot of initiative." Candidates can best answer these types of questions by using the STAR method, meaning they describe the past Situation or Task, explain the Action(s) they took, and describe the Results they achieved. It has been found that responses to questions about candidates' actual, past experiences tend to have high validity.

Situational Interviews
Situational interviews relate more to hypothetical situations that may take place in the future. For example, an employer may present a problem that could occur in the position for which the candidate is interviewing, and ask the applicant how they might handle it. While this type of interview is useful in determining the candidate's suitability for the position, situational interviews can neglect an applicant's past work experience.

Panel Interviews
Panel interviews are conducted by a group of individuals from the organization that may consist of managers, Human Resources representatives, and other future team members, in order to better evaluate whether or not a candidate is suitable. Panel interviews can help to reduce personal biases in the selection decision and are especially useful in work environments where teamwork is an important factor. This type of interview also gives candidates the opportunity to meet more people from the company and see how they interact with each other.

Compensation and Benefits

Compensation and benefits can be an essential element in retaining employees and attracting new candidates. Retaining current employees avoids the additional time and costs associated with training a new candidate altogether, as well as the risk of losing any clients or customers the individual may take along when they exit the organization.

Competitive salary and wages can be important in recruiting and retaining staff. However, unless the difference in salary is significant, it is usually not a factor—especially if the overall compensation package value is comparable. A lower take-home pay paired with a wider selection of healthcare and retirement plans may allow a company to offer a better long-term financial plan to its workers. Bonuses are yet another technique for employers to compensate and reward worthy employees.

Benefits can also assist in retention while saving the company money. Voluntary benefits help employees save money by utilizing group discounts with no added cost to the business. Retention of employees is possible with benefits such as health insurance, because many employees would not be able to afford having medical insurance if they exited their companies.

Terminations, Downsizing, Restructuring, and Outplacement Strategies

There are two main types of employment termination: voluntary and involuntary.

Voluntary termination is made by the choice of the employee. Involuntary termination is made at the discretion of the employer and does not take into account whether the employee wishes to stay. Most commonly, involuntary termination is due to poor employee performance or a directive related to a change in staffing needs.

Some of the more common reasons for an employee voluntarily leaving an organization include:

- Finding a better employment opportunity elsewhere
- General unhappiness with the company
- A health problem
- A desire to further their education
- Retirement

Termination is the final step in the progressive discipline process, where an employee is removed from their job by an employer. Terminations occur for behavioral issues, poor performance, and policy violations. It is imperative that employees receive sufficient warning regarding the seriousness of their offenses prior to their termination. There are two main types of involuntary termination: layoffs due to a change in staffing requirements, which are also known as Reductions in Force (RIFs), and performance-related terminations.

Reductions in Force (RIFs) are the planned elimination of a number of personnel, with the goal of making an organization more competitive. As previously noted, this is typically accomplished by reducing expenses, using technology to replace labor, mergers and acquisitions, or by relocating a company to a more economical location. Although RIFs are often successful at reducing costs in the short term, they often hurt productivity. For an organization to successfully implement a RIF, communication with employees throughout the entire process is essential. Employers should also provide downsized employees with outplacement services to assist them with resume writing, career counseling, interview preparation, and referrals. The management team should also strive to build the trust and commitment of the remaining employees, to help boost their morale.

Once the decision is made to end a staff member's employment, the actual termination takes place in a swift manner and typically during a face-to-face meeting. During the termination meeting with the employee's manager and sometimes with a member of Human Resources, the employee's building and systems access is deactivated while the employee's co-workers are gathered together in a conference room. This allows the terminated employee a few minutes of privacy to gather up their personal belongings under the supervision of building security, Human Resources, or the employee's manager. Then the terminated employee is escorted out of the building as discreetly as possible.

Employees who are laid off are typically asked to sign a document known as a *separation agreement* and *general release*. This document, when signed, is a legally binding agreement that states the employee cannot sue or make any claims against the company in exchange for agreed upon severance benefits. As mentioned, severance pay, although not required by law, is offered by many companies to employees who are laid off. It compensates such employees a set number of weeks of salary and/or healthcare benefits based upon their years of service (typically one or two weeks' pay per year of service), to ease their financial burden and to preserve the organization's image. Separation agreements are given to the employee during their exit meeting and they can take it home and review it with a lawyer. The employee has twenty-one days to sign and return the agreement for an individual separation and forty-five days to sign and return the agreement in cases of a group RIF. Once the agreement is signed, an employee still has seven days to revoke their signature.

Exit/Off-Boarding Process
There are several different aspects that must be addressed when employees exit an organization. First, a manager should ask the exiting staff member to make a list of all of their outstanding work projects, along with a brief description of each item and any associated contact information. This allows for a smooth transition of the workload to remaining team members. The manager will then need to decide how to best cover the staff member's absence, whether that be through allowing existing staff to work overtime, hiring a temporary employee for a short period of time until a replacement is hired, or by some other means.

The manager will need to work with the exiting staff member to ensure that all company property is returned prior to their exit date. This includes all of the following items:

- Company cell phone and/or pager
- Company car
- Company laptop
- Corporate credit card and/or purchasing card
- Office keys
- Remote access secure ID
- Employee badge
- Uniforms
- Completed, final expense reports

The manager should schedule an exit interview to meet with the employee on their last day. Prior to this meeting, the manager will typically arrange to have the employee's system and building access turned off, as they will not be returning to work afterward.

The manager will use this opportunity to review the following points with the exiting employee:

- Collect any outstanding company property
- Address any employee paybacks, if outstanding funds are due to the company
- Obtain the employee's forwarding information for their W-2
- Provide the employee with unemployment compensation information, if required by the state

In addition, the manager will also use this opportunity to discuss the employee's reasons for leaving in order to determine a source of dissatisfaction or perhaps to gain an understanding about why exiting is attractive. This lets the manager know if changes need to be made to increase retention.

A member of Human Resources will also typically meet with the existing staff member to discuss benefits information.

Internal Workforce Assessment Techniques

Skills Testing

A *skills audit* is performed for the purpose of identifying the current skills and knowledge within a company and the skills and knowledge the company will need in the future. A successful skills audit ultimately allows management to build a skills matrix that details the skills and competencies that employees need to fulfill each of their roles.

The skills audit begins by putting together a list of all the major roles within the organization, which is not necessarily every single position found on the organizational chart. Then both the technical and behavioral skills for each of these roles are listed. Surveys are created and distributed to the workforce. It is important to tell employees why they are being asked to participate in the surveys and to explain what will be done with the associated survey results. Depending on the size of the workforce, it may not make sense to survey every employee against every skill. The final steps are to compile the results (knowing what skills are required in each role and knowing what skills each employee has) and to analyze the survey data (identifying skill gaps in roles in the company, as well as determining needs for future skills).

Skills Inventory

A *skills inventory* is a listing of a company's current employees' education, skills, and real-world experience, and is typically tracked in an internal database or a commercial software program. There should be a process in place to prompt employees to update their skills inventory so that it remains current, such as prior to annual review time. The skills inventory loses its value if it is not updated in a timely fashion. Managers use the skills inventory to identify gaps between the existing workforce's education, skills, and experience and what they know will be needed to meet present and future business needs. In addition, the skills inventory assists management with making decisions regarding hiring, staffing internal project teams; assigning employees to different areas; and identifying training and development opportunities for staff.

Workforce Demographic Analysis

Workforce demographics are the statistical characteristics, such as gender, income, and age that make up the human population at work. It is important for individuals working in human resource management to study and analyze trends in the labor force because this will help them recruit the specific types of talent that their organization needs. Current trends in workforce demographics include an aging population. In fact, the fastest growing employee population is those individuals in the age group of fifty-five and older. Many of these workers are interested in a phased retirement approach.

This will affect organizations as they work to control the rising costs of benefits and health care, focus efforts to re-train older workers, and strive to attract, retain, and train younger employees.

Another current trend in workforce demographics is increased diversity in terms of gender, race, and ethnicity. In today's world, there are more women in the paid labor force than in the past, and employees that fall within the Asian and "other groups" categories are experiencing birthrates and immigration rates above the national average. This will affect organizations as they work to comply with the immigration laws and associated audits and paper trails. In addition, companies must strive to create cultures that value diversity and promote career development and advancement for women and minorities.

A third workforce demographics trend is increased skill deficiencies in the workplace. Many computers now perform routine tasks that employees used to do. Therefore, employers are looking for staff that, more often than not, hold college degrees and possess verbal, mathematical, technical, and interpersonal skills. Companies who are unable to find qualified candidates must agree to train employees on basic skills or partner with a community college or university that will offer basic courses for their staff.

Employment Policies, Practices, and Procedures

<u>On-Boarding</u>
On-boarding, also known as *organizational socialization*, is the process by which new hires obtain the knowledge, skills, and behaviors they need in order to become valued, productive contributors to the company. The success of on-boarding programs is crucial because new employees decide whether or not to stay with an organization during their first six months of work. Therefore, it is important for companies to make an effort to ensure that new employees feel supported and get adjusted to the social and performance aspects of their new roles quickly.

On-boarding can begin by having an employee's new managers and teammates reach out to them via email to welcome them even prior to their formal start date with the company. On the first day at work, the manager can introduce the new hire to the team member who will serve as their "buddy," to whom they can feel free to go to with any questions or concerns. Taking the new hire out of the office for a welcome lunch on the first day with a couple of staff members is always a nice gesture, as well as ensuring they have lunch partners for the first couple of weeks on the job.

Other aspects of successful on-boarding programs involve the new hire's manager scheduling meet-and-greet appointments to learn more about the roles that each teammate in the department plays and how the new hire will interact with them. These types of meetings can also be scheduled with individuals throughout the company who have key relationships with the department, such as members of IT, Marketing, Human Resources, etc. Additionally, providing the new hire with an on-boarding schedule that involves various team members who will train on various processes and applications can be helpful. It is also important for the manager to meet with the new hire to discuss their performance and development plans for the first three months, to provide clear expectations. Finally, to help a new hire build contacts throughout the company, it is imperative to get them involved in a cross-functional project.

There is no set time limit for on-boarding programs, but at some companies, these programs can last throughout an employee's first year.

Orientation

Orientation is part of the administrative, transactional aspect of the overall on-boarding process, focused on having employees complete the following types of tasks within their first couple of days of employment:

- Have their photograph taken to create their corporate ID badge
- Take a tour of the building in which they will be working on a daily basis
- Complete I-9 verification
- Register for health care and other company benefits
- Participate in training on the company's time entry system
- Gain an understanding of the payroll process
- Review the company's history, vision, and mission, along with key policies and procedures
- Receive and sign off on a copy of their formal job description

It is also important to note that the workspace for new hires is often set up in advance with the necessary office supplies and a welcome note or card to ensure as smooth of a transition as possible.

Retention

After taking the necessary time to recruit the right employees, it is important for companies to work to retain them. Employee turnover has high costs associated with it—lost time and lost productivity. There are many different ways that companies attempt to retain staff, and not one method works for all employees. For example, some employers feel that offering a competitive benefits package that includes health care, a retirement program, and life insurance is the best way to retain employees. However, sometimes low or no cost options that improve employees' work/life balance, such as flextime, telecommuting, and allowing employees to wear jeans to work every day (unless they are attending customer-facing meetings) are the best way to go. In addition, staff can be grateful for, and tend to stay longer at, workplaces that provide perks that are meaningful to them, such as on-site childcare, tuition reimbursement, dry cleaning pickup, and free doughnuts on Fridays.

Employers can stay in touch with how their employees are feeling about the work environment by conducting what is known as *stay interviews*. During these interviews, topics including why employees came to work for the employer, why the employees have stayed at the employer, what would make the employees consider leaving, and what the employees would want to see changed are discussed. This allows management to make necessary improvements before they find themselves conducting exit interviews.

Finally, in a workplace that is serious about retention, open communication between management and employees about the company's mission and future goals is key. It is also important for management to show concern for employees' continued development and to promote from within when possible.

Employer Marketing and Branding Techniques

A strong company brand is essential to remaining competitive within the workplace and to attracting the most valuable employees. Companies need these employees to increase productivity and grow with the company's interests. Selling the employer's brand and company can be an important tool in attracting potential candidates as well as retaining current employees.

A company's brand is determined by perceptions from employees (both current and former), clients, and customers. It covers all elements of the company, including overall job experience and management practices. For example, a company may be known for providing opportunities for advancement to employees, which in turn enhances its corporate brand. However, a different organization may have a reputation for making staff consistently work long hours in a stressful environment in order to reach their next promotion opportunity, which results in high turnover of existing employees and discourages candidates from applying there.

In order to stand out from the competition, branding and marketing a company to applicants has become essential. The goal is to position the company as an "employer of choice" to candidates by creating an image of what it will be like for them to work there. This is very similar to how they market the products and services that they sell (remaining aligned with the vision, mission, and values).

Some of the techniques that companies employ to create an effective brand image include the following:

- Asking current employees to serve as brand ambassadors and blog or tweet about the company on social media sites, such as LinkedIn, Facebook, and Twitter

- Creating employer profile pages on online job sites

- Creating a company elevator pitch that is simple for employees to use when asked about the company

- Promoting success stories, such as the story of an intern who was promoted through the ranks to a current day team leader

Negotiation Skills and Techniques

Employment Offers and Negotiations
A company goes through the process of analyzing application forms, prescreening, inviting selected candidates to participate in on-site interviews, and conducting any necessary selection tests and background investigations. Then a contingent job offer is made to the top-rated candidate. This is a conditional job offer and may depend on verification of the individual's identity and right to work (under the Immigration Reform and Control Act) and/or the pending results of a medical exam (if it is proven to be consistent with business necessity and is job related).

The next step in the hiring process is extending an employment offer to the top candidate. This is communicated formally through an offer letter. Because time is of the essence, the offer letter is often sent electronically. A job offer can also be extended over the telephone, which is then followed up with a formal offer letter mailed to the candidate. The following items are typically communicated within the offer letter:

- Basic position information: job title, responsibilities, and reporting structure
- Salary information (including guaranteed or discretionary bonuses and signing bonus, if applicable)
- Information about any deferred compensation (i.e., stock option programs)
- Benefits information (i.e., health insurance, short- and long-term disability insurance, retirement plans, etc.)
- Clauses referencing non-compete agreements
- Acceptance details and deadline

An employment-at-will situation is always presumed if there is no written employment contract.

A candidate will frequently reach out to a prospective employer in an attempt to negotiate some terms of the employment offer, such as salary or vacation time. If the employer does not have room to increase the candidate's base salary, a discussion can take place about other perks that the employer may be willing to offer, such as a set number of work-at-home days per month, additional time off during the Christmas holiday or another typical period of down time, use of a company car, relocation assistance (if applicable), or a signing bonus.

If an employer knows there is room to negotiate a base salary with a candidate, it is important for the employer not to offer the highest possible base salary amount in the offer letter, so there is still room to negotiate. Ultimately, it is imperative that the employer be upfront and honest with a candidate about what is possible in terms of negotiation, to stress the value of the corporate benefits that the candidate would receive, and to openly discuss if there is room for growth in the role itself or in other opportunities within the company over time. These can all be convincing reasons for a candidate who is on the fence to choose to accept the employment offer.

It is also important for an employer to know when it is time to stop negotiations with a candidate. Offering a significantly higher salary than what was initially planned to a candidate risks throwing off the internal pay equity of a team and also reducing morale if the other employees find out.

The offer letter is placed in the candidate's personnel file after they have accepted the position and returned a signed hard copy.

Practice Questions

1. Which of the following activities is an example of downsizing?
    a. Implementing a hiring freeze.
    b. Reducing the number of hierarchical levels.
    c. Utilizing contingent workers to fill in.
    d. Outsourcing work to an external service provider.

2. A detailed description of specific qualifications, experience, or education that is needed to perform tasks is known as which of the following?
    a. Job description
    b. Job specification
    c. Job competency
    d. Job analysis

3. A detailed list of broad skills or traits needed for a position is known as which of the following?
    a. Job analysis
    b. Job description
    c. Job competency
    d. Job specification

4. Tasks and responsibilities that are fundamental to a specific position are known as which of the following?
    a. Job competencies
    b. Marginal job functions
    c. Job specifications
    d. Essential job functions

5. Which type of interview occurs when an interviewer has guided conversations with applicants that involve broad questions and new questions that come about from the discussions that take place?
    a. Semi-structured
    b. Structured
    c. Non-directive
    d. Unstructured

6. Which type of interview utilizes questions that are developed from an applicant's answers to previous questions?
    a. Unstructured
    b. Nondirective
    c. Semi-structured
    d. Structured

7. Which of the following pre-employment activities can assist companies with protecting themselves from lawsuits or damage to their reputation?
    a. Interviewing
    b. Selection tests
    c. Reference and background checks
    d. Employment agreements

8. Which of the following items is inferred from an employer's actions or conduct?
   a. Express contract
   b. Employment-at-will
   c. Golden parachute clause
   d. Implied contract

9. Which of the following employers is required to have an affirmative action plan in place?
   a. An employer who has sixty employees and $55,000 in federal contracts
   b. An employer with $40,000 in federal contracts
   c. An employer with fifty-five employees
   d. An employer who is part of the Department of Transportation

10. Which of the following is the major element of an affirmative action plan that examines the internal and external population of women and minorities to determine their theoretical opportunity for employment?
   a. Utilization analysis
   b. Availability analysis
   c. Job group analysis
   d. Organizational profile

11. Which of the following is the major element of an affirmative action plan that compares the availability of women and minorities to their current representation within each job group at the company?
   a. Availability analysis
   b. Job group analysis
   c. Utilization analysis
   d. Organizational profile

12. Under federal guidelines, under what length of time is an employer required to keep employment applications and resumes?
   a. Three years
   b. One year
   c. Three years after creation or following the hire/no hire decision (whichever date is later)
   d. One year after creation or following the hire/no hire decision (whichever date is later)

13. Under federal guidelines, under what length of time is an employer required to keep employee records associated with employment benefits?
   a. Six years
   b. Three years
   c. Five years
   d. One year

14. Under federal guidelines, under what length of time is an employer required to keep employee records associated with family medical leave?
   a. One year
   b. Three years
   c. Five years
   d. Two years

15. Which of the following statements is true regarding Title VII of the Civil Rights Act of 1964?
    a. Equal working conditions must be provided to all employees.
    b. Discrimination against sexual orientation and race is prohibited.
    c. All employees must be provided with an equal opportunity to participate in training.
    d. Sexual harassment training must be provided to all employees.

16. Which of the following would MOST likely be considered an essential job function?
    a. An employee participates in an ongoing employee committee assignment as time permits.
    b. An employee devotes approximately 8 percent of her time to making cold calls to obtain new business.
    c. An employee delegates preparation of a template to their administrative support.
    d. An employee regularly reviews engineering design documents.

17. Which of the following situations would more than likely warrant a written employment contract?
    a. An employee who is a salesperson
    b. A full-time telecommuting employee
    c. An employee who is a department manager
    d. An employee who is a graphic artist

18. Before extending a contingent offer of employment, an employer should obtain which of the following?
    a. Medical records and completion of a physical examination
    b. Signed consent from the candidate to check work references
    c. Verbal consent from the candidate to check work references
    d. Polygraph test

19. Which of the following is an exception to Title VII of the Civil Rights Act of 1964?
    a. An employer with only twenty employees
    b. A new seniority system that is being implemented at a workplace
    c. A bona fide occupational qualification
    d. A work-related requirement that is not truly legitimate

20. The Americans with Disabilities Act applies to which of the following?
    a. An employer with fifty or more employees
    b. All employers regardless of their size
    c. Employers who have at least $50,000 in federal contracts
    d. An employer with fifteen or more employees

21. Which of the following statements is true under the Americans with Disabilities Act?
    a. An employer does not need to make an accommodation for a disabled employee if doing so will result in an undue hardship.
    b. Employers are required to establish affirmative action plans for the disabled.
    c. Drug users who are rehabilitated are excluded by this law.
    d. Pre-employment medical exams may be required before extending a job offer.

22. The Americans with Disabilities Act does not provide protection for which of the following employees?

   a. An employee who is diagnosed with AIDS

   b. An employee who is found using illegal drugs

   c. An employee who suffers from epilepsy

   d. An employee who has serious psychological problems

23. Under the Pregnancy Discrimination Act of 1978, which of the following statements is TRUE?

   a. An employer can refuse to provide a pregnant woman with reasonable accommodation if she is unable to do her job and approaches her manager to that effect.

   b. An employer can ask a pregnant interview candidate when she is due and how much time she will plan to be off of work after the baby arrives.

   c. An employer must give a woman a comparable position to the one that she held prior to her maternity leave (if the company does so with employees on short-term disability).

   d. An employer can discriminate against a female employee who has undergone an abortion if this act is against their personal, religious convictions.

24. A company must set a placement goal when which of the following situations occurs?

   a. Minorities and women are assigned to jobs that are not challenging at the company.

   b. The company experiences adverse impact in its hiring practices.

   c. The company is unable to determine its applicants' ethnicity.

   d. The company is found to employ a smaller number of minorities and women than is indicated by their availability.

25. In which of the following examples is adverse impact demonstrated?

   a. Sixty male candidates were interviewed and thirty were hired. Forty female candidates applied and ten were hired.

   b. Four hundred white candidates applied and two hundred were hired. Two hundred Hispanic candidates applied and one hundred were hired.

   c. Sixty male candidates were interviewed and thirty were hired. Thirty female candidates applied and eighteen were hired.

   d. Four hundred white candidates applied and two hundred were hired. One hundred Hispanic candidates applied and forty-five were hired.

26. Internal employees are able to indicate their interest in an open job position through which of the following?

   a. Succession planning

   b. Job posting

   c. Job analysis

   d. Skill inventory

27. Which of the following scenarios is a violation of the Immigration Reform and Control Act?

   a. A new hire, who is a foreign-looking American citizen, is asked to complete an I-9 form

   b. A job applicant, who is from another country, is asked if he has a legal right to work in the United States

   c. An Asian national, who is hired for an IT position, has a passport but not a right-to-work authorization

   d. A company that does not have an established affirmative action plan

28. Which of the following is held responsible for verifying that a new hire is eligible to work in the United States?
    a. The Social Security Administration
    b. The employee
    c. The U.S. Citizenship and Immigration Services
    d. The employer

29. An employee's identity and right to work can be verified by which of the following documents?
    a. U.S. passport
    b. Social security card
    c. Driver's license
    d. Voter's registration card

30. Which of the following court cases established the "reasonable person" standard for hostile environment sexual harassment?
    a. Faragher vs. City of Boca Raton
    b. Harris vs. Forklift Systems, Inc.
    c. Meritor Savings Bank vs. Vinson
    d. Oncale vs. Sundowner Offshore Service, Inc.

31. Which of the following situations is an example of disparate treatment?
    a. Height and weight restrictions are put in place for all security guards.
    b. All employees at a company are required to take an intelligence test.
    c. Employees who belong to a protected class are subject to stricter attendance rules.
    d. A staffing practice that was neutral when implemented results in discrimination against a protected group.

32. A company received two hundred applicants from an Internet job posting, twenty-five of which were from minority applicants. What is the yield ratio of minority applicants to total applicants?
    a. 25 percent
    b. 4 percent
    c. 87.5 percent
    d. 12.5 percent

33. A company received two hundred applicants from an Internet job posting, twenty-five of which were from minority applicants. It interviewed seventy-five qualified applicants, fifteen of which were minority applicants. What is the yield ratio of qualified applicants to total applicants?
    a. 37.5 percent
    b. 75 percent
    c. 2.67 percent
    d. 62.5 percent

34. Which of the following measures how well a selection tool's subject matter covers the knowledge, skills, and abilities that are required by a specific job?
    a. Construct validity
    b. Content validity
    c. Predictive validity
    d. Concurrent validity

35. Which of the following selection tests is used to measure a candidate's mental abilities, such as verbal and mathematical ability?
    a. Performance
    b. Psychological
    c. Cognitive
    d. Motor

36. Which of the following interview techniques involves asking candidates to use specific examples to describe how they have handled a problem or performed a task in a past work situation?
    a. Panel
    b. Situational
    c. Stress
    d. Behavioral

37. Which of the following statements is TRUE regarding severance packages?
    a. Severance packages are not required by law.
    b. Severance pay increases an employer's contributions to unemployment tax.
    c. Receipt of severance pay guarantees a former employee will not file a lawsuit against the employer.
    d. Severance pay guarantees that an employee will receive other benefits, such as the continuation of health care coverage or outplacement services.

Answer Explanations

1. A: Implementing a hiring freeze is an activity that is an example of downsizing. Reducing the number of hierarchical levels, Choice *B*, is an example of corporate restructuring. Utilizing contingent workers to fill in (Choice *C*) and outsourcing work to an external service provider (Choice *D*) are examples of workforce expansion.

2. B: Job specification is a detailed description of specific qualifications, experience, or education that is needed to perform tasks. Choice *A*, job description, is a detailed breakdown of specific tasks, skills, and knowledge required for a position. Job competency, Choice *C*, is a detailed list of broad skills or traits needed for a position. Finally, job analysis, Choice *D*, is a way of gathering and analyzing information systemically about the context, content, and human resource requirements of jobs within an organization.

3. C: Job competency is a detailed list of broad skills or traits needed for a position. Job analysis, Choice *A*, is a way of gathering and analyzing information systemically about the context, content, and human resource requirements of jobs within an organization. Job description, Choice *B*, is a detailed breakdown of specific tasks, skills and knowledge required for a position. Finally, job specification, Choice *D*, is a detailed description of specific qualifications, experience, or education that is needed to perform tasks.

4. D: Essential job functions are tasks and responsibilities that are fundamental to a specific position. Job competencies, Choice *A*, are detailed lists of broad skills or traits needed for positions. Marginal job functions, Choice *B*, are duties that are ancillary or incidental to the nature or purpose of a job. Finally, job specifications, Choice *C*, are detailed descriptions of specific qualifications, experience, or education that is needed to perform tasks.

5. A: A semi-structured interview occurs when an interviewer has guided conversations with applicants that involve broad questions and new questions that come about from the discussions that take place. A structured interview, Choice *B*, is controlled by the interviewer, who has a list of specific, job-related questions prepared prior to the start of the interview. The same questions are asked of all applicants. A non-directive interview, Choice *C*, utilizes questions that are developed from an applicant's answers to previous questions. Finally, Choice *D*, an unstructured interview, takes place when an interviewer improvises and asks applicants questions that were not prepared prior to the start of the interview.

6. B: A non-directive interview utilizes questions that are developed from an applicant's answers to previous questions. An unstructured interview, Choice *A*, takes place when an interviewer improvises and asks applicants questions that were not prepared prior to the start of the interview. A semi-structured interview, Choice *C*, occurs when an interviewer has guided conversations with applicants that involve broad questions and new questions that come about from the discussions that take place. Finally, a structured interview, Choice *D*, is controlled by the interviewer, who has a list of specific, job-related questions prepared prior to the start of the interview. The same questions are asked of all applicants.

7. C: Reference and background checks are pre-employment activities that can assist companies with protecting themselves from lawsuits or damage to their reputation (for example, in the event of negligent hiring claims). Interviewing candidates, Choice *A*, may not reveal all pertinent information. Choices *B* and *D*, selection tests and employment agreements, do not provide information that would protect the company's interests.

8. D: An implied contract is inferred from an employer's actions or conduct. An express contract, Choice A, is based on an employer's written or oral words. Employment-at-will, Choice B, is a common-law doctrine that states employers have the right to hire, promote, demote, or fire whomever they choose, provided there is not a law or contract in place to the contrary. Under this doctrine, employees are also free to leave an employer whenever they choose to seek other employment. Finally, a golden parachute clause, Choice C, is an agreement between an employer and an executive that guarantees the executive the right to certain benefits if their employment is terminated.

9. A: Employers with fifty or more employees and $50,000 in federal contracts are required to have affirmative action plans in place, as well as employers who are a member of the federal banking system and employers who issue, sell, or redeem U.S. Savings Bonds.

10. B: An availability analysis is the major element of an affirmative action plan that examines the internal and external population of women and minorities to determine their theoretical opportunity for employment. A utilization analysis, Choice A, compares the availability of women and minorities to their current representation within each job group at the company. A job group analysis, Choice C, is a list of all titles that comprise each job group. Jobs are grouped according to whether they have similar content, responsibilities, compensation, and opportunities for advancement. Choice D, an organizational profile, is a snapshot of an organization and organizes the key components and competitions within that organization.

11. C: A utilization analysis is the major element of an affirmative action plan that compares the availability of women and minorities to their current representation within each job group at the company. An availability analysis, Choice A, examines the internal and external population of women and minorities to determine their theoretical opportunity for employment. A job group analysis, Choice B, is a list of all titles that comprise each job group. Jobs are grouped according to whether they have similar content, responsibilities, wage rates, and opportunities for advancement. Finally, an organizational profile, Choice D, depicts the organization's staffing patterns to determine if any barriers exist to equal opportunity employment.

12. D: Under federal guidelines, an employer is required to keep employment applications and resumes for one year after creation or following the hire/no hire decision (whichever date is later).

13. A: Under federal guidelines, an employer is required to keep records associated with employment benefits for a period of six years.

14. B: Under federal guidelines, an employer is required to keep records associated with family medical leave for a period of three years.

15. B: Title VII of the Civil Rights Act of 1964 prohibits discrimination against sexual orientation and race.

16. D: When an employee regularly reviews engineering design documents, this would most likely be considered an essential job function.

17. A: An employee who is a salesperson would more than likely warrant a written employment contract to outline information, such as salary (including guaranteed or discretionary bonuses), commission structure and payment processes, and clauses referencing non-compete agreements.

18. B: An employer should obtain signed consent from the candidate to check work references before extending a contingent offer of employment. This is due to the fact that many companies have been sued by job applicants who have discovered that they have been given poor references. Physical examinations cannot be required by an employer until after a job offer has been made. Finally, polygraph tests cannot be required by the majority of employers.

19. C: A bona fide occupational qualification is an exception to Title VII of the Civil Rights Act of 1964. This act applies to most employers with fifteen or more employees. A new seniority system implement in the workplace and work-related requirements that are not truly legitimate are not exceptions to Title VII of the Civil Rights Act of 1964.

20. D: The Americans with Disabilities Act applies to employers with fifteen or more employees. The number of value of federal contracts an employer has is irrelevant.

21. A: Under the Americans with Disabilities Act, an employer does not need to make an accommodation for a disabled employee if doing so will result in an undue hardship. Employers are not required to establish affirmative action plans for the disabled (but may choose to do so). This law does not exclude rehabilitated drug users. Pre-employment medical exams cannot be required before extending a job offer.

22. B: The Americans with Disabilities Act does not provide protection for an employee who is found to be using illegal drugs. Employees who are diagnosed with AIDS, those who suffer from epilepsy, and those with serious psychological problems are protected under this act.

23. C: Under the Pregnancy Discrimination Act of 1978, an employer must give a woman a comparable position to the one that she held prior to her maternity leave (if the company does so with employees on short-term disability).

24. D: A company must set a placement goal when it is found to employ fewer minorities and women than is indicated by their availability. This is known as underutilization.

25. A: Adverse impact is demonstrated in the example where sixty male candidates were interviewed and thirty were hired (50 percent), and forty female candidates applied and ten were hired (25 percent). 80% of 50 = 40. Therefore, female candidates must be hired at a selection rate of 40 percent (and instead, they are only being hired at a selection rate of 25 percent).

26. B: Internal employees are able to indicate their interest in an open job position through job postings. Succession planning, job analysis, and skill inventory are other types of human resource activities and have nothing to do with an employee stating their interest in an open job position.

27. C: An Asian national who is hired for an IT position with a passport but without having a right-to-work authorization is a violation of the Immigration Reform and Control Act. Under this act, both identity and right-to-work in the U.S. have to be verified. Documents that can accomplish these tasks include a U.S. passport and an I-9 form.

28. D: The employer is held responsible for verifying that a new hire is eligible to work in the United States. Verification is not the responsibility of the Social Security Administration, the employee, or the U.S. Citizenship and Immigration Services.

29. A: A U.S. passport is the only document that can verify both an employee's identity and right to work. Choices *B*, *C*, and *D*, a social security card, driver's license, or voter's registration card, do not provide enough proof of identity or authorization to work in the United States.

30. B: Harris vs. Forklift Systems, Inc. is the court case that established the "reasonable person" standard for hostile environment sexual harassment. Faragher vs. City of Boca Raton is the court case that stated that employers can be held liable for supervisory harassment that results in an adverse employment action. Meritor Savings Bank vs. Vinson is the court case that held that sexual harassment violates Title VII. Finally, Oncale vs. Sundowner Offshore Service, Inc. is the court case that ruled that same-gender sexual harassment is actionable.

31. C: Employees who belong to a protected class and are subject to stricter attendance rules is an example of disparate treatment because they are being held to a different standard than the rest of the employee population. Placing height and weight restrictions on security guards, Choice A, requiring employees to take an intelligence test, Choice B, and employers who were neutral when implementing results in discrimination against a protected group, Choice D, are not examples of disparate treatment.

32. D: The yield ratio of minority applicants to total applicants in this example is 12.5 percent, which is calculated by dividing the number of minority applicants by the number of total applicants $\frac{25}{200} \times 100 = 12.5\%$.

33. A: The yield ratio of qualified applicants to total applicants in this example is 37.5 percent, which is calculated by dividing the number of qualified applicants by the number of total applicants ($\frac{75}{200} \times 100 = 37.5\%$). The number of minorities who applied is irrelevant for this example.

34. B: Content validity measures how well a selection tool's subject matter covers the knowledge, skills, and abilities that are required for a specific job. Construct validity, Choice A, determines if a screening tool effectively tests and measures the characteristic it claims to measure and that the characteristic in question is important for successful performance on the job. Predictive validity, Choice C, is a measure of whether an individual will possess the required skills, knowledge, or behavioral traits in the future. Finally, concurrent validity, Choice D, determines if an individual currently possesses a required skill, knowledge, or behavioral trait.

35. C: Cognitive selection tests are used to measure a candidate's mental abilities, such as verbal and mathematical ability. Performance selection tests, Choice A, are designed to have a candidate complete a simulated task that is part of the target job for which they are applying. Psychological selection tests, Choice B, are used to explore candidates' personalities to determine if they are the right fit for open positions in certain situations. Finally, motor selection tests, Choice D, are used to assess the muscular movement, strength, endurance, range of motion, posture, and cardiovascular fitness of candidates for roles that require a high level of physical activity.

36. D: Behavioral interviews ask candidates to use specific examples to describe how they have handled a problem or performed a task in a past work situation. Panel interviews, Choice A, are conducted by a group of individuals from the organization that may consist of managers, Human Resources representatives, and other future team members in order to better evaluate whether or not a candidate is suitable. Situational interviews, Choice B, relate more to hypothetical situations that may take place in the future. Finally, stress interviews, Choice C, are used to see how candidates react to unusual circumstances under pressure.

37. A: Severance pay is not required by law. Receipt of severance pay does not guarantee that a former employee will not file a lawsuit against the employer. Severance pay does not increase an employer's contributions to unemployment tax. Finally, severance pay does not guarantee that an employee will receive other benefits, such as the continuation of health care coverage or outplacement services.

Human Resource Development

Human resource development (HRD) is the area of human resource management that deals with employee training and development. It includes initial training programs for new hires; ongoing learning opportunities for existing employees to develop their knowledge, skills, and abilities; performance management; career development; and succession planning. All of these aspects are done in an effort to improve the overall effectiveness of individuals, groups, and the organization as a whole.

Federal Laws and Regulations

Copyright Act of 1976

The Copyright Act of 1976 is the foundational law in the United States regarding property ownership of film, radio, musical and dramatic works, literary and pictorial works, and architectural structures. Superseding local and state copyright laws, the statute establishes a standardized and universally applied measure to the country's major social and technological transformations in media. Hitherto the act, there were deficient authorship protections that had the capacity to safeguard creative works and lawfully secure remunerative rewards. Written with a broad intent, the landmark legislation is applicable to "original works of authorship fixed in any tangible medium of expression."

In order to lawfully reproduce, disseminate, modify, publicly display, or perform copyrighted material, one must hold a copyright over such material – published or unpublished. Stipulated by the Copyright Act of 1976, a copyright lasts for the duration of the author's life, plus an additional seventy years after his or her death. However, the law incorporates a policy of "fair use." Fair use enumerates some instances in which a person may use copyrighted material.

Fair Use

The Copyright Act of 1976 specifies instances in which protected material can be used without threat of infringement. These selective requirements fall into the jurisdiction of "fair use." The first qualification is the intended purpose of the work. Is it intended for commercial gain or for non-profit education? Secondly, fair use is determined by the nature or type of work in question. Thirdly, the amount or proportion of the copyrighted work is evaluated. Lastly, the potential variation in market value of copyrighted material is determined. Educational purposes, research, criticism, scholarship, comment, teaching, or news reporting are the categories specifically noted that would determine the applicability of fair use.

Public Domain

When any of the works delineated have no copyright, they enter into the public domain. In the public domain, any person can use these works freely. In order for a work to not be protected by federal copyright law, it needs to meet one of two conditions. If the federal government publishes the work, it is regarded as public, and therefore is exempt from copyright infringement. Expiration is the only other way an article would lose copyright protection. Works created on or after January 1, 1978, are protected for the life of the author and seventy years after his or her death; anonymous works, works-made-for-hire, and articles are protected for ninety-five years from the date of creation or 120 years after being published. Works-made-for-hire includes works made by employees or works that are specially ordered or commissioned.

Title 17

Title 17 is a United States copyright law enacted in 1947. It applies to authorship of any tangible medium of expression. Specific works that fall under Title 17 are literary works, architectural works, musical recordings, pictures and graphics, choreographic works, musical works, motion pictures, and audio works.

U.S. Patent Act
The U.S. Patent Act expressly prohibits the unauthorized use, sale, reproduction, or distribution of the product without the consent of the patent holder. The legislation's broad composition is designed to preserve and protect the property of inventors. Furthermore, one of two conditions must be met in order for protections to be granted by the act to apply: the invention in question must be created in the United States or the invention must be imported into the country. Although the law explains several prohibitions regarding the unsanctioned use, sale, reproduction, or distribution of an invention, it does not specify any legal recourse in the event of infringement of a particular patent.

Patent Types
There are three types of patents in the United States: utility, design, and plant. The most common type of patent is a utility patent. A utility patent involves anything technological, mechanical, chemical, pharmaceutical, or software-related. Utility patents are valid for twenty years after the date the patent is filed. In order to obtain a utility patent, one must provide a written and meticulously detailed description of the product. The second type of patent is a design patent. These patents are valid for fourteen years after the date they are filed. Unique to the United States, this patent comprises ornamental design –specifically, the way a product looks (aesthetics) and how it actually works. For instance, when applying for a design patent for a bookcase, the inventor must exhibit how it is assembled, how much weight it can withstand, and the size screws that must be used to give it requisite support. A plant patent can be filed for an asexually reproducible plant discovered in a cultivated area. These patents last for twenty years after the date they are filed. Plant patents are the least common type of patent.

Trademark Act
The Trademark Act was created to provide for the protection and registration of trademarks and service marks.

Title VII
Title VII is a federal law within the Civil Rights Act of 1964. It stipulates that no person shall be discriminated against on the basis of sex, race, color, national origin, and religion. Although Title VII is a federal law, it applies to state and local governments as well. Moreover, the law applies to private and public colleges and universities, private sector employment, and labor unions. Under this law, all employees are guaranteed equal access to career development and training.

Americans with Disabilities Act
The Americans with Disabilities Act (ADA) is a federal law that outlaws discrimination based on disability. The ADA precludes discrimination based on race, sex, national origin, and religion. Moreover, the law requires that employers provide reasonable accommodations to employees who have a disability. For instance, this could require employers to build a wheelchair accessible ramp for disabled employers to enter and leave the building. Also, the ADA stipulates that public spaces be accessible for disabled persons. Under this law, all employees are guaranteed equal access to career development and training.

Additionally, all employees are also guaranteed equal access to career development and training under the Age Discrimination in Employment Act (ADEA) and the Uniformed Services Employment and Reemployment Rights Act (USERRA).

ADDIE Model

The most commonly used framework that organizations and training developers use to enhance human resource development programs is the ADDIE model. Each step in the multi-dimensional and adaptable ADDIE model is intended to bolster programs that bolster systems of personal development and training. As an acronym, each step characterizes a different phase: *A* denotes the Analysis phase, *D* denotes Design, *D* denotes Development, *I* denotes Implementation, and *E* denotes Evaluation. The ADDIE model is not limited to strictly training programs and is widely accepted by educators, instructional designers, industry leaders, and the U.S. Armed Forces. ADDIE is noted for being highly applicable to any project and for its flexibility in practice.

The initial phase of ADDIE is analysis wherein the course and primary learning objectives are evaluated and determined. The trainees' potential and aptitude for the subject are assessed and determined, along with any significant learning limitations. The timeline for project completion is also determined during this initial phase.

The second phase in the ADDIE model is the design phase where the principal architecture of the training course is constructed. Aside from just learning objectives, relevant subject matter is gathered and determined while exercises are planned. After these are considered, a lesson plan must be carefully fashioned that synthesizes the objectives of the course and the specific abilities or constraints of the subject.

The third phase in the ADDIE model is the development phase. After the design of the course is constructed, its methodological efficacy needs to be tested. Creating the content that is drafted in the previous phase performs this test. Development encompasses creating and distributing tangible tools or courseware for successfully engaging the program. For instance, graphics, handouts, or any other learning technologies would be circulated.

The fourth phase in the ADDIE model is the implementation phase. The implementation phase consists of establishing a procedure for training both facilitators and learners. Facilitators should continuously amend the course in order to maximize efficiency. After extensive analysis, the course should be amended and redesigned accordingly. For learners, this phase embodies preparation and gaining increasing familiarity with the course and content. In addition, learners should also develop an acute knowledge of the course materials and tools.

The fifth phase of the ADDIE model is the evaluation phase. Although the course is constantly being evaluated, this is a designated phase that empirically studies the efficiency and productivity of the course and material. Some of the questions that may be asked include: Were the course's primary objectives met? Were the learners' specified goals achieved? What (if any) were the most arduous aspects of the course or its materials, and how could any problems be appropriately addressed?

Needs Assessment

A training needs assessment is conducted to determine whether a training program will be an adequate solution to correct a performance issue. A training program might be an appropriate solution when poor performance is due to an employee's lack of knowledge or skills, legislation requiring new knowledge or skills, higher performance standards, new technology, or placement in new jobs. On the flip side, the creation and implementation of a training program will not be effective in resolving poor performance that results from a recruiting, selection, or compensation issue, failure to provide proper coaching and feedback to an employee, problems with an employee's physical work environment, or a lack of employee motivation. These particular issues are best addressed through a non-training intervention, such as job redesign, improved communication and employee feedback, and goal-setting.

A thorough training needs assessment involves an organizational analysis, a task analysis, and a learner analysis. The organizational analysis is conducted to ensure that the company is on board with the training initiative and will be supportive. The goal is to ensure that the training is aligned with the overall business strategy, supported by the necessary stakeholders, and that available resources are committed to the training program. Data is gathered for this analysis from holding focus groups of mid-level and senior-level managers, since they are the individuals who make decisions regarding training budget allocations and strategic planning. The organizational analysis is performed first, as there is no reason to move forward with the task and learner analyses if low interest or support for the training is found.

It is important to note that the task analysis and learner analysis can be completed simultaneously. The task analysis focuses on the specific tasks employees must complete to successfully perform their jobs. Data is gathered through interviews with or surveys of individuals, such as managers, top-performing employees, or subject matter experts (SMEs), who have direct knowledge of the work tasks and the associated, expected level of performance. The overall goal of a task analysis is to define what good performance looks like in the jobs that are chosen to be analyzed. A list of tasks that are performed in each of the jobs that are being analyzed is created. The individuals being interviewed/surveyed are asked to rate the frequency with which the tasks are completed, the importance each task has to the overall work, and the difficulty of each task. The results from this analysis are used to identify performance gaps in either desired or actual employee performance and to then decide if training can be used to address those gaps. If the decision is to move forward with a training program intervention, then the information from this analysis can also be used in the training design process.

The learner analysis identifies if the employees' performance issues are occurring due to a lack of knowledge, skills, and abilities, or due to some other issue, such as a lack of motivation or insufficient tools. During this analysis, it is important to determine if the learners are cognitively and physically able to complete their assigned tasks. Moreover, it is crucial to ascertain if the learners understand the level of performance that is expected of them and to determine if they are indeed receiving accurate and timely feedback regarding their performance. Additionally, the learner analysis identifies which employees are in need of the training and determine their readiness for training. Data is gathered from managers, learners, and document reviews, such as personnel records and previous training records.

Data gathering methods that are used during a training needs assessment include: observation, questionnaires (surveys), interviews, focus groups, and document reviews. Each method has its pros and cons, and some methods may be more realistic to use than others considering time and resources constraints. It can also be helpful to collect data using multiple methods, such as using a questionnaire (survey) format that is followed by a one-on-one interview to clarify and expand upon responses.

Management personnel in some organizations do not want to take the time to conduct a formal training needs assessment. However, the information gathered during the training needs assessment will ultimately influence how a training program is designed, developed, implemented, and evaluated. Therefore, although there can be challenges associated with performing a training needs assessment, such as time constraints and lack of management support, when the proper information is not gathered, a training program may not be properly designed to address the true performance issue at hand.

Implementing Employee Training Programs

Learning Techniques
Organizations often employ several methods when attempting to teach new knowledge, capacities, or skills. A few of the principal methods instructors use to train subjects are lectures, group discussions, case studies, and demonstrations. A lecture is the act of an educator verbally articulating how to perform a task or a branch of knowledge. Educators plan a group discussion when they want students to work cooperatively. These permit students to engage collectively, verbalize key concepts, and improve aptitudes for listening and comprehension. Case studies give students the opportunity to situate themselves into real world, tangible scenarios. This brand of training allows students to think critically about how they would approach problem solving. A demonstration is a type of training that presents students with the opportunity to observe an educator in the act of performing a task.

Learning Styles
When considering a particular avenue of training, it is important to determine which will create an experience that will be conducive to learning. It is important to create in-class activities that will appeal to the various learning styles: visual, auditory, and kinesthetic. Visual learners prefer to associate information with images (e.g., watching videos or looking at PowerPoint slides) while auditory learners depend on hearing and speaking to learn (e.g., listening to lectures and participating in group discussions). Kinesthetic learners benefit most from participating in physical, hands-on activities (e.g., looking at the inside of an automobile or taking apart some type of model).

The most crucial objective for the educator is not to strictly possess understanding and expertise of the particular subject matter, but to also be able to articulate and impart those skills in an effective manner to others. A useful barometer for evaluating the efficacy of an instructor is to conduct a thorough evaluation of his or her students. If students demonstrate an aptitude for the particular knowledge, ability, or skill being taught, then one can safely assume that the faculties and techniques of the instructor can be considered proficient. Discussion, demonstration, and communication are all equally integral components of training.

Seating Arrangements
Seating arrangements are an important configuration that can severely impact the flow of ideas within a training program.

Theater-style seating reflects a movie theater setting; all seats are facing the same direction. However, there is no room for taking notes or consuming food or beverages. In addition, without adequate space, leaving while a meeting is in progress can be distracting and cumbersome.

Classroom-style seating remedies the problem of the lack of ability to take notes and consume food and drink, but such a close seating arrangement leaves room for distractions.

Herringbone-style seating may be a more effective solution to prevent chatter during a meeting, but the problem of navigating the boardroom is still present.

U-shape-seating style is frequently used when presentations are being given. Allowing presenters to more easily interact and engage audience members. However, since a majority of audience members are not facing the presenter, keeping the focus on the presenter can be difficult.

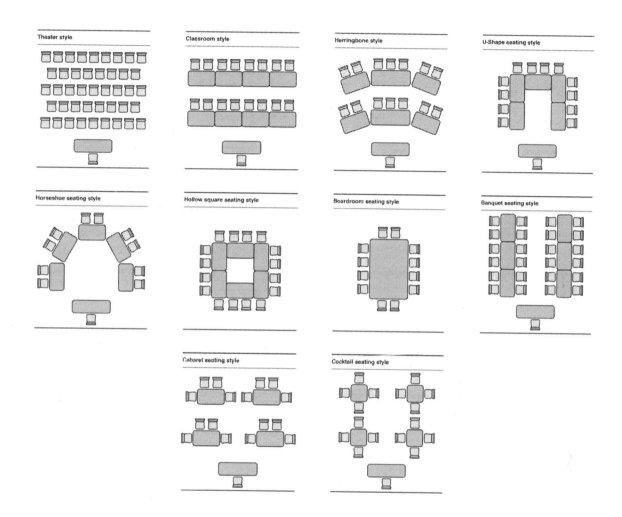

Horseshoe-seating style resembles the U-shape-seating style, but without desks. This allows the audience to focus on the presenters more easily, but without desks, there is inadequate space for audience members to take notes.

Hollow square-seating style is similar to the U-shaped-seating style, but it is fully enclosed on all four sides. This permits all audience members to face each other and for a presenter to fully engage them, but it fails to provide a focal point for a presenter.

Similar to the hollow square seating style, the boardroom-seating style features long tables for audience members to lean on. Permitting audience members to face each other encourages interactions and exchanges. Unfortunately, this arrangement does not allow presenters to engage with and approach the audience.

Banquet-seating style provides circular tables for audience members to lean on and is designed to encourage discussion and dialogue. However, this style places audience members at different tables, which precludes a unified discourse.

Cabaret-seating style is slightly more attractive than banquet-seating style because it leaves an open space at each table as a focal point for a presenter. However, it does not sufficiently address the issue of separate tables.

Cocktail-seating style allows for audience members to move freely and roam as they wish. However, in the absence of desks or tables, there is no room to take notes or consume food or drink.

Pilot Programs
In order for an organization to develop a large-scale project, it must launch a pilot program in order to test the feasibility of the intended project. Also called a feasibility study or an experimental trial, pilot programs are small-scale and should not be of significant cost. Before investing substantial time, financial, or human resources into a project, organizations need to determine its revenue-wielding potential, logistical considerations, and possible planning or structural deficiencies. Pilot programs are tests or trials that sample a small group of people and use empirical analyses to improve strategies.

Types of Training Programs
Harassment Prevention
In order to for an organization to successfully meet its goals, it must preclude any form of harassment from occurring. Aside from moral incentives, there are also major financial incentives for employers preventing harassment of all forms. From burdensome legal costs to potential loss of clients, harassment suits can incur significant costs for an organization. In order to abate the possibility of situations of harassment, employers should design programs in which employees must participate and establish a policy of zero tolerance.

Leadership Skills
Quality leadership skills are essential to any organization, and thus, leadership training is typically provided to mid and upper management. Signs of effective leadership skills are strategic thinking, solving problems as they come, and managing time in the most financially responsible manner. While these skills are essential, there are also more human characteristics that must be mentioned. A successful leader must have the ability to: build confidence within his or her organization, obtain the trust of others, inspire others, and engender a sense of pride and purpose within his or her company.

Computer Skills
In a world of increasing competition where technology has become integral, it is imperative that employers invest in research and technology in order to constantly find cheaper and more efficient ways to increase productivity. In addition, employees should be well trained in the latest technological machinery. The task to remain competitive must lay with employers and employees. While employers must provide the tools, employees need to be proficient in the proper use of those tools in order to be productive.

Talent and Performance Management Programs

Career Development
Career development encompasses six primary stages: assessment, investigation, preparation, commitment, retention, and transition. Career development is an important process when attempting to make a person attractive to prospective employers. During the assessment stage, a person begins to

realize that he or she is unsure about his or her values, weaknesses, interests, and strengths. This stage requires a conscious effort on behalf of the person to begin an exploration process. In the investigation phase, a person begins to search for opportunities that the world of work has to offer. After the investigation stage, a person has acquired knowledge about what best suits him or her and begins preparation. The commitment stage comes after a person recognizes his or her talents, prompting a commitment to a particular job or career. After a person feels most comfortable in his or her career, he or she begins to sharpen his or her skills and become acclimated with his or her industry – this is the retention stage. Lastly, the transition stage forces a person to assess his or her happiness and make connections to a new career (if necessary).

In addition to career development, there are other ways that enable a person to advance his or her career. Other methods include support programs, employee counseling, training workshops, and coaching programs. Support programs, which attempt to remedy personal and utility problems, create channels for employers to assist employees who are not maximizing their potential with training or counseling. Similarly to support programs, employee counseling is an institutional program used by employers to maximize productivity within the organizational structure. Training workshops enable employers and employees to identify particular skills and ensure that they are placed in a position of maximum utility. Coaching workshops place workers under the supervision of a counselor in order to equip them with the tools to solve problems that may be inhibiting their work capacities.

In order to create an environment that allows all workers to maximize their potential in an organizational structure, employers offer programs that are designed to benefit the career development of employees. A few of these methods are evaluating, mentoring, counseling, and coaching. A proper evaluation of the deficiencies, skills, and psychological health of employees is important to identify their strengths and weaknesses, while determining their most efficient roles in the organization. Mentoring programs for employees is a critical component to making sure that they are under guardianship at a professional and emotional level. Counseling in the workplace permits employees to be given additional personal and professional support. Under the supervision of professional counselors, workshops that offer coaching to employees can bolster both organizational and personal health.

Over the course of their careers, individuals often use various methods to enrich their careers. Some of these methods include networking, pursuing supplementary formal education, and attending training workshops. Networking permits individuals to build beneficial connections with people who may be able to help them obtain employment. At networking events, an individual will attempt to speak to as many people as possible to establish relationships. When job searching, individuals may discover that many opportunities require more skills than they possess. To remedy this problem, many people pursue additional education to make them more marketable and attractive to prospective employers. Training workshops are events designated to let individuals discover their skills, allowing them to pursue careers that correspond to them.

Management and Leadership Development
Management and leadership development is a critical component for organizations to invest in. For this practice to be effective, managers must exercise their capacities to establish objectives and means of attainment. Concurrently, management and leadership development is designed to equip the workforce with the requisite tools and skills to compete in a functional organization. The primary purpose of management and leadership development is to provide a holistic approach for individuals, managers, and leadership. Individuals are able to increase their skills and knowledge working within an organizational apparatus. Managers find more efficient ways to execute predetermined objectives.

Leaders improve their ability in a decision-making process that incorporates creative input from the organization's members and accomplishes mutually shared goals.

Succession Planning

Succession planning is the practice of identifying and evaluating specific employees to fill leadership positions within an organization. Once identified, the employees selected need to be trained to fill these capacities. Because of the chronically evolving nature of organizations, succession planning is critical. There are many reasons why positions would open, such as promotions, firings, and retirements.

Dual Career Ladders

A dual career ladder is a specific type of program employed by organizations that allow room for advancement without promoting an individual into a supervisory or managerial role. Dual career ladders can be useful for an employee who may not be interested in a managerial position, and they give employers the latitude to offer valuable employees alternative choices of advancement. Within this paradigm, employees do not need to become supervisors to receive a pay increase.

Managing the Placement of High-Potential Employees

High-potential employees, also known as high-pos, are individuals who fall in the top 10 percent of talent. Many companies struggle to keep high-pos engaged and satisfied in the workplace. Several key practices that organizations can use to manage high-pos include:

- Recognizing the talents these individuals possess
- Including these individuals in more of an ongoing development process
- Providing these employees with qualified mentors
- Making flexible and substantial opportunities available to these individuals, which will allow them to obtain more visibility and responsibility in the company.

Performance Appraisal

Performance appraisal is a process that is integral to maintaining standards that are essential to consistent productivity in an organization. An intricate process, performance appraisal measures and evaluates the quality of work that is performed by employees. It is a barometer by which employees must exceed pre-established benchmarks and simultaneously uphold organizational protocol. Moreover, managers and administrators compare performance appraisal results with other employees and expectations while making rational decisions regarding efficacy and value. From the process, management crafts a compilation of results and data with the intention of performing a cost-benefit analysis. After these analytical methodologies are conducted, management and administrators will enact appropriate changes for improvement.

After a performance appraisal, management will effect these improvements through incentivizing programs. Increasing salaries or rewarding promotions are typically two strategies that are used to reinforce desired behavior. For employees who are found to be less efficient or productive, training or counseling programs are a means of providing underperforming individuals with the tools to improve. In some instances, management will pursue punitive responses to underperformance: demotions, reductions in pay, or termination of employment. Essential to performance appraisal is the establishment of firm standards and procedures for an organization in which underperformance will be quickly rectified. An inflexible organizational infrastructure forces employees to conform to the institution, rather than institutional codes being disregarded and ignored.

Communicational development is a crucial advantage of performance appraisal. A channel of communication is clearly delineated through two principal means: organizational rules and regulations, and explicit managerial examinations. Organizational policies offer nonverbal guidance to employees by consistently challenging them to assimilate to protocol while sustaining maximal productive capacities. After performance appraisals are conducted, managerial expectations can be developed, and solutions to remedy underperformance can be pursued. Any disputes between labor and management can quickly be softened by maintaining stringent channels of communication, where both sides have assigned responsibilities and coordinate to meet shared goals.

Instruments
Some types of performance appraisals are the 360-degree feedback, general appraisal, employee self-assessment appraisal, and the technological/administrative performance appraisal. The 360-degree feedback method is a way for employees to receive feedback about their performance in an anonymous manner from individuals they frequently work in close contact with, such as their managers, peers, direct reports, customers, and suppliers. The employee self-assessment appraisal forces employees to examine their own work, while management conducts a concurrent appraisal. After these are completed, the two are jointly compared. The technological/administrative performance appraisal concentrates on employees who perform technical jobs. The type of work they do, productivity levels, output, and other important tasks are barometers by which employers measure.

Ranking/Rating Scales
Another system for rating employees is the behaviorally anchored rating scales, or (BARS). BARS is a unique system because it specifically focuses on behaviors that are necessary for performing a task successfully, rather than evaluating more analytical employee habits. Instead of appraising general behaviors that are required to be present in all employees, BARS examines precise behaviors that are unique to a certain job or task. After an investigation has taken place, management will employ a designated rating scale that appropriately locates an employee based on performance. On the rating scale, a "1" designates unsatisfactory performance, a "2" designates marginal performance (troublesome employees), a "3" designates fully competent performance, a "4" designates excellent performance, and a "5" designates exceptional performance.

The 1 – 5 rating scale method demonstrated above is just one of the numerous varieties. In addition to the 1 – 5 rating scale, they can also express a 1 – 3 model, 1 – 4 model, 1 – 5 model, or 1 – 10 model. These models are known as rating scale methods. Moreover, another prominent method of appraisal is the checklist method. The checklist method features a series of questions that determine a specific level of performance, with the participant placing a check next to applicable statements.

Goal Setting
A robust system of planning can be incorporated into an organization's agenda to set expectations and devise strategies to meet them. Monitoring performance levels enables organizations to ensure that operations harmonize with expectations. If specific goals are not met, this indicates an error in planning or execution. Identifying any unmet goals makes organizations more likely to become more productive by constantly improving.

Relationship to Compensation
Rating is a tactic that employers use to incentivize employees to efficiently fulfill tasks in a timely manner. In addition, rating is a way that employers can measure and identify their productive, talented, and best workers. After employees are rated, the highest-performing individuals will be rewarded. Similarly to rating, rewarding is a mechanism used to incentivize and reinforce positive behavior. In all

successful organizations, employers have discovered the most efficient means of regulating, monitoring, and sculpting maximal performance strategies.

Training for Evaluators

One key reason why performance appraisals tend to be ineffective is that most individuals who evaluate employee performance have received little or no training on how to do so, and they are not adequately supported throughout the performance appraisal process.

Therefore, many types of performance appraisal errors may result. Evaluators make the similar-to-me error when they rate employees more favorably who are like themselves. Contrast errors come into play when an evaluator focuses on a particular stereotype, such as age or race, instead of on performance when rating employees, or when an evaluator compares two employees who have similar performance records and rates one of the employees higher than the other due to his or her likeability. Excessive leniency or excessive strictness occurs when performance appraisals are written to be too accommodating or too harsh and tend to be more about the evaluators temperament than about the employee's job performance. The halo effect takes place when an employee receives a glowing performance appraisal (is rated highly in all areas regardless of actual job performance), after the evaluator notices that he or she is really very good at performing one aspect of his/her job (perhaps something that the evaluator values personally).

The opposite of halo effect is what is known as the horn effect. The horn effect takes place when an employee receives a negative performance appraisal (is rated poorly in all areas regardless of actual job performance), after the evaluator notices that he or she is poor at performing one aspect of his/her job (perhaps something that the evaluator values personally). In addition, central tendency error takes place when the evaluator gives all employees a middle of the range performance appraisal score (i.e., a 6 out of 10), so he or she cannot be perceived as "the bad guy" if the truth about employees' job performance is told. The recency effect takes place when an evaluator bases an employee's performance appraisal solely on a recent event (good or bad) instead of on the employee's entire performance history during the established rating period. The opposite of this is what is known as the primacy error. This error takes place when an evaluator bases an employee's performance appraisal solely on his or her initial impression of the employee (good or bad) instead of on the employee's performance history during the established rating period.

Evaluators should receive the necessary training to ensure that employees' performance appraisals are free from all bias and discrimination. This involves training on how to use the performance tool, training on the various types of performance appraisal errors listed above and how to avoid them, along with how to manage difficult conversations with employees. Performance appraisals should be based on formal evaluation criteria that has been previously set and on evaluators' personal interactions with the employees. Evaluators should accurately describe employees' behavior by citing specific examples using objective criteria and to document situations as they occur. Additionally, equitable treatment should be provided to all employees during the performance appraisal process.

Outcomes of Performance Management Programs
There are several outcomes of the performance management process, including:

- Disciplinary actions that can be taken for underperforming employees
- Pay increases and incentive rewards
- Opportunities for employee advancement and promotions

- Employee development plans
- Career/succession planning

Performance management gives organizations the opportunity to identify the most suitable jobs for the most qualified people. After analyzing the results of goal setting, if certain individuals possess skill sets that indicate that they would be more productive in other areas of the business, this phase allows those transitions, or transfer assignments, to occur. Furthermore, promotions can be used to reinforce positive behavior. Another strategic use of promotions is to maximize each individual's utility by encouraging them to take positions that they may not have otherwise been interested in. These types of employment moves should be properly documented through the employees' performance appraisals to ensure that the organization is protected should any legal concerns arise.

Organizational Development Theories and Application

Kurt Lewin's Change Process Theory
Kurt Lewin's change process theory is a three-step organizational program that seeks to explain how entities change, the catalysts that precipitate change, and how change can be successfully accomplished. Fundamental to the theory is the notion that an entity will respond to the need for change when there is an external stimulus that compels it.

The first phase of the theory is unfreezing. Unfreezing means that there is immense importance for an organization to understand the need for change and to brace for the anticipated impact of change. The second phase is transition. Transition stipulates that for any entity to change, there must be a transitory period in which inner motivating factors come to terms with the need for change. The final phase is freezing, in which the new adjustments are solidified and cemented into the functions of an entity. Freezing is the reestablishment of new compositions, norms, rules, and procedures.

Implementation Theory
Implementation theory is the study of the goals that can be achieved in the change phase when rational agents work cooperatively. When agents work cooperatively, the ability and degree of modification, adaptability, identification, and improvement of malfunctions of an organization is augmented. The implementation of these changes is designed to benefit the entire organization. This theory is imperative to Kurt Lewin's process change theory, since it identifies and targets areas of unfreezing, transition, and freezing to maintain the intended function of an organization.

Change Management and Organization Development
Change management refers to an organization's ability to implement changes in a diligent and comprehensive manner. This concept of change is holistic and encompasses sweeping change of an organization. Equally important is how the changes made will affect pre-existing institutions (regulations, hierarchies). Similarly, organization development is a strategy of systematically planned interventions that are employed by an organization. The primary purpose of organization development is to raise the infrastructural efficiency of bureaucracies by devising more operative processes. Change management and organization development are two concepts that focus on evaluation, implementation, and development strategies that are complementary and, in many ways, similar to one another.

Organization Development Intervention
An organization development intervention outlines various strategies that an organization employs to effect a desired change. After identifying a problem, organizations target it by employing systematic and

designated institutional processes that endeavor to maximize productive potential. An organization development intervention is instrumental in analyzing, directing, and restructuring any underperforming phases in an organizational process. Within this process, there are three primary types of interventions: human process interventions, sociotechnical interventions, and techno-structural interventions.

Human process interventions are specific types of interruptions in an organization model through human interactions. Specific techniques used in human process interventions are coaching, large-group interventions, and training and development. Coaching typically involves working interpersonally (with a supervisor) to enhance techniques for self-management, strategy development, customizing strategies that are proximate to client needs, and meeting core objectives. Third-party interventions occur when an agent located outside of the organization mediates or manages disputing parties in problem solving. In order to sharpen educational capacities and skills, organizations develop key training and development programs. An example is a program that will instruct employees on how to use a specific piece of machinery that is integral to performance.

A sociotechnical intervention is a process undertaken by organizations to maximize productivity by integrating machinery and technology into a pre-existing organizational structure. Since organizations are immensely affected by technological performance and change, it is imperative that strategies are designed to assimilate it, rather than cause institutional shock. Job rotation is one method organizations use to cope with technological change by ensuring that employees are equipped with the physical and cognitive capacities to perform a variety of disparate tasks. By delegating new tasks to meet expanding needs, job enrichment is a strategy that increases responsibilities and authority. Lastly, process improvement is an approach that investigates and alters the way a group performs specific tasks.

Techno-structural interventions represent a type of organization development intervention that focuses on how to most efficiently incorporate and use a piece of technology to maintain maximum productivity. These interventions describe a technique in which an organization redesigns and restructures by implementing more efficient methods. One of the most well-known examples of a techno-structural intervention is total quality management (TQM). Total quality management evaluates and changes an organization's dominant attitudes and culture if they are incongruent with the needs of customers. More precisely, styles of communication, leadership, ethical considerations, trust, training, and teamwork are examples of what total quality management reconsiders, if needed.

Coaching and Mentoring Managers and Executives

To improve their leadership abilities and the performance of their companies, managers and executives may enlist a group of coaches. Different than trainers, coaches provide a level of self-improvement and teach leaders how to identify and solve problems. In addition, executive coaching also gives business leaders the occasion to receive crucial feedback that only outside coaches could provide. Having the opportunity to receive expert and unbiased analysis from trained professionals is advantageous to develop long-term strategies and thinking that will allow greater prosperity within a firm.

Mentoring is a specific process that involves influencing the way managers approach and think about solving problems. Specifically, it does not involve a rigid structure; it is long-term commitment on behalf of mentors and management. Mentoring is also vague and does not deal with specific accomplishments. Different kinds of problems that mentors deal with are preparing for a prospective promotion, personal growth, life transitions and adjustments, and developing an individual personally or professionally.

Facilitation Techniques, Instructional Methods, and Program Delivery Systems

William Edwards Deming

William Edwards Deming is one of the most discussed and influential proponents of quality control management. Deming developed fourteen core principles for improving efficiency and productivity of an organization. Among his principles, Deming emphasized a stringent dedication to constant improvement, firm and active leadership, establishing long-term relationships with suppliers and financial institutions, high levels of job security for employees in order to raise morale, and diminishing costs while increasing productive value. In addition, Deming prescribed that barriers between departments be minimal. For example, sales, production, and design must communicate without obstruction. Lastly, Deming felt it was important to encourage self-improvement, eliminate quotas, cultivate a unifying sense of pride throughout the organization, and ensure that all employees familiarize themselves with the fourteen core principles.

Joseph Moses Juran

Joseph Moses Juran was an engineer and a pioneer of quality control management. Similar to William Edwards Deming, Juran has been heralded for resuscitating Japanese industry after World War II. Juran is also responsible for developing the Pareto principle, which identified the disproportionality between input and output. Also known as the 80-20 rule, the principle observes that 80 percent of output can be generated by 20 percent of the population. For instance, if an employee managed their time effectively, 80 percent of his or her output could be produced by 20 percent of time spent actually working.

Juran Trilogy

According to Juran, there are three areas of quality management: quality planning, quality improvement, and quality control. These three principles are known as the Juran Trilogy. Quality planning is focused on the needs of customers—determining the customers, the principal needs of the customers, and figuring out how to develop a product that is congruent to the needs of the customers. Quality improvement is a process that revolves around designing a strategy that allows an organization to meet the needs of the customers. It involves creating an organizational infrastructure that serves the demands of customers. Quality control is the phase where the process is tested, ensuring that it can suit customer needs with minimal inspection. It is the phase that tests organizational efficiency. Intrinsic to Juran's philosophy is apt leadership, once stating, "It is most important that top management be quality-minded. In the absence of sincere manifestation of interest at the top, little will happen below."

Pareto Analysis System

Developed by Italian Vilfredo Pareto, the Pareto analysis system is a statistical model used for decision-making in an organization. The Pareto Principle articulates that 80 percent of the output of an organization emanates from 20 percent of the input. In effect, 80 percent of the consequences are brought to fruition by 20 percent of the causes. The Pareto analysis system is a methodological process employed by business leaders to effectively determine their most revenue-raising technologies, workforce, and resources. After this evaluation, targeted and sustained investments will be made into the most valuable 20 percent. In order to satisfactorily identify factors that least and most heavily influence revenue, the Pareto analysis system is typically accompanied by a bar chart. Used for quality control issues, the bar chart is a thorough analysis of a company's net input and net output, used to find more efficient ways of employing scarce resources.

Philip B. Crosby

In the field of quality management, Philip B. Crosby introduced several important ideas that remain highly consequential in organizations attempting to solve quality control issues. One of his principal ideas is "Zero Defects." Zero Defects is not just a program that is directed by an organization, but a philosophy of business and pedagogy. It requires one to assess the high cost of quality failures and then realize the relation to deflated revenues. If one is chronically wary of these damaging costs, they are more likely to advocate a Zero Defects philosophy, where errors are scrutinized as much as proficiencies. In conjunction with Zero Defects, Crosby advanced "doing it right the first time," or DRIFT.

DRIFT consists of four basic tenets:

- The need to conform to requirements
- The management system is responsible for preventing errors
- The standard of performance is zero defects
- The quality costs are the standard of measurement.

An enduring emphasis throughout Crosby's thoughts focuses on powerful managerial operations. The four principles of DRIFT are contingent upon firm and authoritative management that establishes rules and standards. Throughout the production process, management is responsible for preventing costly glitches and backing a zero defects philosophy. Additionally, management bears responsibility for making the barometer of all decision-making subordinate to quality costs and the organizational conformation to firm requirements.

DRIFT is a system of managerial accounting that works closely with just-in-time production. Just-in-time (JIT) is a management technique where a business will only receive goods according to effective demand, rather than maintaining a stockpile inventory of unused supplies. In order for JIT to be a cost-saving program, DRIFT ensures that demand, inventory, and supply chains are congruent to business accounting expectations. If there is any error in JIT, it no longer becomes a cost-saving proposition, but rather it increases the costs of production. The stringent philosophy of DRIFT enables businesses to increase revenues, keep production costs low, and manufacture low-cost commodities.

Dr. Kaoru Ishikawa

Dr. Kaoru Ishikawa is a central figure in the rebuilding of the Japanese industrial base after the Second World War. He introduced several invaluable ideas, one of the most prominent is that production does not end after the commodity is purchased, but rather it continues to ensure maximum customer satisfaction. If a customer is not satisfied with the product, the organization must mobilize itself to resolve the problem and create a better product. A forerunner in quality assessment, Ishikawa introduced numerous statistical analyses to improve productive processes, ranging from charts, graphs, diagrams, and algorithmic equations. Throughout his career, Ishikawa was a proponent of standardization in quality control. Standardization, according to Ishikawa, did not mean a set of rigid and unchangeable rules, but rather rules that are mutable and constantly subject to improvement.

Another one of Ishikawa's innovations is the Fishbone, or Ishikawa Diagram. The fundamental objective of the Ishikawa Diagram is to identify the principal causes of an effect of a particular problem to give an assessment of quality. Once there is a consensus on a problem (cause), a focus group can mobilize to identify all of its potential causes. These causes could range from employee performance, underperforming machinery, unsatisfactory calculations or methods, or responses to external stimuli. The Ishikawa Diagram is an efficient way of problem solving by isolating specific components and deconstructing positive or negative consequences through an investigatory lens. When a group employs an Ishikawa Diagram, it can be easily thought of as a brainstorming session, where each member offers contributions to amend and resolve current organizational processes.

Also used in quality assessment are histograms and stratification charts. Resembling a bar chart, a histogram incorporates bars and groups numbers into ranges. A histogram includes a horizontal distribution of data and is designed to give a visual representation of a certain distribution. For instance, if one were to calculate a histogram of the federal budget of the United States, the y-axis would measure the amount of money spent and the x-axis would parcel the different areas of spending (military, education, social programs, infrastructure, etc.). As histograms, stratification charts also use bars. However, the purpose of a stratification chart is to separate concentrated data to make identifiable patterns.

Six Sigma

Six Sigma is a methodological strategy that is used by organizations to devise more productive ways to organize processes. The principal reason for employing Six Sigma is to eliminate defects in organizational protocol that impede the ability to maximize profitability. In many instances, those people involved in the method must be highly trained in project management and statistics. The goal of organizations that incorporate Six Sigma into production is to maintain a rationally driven, scientific approach to output. As a preventive strategy, a key concept is to preclude wasteful, defective, and time-consuming policies by improving techniques.

DMAIC is the primary process that incorporates Six Sigma. An acronym, DMAIC stands for define, measure, analyze, improve, and control. The first step is to define problems, deficiencies, or areas of improvement. Second, measure means to simply measure the process performance. The third step instructs the group to analyze the process to ensure that it is the most effective strategy in solving the root cause of the problem. Fourth, the organization needs to improve process performance and gauge how successfully it targets and eliminates the root causes of defects. Finally, control requires that the most resourceful process be improved and salvaged for future use.

Practice Questions

1. What is the purpose of a pilot program?

    a. The purpose of a pilot program is to assign leadership and decision-making roles to a program, designating leaders as "pilots."

    b. The purpose of a pilot program is to function as a test program, in which leadership conducts analyses to assess the program's feasibility and revenue-wielding potential.

    c. The purpose of a pilot program is to rescue a pre-existing project from certain failure.

    d. The purpose of a pilot program is to validate the success of a project by awarding higher salaries and bonuses to leadership.

2. One of the six stages of career development is assessment. What occurs during this stage?

    a. The assessment stage demands that people assess their new occupation and begin working on assignments.

    b. The assessment stage requires that people begin looking for opportunities that reflect their interests and skills.

    c. The assessment stage occurs when people begin to feel a comfort and familiarity with their careers and become acclimated.

    d. Assessment is an introspective stage that requires that one be aware of their values, interests, and skills to discover a career that is most suitable.

3. Kinesthetic learning is accomplished most efficiently through which of the following?

    a. Kinesthetic learning is learning that is done by listening to lectures or group discussions.

    b. Also called spatial learning, kinesthetic learning is learning that is best done by watching videos, looking at maps, or copying notes from a blackboard.

    c. Kinesthetic learning is learning that takes place through physical touching or moving. Examples of kinesthetic learning are using building blocks or drawing.

    d. Kinesthetic learning is learning that is best done by reading text and writing down an alternate interpretation of that text.

4. What does a plateau learning curve indicate?

    a. A plateau learning curve represents initially slow learning but then a rapid acceleration.

    b. A plateau learning curve indicates quick initial learning followed by a stoppage.

    c. A plateau learning curve indicates sluggish learning, acceleration in learning activity, and then a deceleration.

    d. A plateau learning curve represents quick initial learning followed by a slowdown.

5. What are the three types of organization development interventions?

    a. Human process intervention, sociotechnical intervention, techno-structural intervention

    b. Human process intervention, managerial intervention, techno-structural intervention

    c. Managerial intervention, human process intervention, techno-structural intervention

    d. Employer intervention, sociotechnical intervention, techno-structural intervention

6. Which statement is most reflective of the Pareto analysis system?

    a. 20 percent of output is generated by 80 percent of input.

    b. 80 percent of output is generated by 20 percent of input.

    c. Decisions should be made democratically rather than statistically.

    d. Resources need to be allocated according to need rather than according to productivity.

7. Which is a primary principle of DRIFT?

    a. One primary purpose of DRIFT is to distribute high profits to employees so that they will be more loyal.

    b. One primary purpose of DRIFT states that as long as they are dealt with immediately, errors can be tolerated.

    c. One primary purpose of DRIFT is that stockpiling commodities can be profitable because supplies are easily accessible.

    d. One primary purpose of DRIFT is that supply and demand must be congruent with management expectations.

8. Public domain is a copyright provision that posits which of the following?

    a. Under no circumstances can a previously copyrighted work be used without authorization.

    b. Any work published by the federal government can be used freely without authorization.

    c. Items that are considered to be works-made-for-hire never fall into the public domain.

    d. Works protected by a copyright can be used without consent if they are used for a public purpose.

9. Which of the following pieces of legislation guarantee that all employees have equal access to career development and training?

    a. Title VII of the Civil Rights Act of 1964

    b. Fair Labor Standards Act (FLSA)

    c. Older Workers Benefit Protection Act (OWBPA)

    d. Davis Beacon Act

10. Which of the following statements is true regarding a learner analysis in the needs assessment process?

    a. Data is gathered from both mid-level and senior level managers.

    b. It will ensure the company is on board with the training.

    c. It can be completed in conjunction with the task analysis.

    d. Data is gathered from individuals who have direct knowledge of the work.

11. Which of the following best represents 360-degree feedback?

    a. A method by which employees receive anonymous feedback from their managers, peers, direct reports, and customers.

    b. A method by which employees perform a self-appraisal regarding their own performance at several different points over the course of a year.

    c. 360-degree feedback features reviews only by fellow employees. This is most effective because learning how employees interact with each other is indicative of their attitudes and efforts.

    d. 360-degree feedback uses reviews only by management. Only management can assess an employee's suitability in an organization by evaluating productivity levels.

12. In performance management, what is a principle function of rating?

    a. Rating allows management to identify their most productive workers and provide them incentives to retain them.

    b. Because of its narrow statistical application, rating is generally an infrequent practice by management.

    c. To provide a way for management to designate their most favored employees.

    d. By employees rating management, they can more accurately decide for whom and under which conditions they wish to work.

13. Peter Senge postulated that there are five disciplines that complete a learning organization. When appropriately used in an organization, what is the purpose of these disciplines?

a. The purpose of Peter Senge's five disciplines is to permit an organization to function more comprehensively by augmenting communication and establishing common goals.

b. The purpose of Peter Senge's five disciplines is to articulate management's exact expectations to employees.

c. The purpose of Peter Senge's five disciplines is for employees to compete for the best ideas and to incorporate them into a productive strategy.

d. The purpose of Peter Senge's five disciplines is discovering different modes of innovation and to force employees to conform to them without engaging in dialogue.

14. Which of the following accurately represents the Fishbone Diagram?

a. The Fishbone Diagram is centered on the analysis of management and does not consult the entire organization.

b. The Fishbone Diagram identifies the effects and works to determine causes.

c. The Fishbone Diagram investigates the causes of problems. It is crafted after comprehensive brainstorming, determines positive and negative consequences, and isolates various components.

d. The Fishbone Diagram is a way to provide a visual representation of a distribution of data.

15. Which of the following best represents the purpose of Six Sigma?

a. Six Sigma is a rationally motivated and methodological process that seeks to eliminate ineffective and wasteful techniques that diminish productivity.

b. Six Sigma is a process that seeks to terminate wasteful programs through organizing management and employee councils.

c. The major purpose of Six Sigma is to use brainstorming techniques to gain valuable feedback from employees to determine the most ineffective use of company resources.

d. To increase productive capacities, organizations employ Six Sigma. Six Sigma recruits employees with the most experience, not necessarily the most highly trained in Six Sigma methodology or statistics.

16. DMAIC is a process that incorporates Six Sigma. Which of the following is the accurate order of its steps?

a. Control, measure, analyze, improve, define

b. Measure, define, control, analyze, improve

c. Define, measure, analyze, improve, control

d. Control, improve, measure, analyze, define

17. Which of the following items is now in the public domain according to the Copyright Act of 1976?

a. A pamphlet that is produced by the federal government

b. A science textbook that was written in 1998

c. A song that was written in 1992

d. An article published in an organizational behavior magazine in 1980

18. Kurt Lewin's change process theory features three steps. What is the correct order of these three steps?

a. Freezing, transition, unfreezing

b. Unfreezing, transition, freezing

c. Change, unfreezing, holding

d. Unfreezing, holding, freezing

19. Which of the following best describes William Edwards Deming's 14 points?

   a. Walls between bureaucracies should be solidified to increase specialization and expertise; low wages are important to motivate workers; a single successful strategy should be cemented without amending it.

   b. Short-term relationships with suppliers increase a firm's flexibility; low wages increase a firm's ability to invest in competent leadership.

   c. Job security does not matter because workers are expendable; establishing long-term relationships is costly and time-consuming; bureaucrats should focus exclusively on their departments.

   d. Walls between bureaucracies should be minimal; job security increases workers' loyalty and morale; establishing long-term relationships with suppliers and financial firms is crucial to development; cut costs and increase productivity.

20. Which of the following is the appropriate order of the Juran Trilogy?

   a. Quality planning, quality improvement, quality control

   b. Quality control, quality planning, quality improvement

   c. Quality planning, quality control, quality improvement

   d. Quality improvement, quality control, quality planning

Answer Explanations

1. B: Also known as an experimental trial or feasibility study, a pilot program is designed to be small-scale. A pilot program's purpose is to enable an organization to test new methods, new products, or engineer new methods or techniques without incurring significant cost. Tremendously important to research, pilot programs can be considered laboratories of innovation and experimentation because they allow logistical considerations, structural efficiencies and deficiencies, and profitability to be evaluated and determined. Pilot programs are widely used in application by many companies, notably Microsoft Corporation, Pfizer Inc., The Dow Chemical Company, and Xerox Corporation.

2. D: Assessment is the first stage of career development. This stage asks that an individual do soul-searching. It demands that a person discover their values, interests, skills, and passions in order to find a career that is most suitable. It can be seen as a stage of self-affirmation that precedes the journey of job searching. During this stage, a person may ask: "What inspires me?" and "What is my purpose?" Assessment is unique to the other stages of career development because it is independent and exists outside of the workplace.

3. C: Kinesthetic learning can most easily be described as learning by doing. Whereas auditory learning occurs by listening, visual learning occurs through sight, and reading/writing learning occurs through interacting with text, kinesthetic learning occurs distinctly through touch and movement. Kinesthetic learners may grasp concepts more easily by physical activity – playing sports, laboratory exercises, drawing, charades, building, or role-play. To properly accommodate kinesthetic learners, one may use field trips, memory games, or flash cards. Studying while loud music is playing, poor penmanship and spelling, inability to sit still for long periods of time, and emphasis on breaks while studying are a few of the signs of a kinesthetic learner.

4. B: A learning curve is a graphical representation of a person's learning progress. A plateau learning curve indicates that learning takes place at an accelerated rate and then comes to a halt. Out of the four types of learning curves discussed, the plateau learning curve is unique. It is the only learning curve that indicates a stoppage in learning. A positively accelerating learning curve represents slow initial learning, but then a rapid increase. A negatively accelerating learning curve depicts an accelerated beginning followed by a slowdown. Lastly, an S-shaped learning curve denotes initial sluggishness, heightened learning activity, followed by a return to lethargy.

5. A: The three types of organization development interventions are human process interventions, sociotechnical interventions, and techno-structural interventions. Human process interventions are coordinated efforts to correct inefficiencies through human contact. Specific types of human process interventions are coaching, mentoring, training, or using a third party to mediate disputes. Sociotechnical interventions attempt to integrate new machinery and technology into pre-existing organizational models. Lastly, the goal of techno-structural interventions is to use technology to its most productive capacities.

6. B: The Pareto analysis system is a statistical model that postulates that 80 percent of output is generated by 20 percent of input. Management can use this rule to identify where to invest scarce resources. Other names for this rule are the "80-20 rule" and "law of the vital few." Remembering these other names can be helpful because they highlight the essential functionality of the rule. By constantly searching for the most productive members of an organization or the resources that yield the most revenue, management personnel are able to prioritize employees or investments over others. This analysis can be useful when restructuring an organization, rating employee performance, capital investment, and much more.

7. D: DRIFT is a technique that organizations adopt to harmonize supply and demand. In practice, DRIFT can only be successful if the costs of production are in accordance with expectations. Just-in-time is a concept that is accompanied with DRIFT. In order to control the costs of stockpiling unused wares, long-term and close-knit relationships with suppliers and creditors are imperative. If an organization did not have easy access to supplier and financial institutions, then its ability to respond to the vacillations of the market would not be as swift.

8. B: Public domain is a provision in federal copyright law stating that work that meets designated criterion can be used without authorization. There are two possibilities where one can use material without obtaining consent. First, if the federal government publishes a work, then it is considered to be public, thus falling into the public domain. Second, copyrights can expire. Material that is created on or after January 1, 1978 is protected for the remainder of the author's life plus seventy years after death. Anonymous material, works made for hire, and articles are protected for ninety-five years from the date of creation or 120 years after being published.

9. A: Title VII of the Civil Rights Act of 1964 guarantees that all employees have equal access to career development and training. The Fair Labor Standards Act (FLSA) was put into effect to establish employee classification (exempt/non-exempt) and regulate minimum wage, overtime pay, on-call pay, associated recordkeeping, and child labor. Under the Older Workers Benefit Protection Act (OWBPA) it is illegal for employers to discriminate based on an employee's age in the provision of benefits, such as pension programs, retirement plans, life insurance, etc. Finally, the Davis Beacon Act requires contractors and subcontractors working on federally funded contracts in excess of $2,000 to pay all laborers at construction sites associated with such contracts at least the prevailing wage and fringe benefits that individuals working in similar projects in the area are receiving.

10. C: A learner analysis can be completed in conjunction with a task analysis during the needs assessment process. Data is gathered from both mid-level and senior level managers during an organizational analysis, and the point of performing this type of analysis is to ensure that the company is on board with the training. Data is gathered from individuals who have direct knowledge of the work during a task analysis.

11. A: 360-degree feedback is a method by which employees receive anonymous feedback from their managers, peers, direct reports, and customers. Choice *B* is incorrect since 360-degree feedback involves much more than employee self-appraisals. Choice *C* is incorrect since 360-degree feedback involves much more than reviews by only fellow employees. Choice *D* is also incorrect since 360-degree feedback involves much more than reviews only by management.

12. A: There are multiple functions for rating in performance management. The first purpose of rating is to give management the opportunity to identify the best performing employees. Once this is done, these employees can be rewarded in various ways. Conversely, rating is a technique used by management to distinguish poorly performing employees. Underperforming employees can be dealt with in many ways: they can receive a decrease in pay, be forced to attend additional training programs, or ultimately have their employment terminated.

13. A: The intended purpose of the five disciplines outlined by Peter Senge is to enable organizational apparatuses to remain adaptable and capable of change. Essential to the five disciplines are communication, dialogue, team learning, and establishing common goals. Individuals must develop personal skills and mastery, but there remains an equal focus on the organization itself. It must be able to adapt to extemporaneous circumstances, adopt innovative tactics, and embrace participatory approaches that permit the fluidity of ideas. By compelling members of an organization to communicate and work cooperatively, the concept of systems thinking is critical to Senge's five principles.

14. C: The Fishbone Diagram is a tool that seeks to analyze the primary causes of an effect of a problem. Ultimately, the diagram engages problems and investigates remedial efforts for improvement. In a group formation, a consensus is gathered to identify possible causes, which could range from employee performance or outdated technology to inefficient methods of production or environmental implications. By isolating each factor, the diagram details organizational procedure to scientifically diagnose potential inefficiencies.

15. A: Six Sigma is a method used by organizations to reduce inefficiencies and other cumbersome techniques that diminish profitability. It is a rationally organized process that is enlisted to constantly increase productive capacities by eliminating antiquated or outdated machinery and technology. Furthermore, Six Sigma may scrutinize opaque bureaucratic structures or wasteful practices that obstruct maximum profitability. Grounded in statistical analysis, this methodology exhibits a scientific and technical approach to solving critical problems facing an organization.

16. C: The process of incorporating Six Sigma is DMAIC. The correct order of operations of DMAIC is define, measure, analyze, improve, and control. Define means to give affirmation to the specific problems or deficiencies that are not yielding expected results. Measuring specifies an analysis of the process performance. Sufficient analysis occurs when a group examines the process to determine the most sensible strategy. To improve the strategy and conclude the value of process performance is an extremely important step in DMAIC. Finally, after extensive analysis, control enables the most successful process be continuously improved and sustained.

17. A: If the federal government publishes the work, it is regarded as public and therefore is exempt from copyright infringement. For instance, a government pamphlet is considered to be in the public domain according to the Copyright Act of 1976. Expiration is the only other way an article would lose copyright protection. Works created on or after January 1, 1978, are protected for the life of the author and seventy years after his or her death; anonymous works, works-made-for-hire, and articles are given protection for ninety-five years from the date of creation or 120 years from being published. The copyrights of the science textbook written in 1998, the song written in 1992, and the article published in a magazine in 1980 have not yet expired, and so these items are not yet considered to be in the public domain.

18. B: Kurt Lewin's theory features three phases: unfreezing, transition, and freezing. During the unfreezing phase, an organization realizes the necessity to change. The transition phase forces the organization to implement strategies to alleviate problems. Lastly, the third step (freezing) solidifies and cements these new strategies into organizational processes. When synthesized, the pith of the theory functions as a model for orderly and stable change.

19. D: One of William Edwards Deming's most prominent contributions is the 14 points. The 14 points illustrate a cohesive and secure approach to organizational development. Although there are a variety of factors that embody Deming's principles, the central features are development of long-term relationships with suppliers and creditors, increasing job security to cultivate worker morale and loyalty, management that maintains a strong and active role in leadership, and inoculating a pervasive feeling of unity and employee pride. Moreover, organizations must prioritize decreasing barriers between bureaucracies and cut costs while raising productivity levels. According to Deming, these properties present a firm orientation that permits an organizational structure conducive to firmness and innovation.

20. A: The Juran Trilogy features three components: quality planning, quality improvement, and quality control. Quality planning is the first step and focuses on the goal of discerning the needs of customers. Secondly, quality improvement relates to improving organizational abilities to meet the requirements demanded by customers. In this phase, leadership may ask, "How may we craft a strategy that most suitably accommodates the needs of customers?" Lastly, quality control is a phase where new organizational methods are inspected and tested for efficacy.

Compensation and Benefits

Federal Laws and Regulations

A company's total rewards strategy is used to attract, motivate, engage, and retain employees through compensation packages made up of pay, incentives, and benefits. This rewards system should be aligned with the company's mission, strategy, and corporate culture, and it must comply with all applicable laws and regulations.

Davis Bacon Act (1931)
This piece of legislation applies to contractors and subcontractors working on federally funded contracts in excess of $2,000. The act requires employers to pay all laborers at construction sites—associated with such contracts—at least the prevailing wage and fringe benefits that individuals working in similar projects in the area are receiving. Employers who fail to comply with this act risk losing their federal contracts and the ability to receive new federal contracts for a period of up to three years.

Walsh-Healy Public Contracts Act (1936)
This federal law applies to contractors working on federally funded supply contracts in excess of $10,000. Under this act, employers associated with such contracts must pay employees at least the federal *minimum wage*—currently set at $7.25 per hour—and overtime pay. Overtime pay is calculated as one and one-half times an individual's regular rate of pay for any hours worked in excess of eight hours in a single workday or any hours worked in excess of forty hours in a single workweek.

The employment of youth under the age of sixteen and convicts is also prohibited under this legislation. Additionally, the act calls for job safety and sanitation protocols. Failure to comply with this law may result in the withholding of contract payments to reimburse any underpayment of wages or overtime pay due to employees. There is also a penalty of $10 per person per day for any employer who is found to be employing youth or convicts, along with possible additional legal action. Employers may ultimately face losing their federal contracts and the ability to receive new federal contracts for a period of up to three years for non-compliance.

Fair Labor Standards Act (1938)
The Fair Labor Standards Act (FLSA) is also known as the *Wage and Hour Law*, and it covers most governmental agencies and private-sector employers. This includes companies with employees involved in interstate commerce, employers with $500,000 or more in annual sales or business completed, and organizations caring for the physically and mentally ill, the aging population, and educational institutions. The act does not apply to employers working in industries who are covered under other labor standards that are specific to those industries. The law was put into effect to establish employee classification and to regulate minimum wage, overtime pay, on-call pay, associated record keeping, and child labor, as discussed in detail below.

Employee Classification
The FLSA requires employers to classify all employee positions into two categories, exempt and non-exempt, depending on the type of work the employees do, the amount of money the employees are paid, and how the employees are paid.

- *Non-exempt* positions fall directly under the FLSA regulations. These employees earn a salary of less than $23,600 per year or $455 per week. Non-exempt positions do not involve the supervision of others or the use of independent judgment; they also do not require specialized education.

- *Exempt* positions do not fall under the FLSA regulations. These employees are paid on a salary basis and spend more than 50 percent of their work time performing exempt duties. Exempt level duties fall into three main categories: executive, professional, and administrative.

  o *Executive employees* are responsible for directing the work of two or more full-time employees. Management is a key focus of their role, and they have direct input into the job status of other employees, such as hiring and firing.

  o *Professional employees* can fall into the category of learned professionals, meaning their positions require knowledge in a specific field of science or learning, such as doctors, lawyers, engineers, and accountants. Professional employees can also fall into the category of creative professionals, meaning their positions involve the invention, imagination, originality, or talent in a recognized field of artistic or creative endeavor—e.g., writing, acting, and graphic arts.

  o *Administrative employees* are responsible for exercising discretion and judgment with respect to matters of significance, which can be directly related to management of the general business or in dealings with the customers of the business.

Minimum Wage
Under this act, employers must pay nonexempt employees at least the federal minimum wage. However, if the state in which an employee works pays a higher minimum wage than the current federal minimum wage, the employee will receive the higher state minimum wage. Additionally, employers must pay $2.13 per hour in direct wages to employees who receive tips as their form of salary. The total of the employer's wage and the employee's tips should then equal the minimum wage.

Overtime
Under this law, employers must pay nonexempt employees overtime pay at the rate of one and one-half times an individual's regular rate of pay for any hours worked in excess of forty hours of work in a single workweek. The act does not require that overtime be paid to employees for work performed on Saturdays, Sundays, or paid time-off days, such as sick days, vacation days, or holidays. Overtime pay that is earned in a specific workweek must be paid out in the pay period during which it was earned, instead of averaging overtime hours across multiple workweeks.

On-Call
Under this act, employers must pay nonexempt employees their regular rate of pay for *on-call time*—the time that they are required to remain at the employer's place of business while waiting to engage in work as required by their employer. An example of this would be medical employees who are asked by their employer to wait to engage in work in an on-call room at a hospital. Since they are not free to leave the hospital and are expected to work if called upon, they must be compensated for their time spent on-call.

Record Keeping

Under this law, employers are required to keep specific records as defined by the Department of Labor. In regard to nonexempt employees, employers must specifically keep track of the following personal information for an employee:

- Name, address, occupation, gender, and date of birth, if employee is under the age of nineteen
- Day and time of the start of the workweek
- Total hours an employee worked during each workday and for the workweek as a whole
- Employee's daily and weekly straight-time earnings
- Employee's regular hourly rate of pay for weeks when any overtime is worked
- Total overtime pay for the workweek
- Any additions or deductions to an employee's wages
- Total wages paid to an employee during each pay period
- Date the employee received payment for work performed and the pay period that payment covered

Child Labor

This legislation also put provisions in place—commonly referred to as *child labor laws*—to ensure that working youth were guaranteed a safe workplace environment that did not pose a risk to their overall health and well-being or prevent them from pursuing additional educational opportunities.

Youth under the age of fourteen are only allowed to perform such functions as newspaper delivery, babysitting, acting, and assisting in their parents' business, as long as that business is non-hazardous in nature. They may also perform non-hazardous agricultural work on a farm that employs one of their parents. Youth ages fourteen and fifteen are allowed to perform non-hazardous work, such as positions in retail, some yard work, and some kitchen and food service work. Youth in this age group are not allowed to work more than three hours a day or eighteen hours a week when school is in session. However, when school is not in session, these youth can work up to eight hours a day and up to forty hours a week.

Youth in this age group do have restricted work hours of 7:00 am to 7:00 pm during the school year. The evening time is extended to 9:00 pm during the period of June 1 through Labor Day. Youth ages sixteen and seventeen can work unlimited hours. However, youth in this age group are still prohibited from working on hazardous jobs, such as operating trash binders, shredders, or material-handling equipment.

Age	Legal Requirements
Under 14	Children under fourteen years of age may not be employed in non-agricultural occupations covered by the FLSA, including food service establishments. Permissible employment for such children is limited to work that is exempt from the FLSA (such as delivering newspapers to the consumer and acting). Children may also perform work not covered by the FLSA such as completing minor chores around private homes or casual baby-sitting.
14 & 15	Fourteen and fifteen-year-olds may be employed in restaurants and quick-service establishments outside school hours in a variety of jobs for limited periods of time and under specified conditions. Child Labor Regulations No. 3, 29 C.F.R. 570, Subpart C, limits both the time of day and number of hours this age group may be employed as well as the types of jobs they may perform. **Hours and times of day standards for the employment of 14- and 15-year-olds:** • outside school hours; school hours are determined by the local public school in the area the minor is residing while employed; • no more than three hours on a school day, including Fridays; • no more than eight hours on a non-school day; • no more than eighteen hours during a week when school is in session; • no more than forty hours during a week when school is not in session; • between 7 a.m. and 7 p.m., except between June 1 and Labor day when the evening hour is extended to 9 p.m. **Occupation standards for the employment of 14- and 15-year-olds:** • They may perform cashiering, shelf stocking, and the bagging and carrying out of customer orders. • They may perform clean up work, including the use of vacuum cleaners and floor waxers. • They may perform limited cooking duties involving electric or gas grills that do not entail cooking over an open flame. They may also cook with deep fat fryers that are equipped with and utilize devices that automatically raise and lower the "baskets" into and out of the hot grease of oil. They may not operate NEXCO broilers, rotisseries, pressure cookers, fryolaters, high-speed ovens, or rapid toasters. • They may not perform any baking activities. • They may not work in warehousing or load or unload goods to or from trucks or conveyors. • They may not operate, clean, set up, adjust, repair, or oil power driven machines including food slicers, grinders, processors, or mixers. • They may clean kitchen surfaces and non-power-driven equipment, and filter, transport, and dispose of cooking oil, but only when the temperature of the surface and oils do not exceed 100 degrees Fahrenheit. • They may not operate power-driven lawn mowers or cutters, or load or unload goods to or from trucks or conveyors. • They may not work in freezers or meet coolers, but they may occasionally enter a freezer momentarily to retrieve items.

	• They are prohibited from working in any of the Hazardous Orders.
16 & 17	Sixteen and seventeen-year-olds may be employed for unlimited hours in any occupation other than those declared hazardous by the Secretary of Labor. Examples of equipment declared hazardous in food service establishments include: **Power-driven meat and poultry processing machines** (meat slicers, meat saws, patty forming machines, meat grinders, and meat choppers), commercial mixers and certain power-driven bakery machines. Employees under eighteen years of age are not permitted to operate, feed, set-up, adjust, repair, or clean any of these machines or their disassembled parts. **Balers and Compactors.** Minors under eighteen years of age may not load, operate, or unload balers or compactors. Sixteen and seventeen-year-olds may load, but not operate or unload, certain scrap paper balers and paper box compactors under certain specific circumstances. **Motor Vehicles.** Generally, no employee under eighteen years of age may drive on the job or serve as an outside helper on a motor vehicle on a public road, but seventeen-year-olds who meet certain specific requirements may drive automobiles and trucks that do not exceed 6,000 pounds gross vehicle weight for limited amounts of time as part of their job. Such minors are, however, prohibited from making time sensitive deliveries (such as pizza deliveries or other trips where time is of the essence) and from driving at night.
18	Once a youth reaches eighteen years of age, he or she is no longer subject to the federal child labor provisions.

Employers who fail to comply with the FLSA may face lawsuits from both the Secretary of Labor and wronged employees for the repayment of backpay of proper minimum wages and/or overtime pay. If it is found that an employer willfully violated this law, the Department of Labor can also impose a $1,100 penalty per violation for repeated offenses.

Employees and Independent Contractors
It is important for employers to be able to discern between employees and independent contractors who are performing work for them for the purpose of withholding taxes, paying overtime and on-call pay with regard to the Fair Labor Standards Act (FLSA), providing benefits, and granting legal protection to the appropriate individuals, all of which apply only to employees.

Employers are able to use independent contractors as a way to grow and reduce their workforce as needed while reducing their legal liability. There can also be a significant cost savings associated with having independent contractors complete work as they can typically be paid less than regular, full-time staff, and they do not receive healthcare benefits.

The Internal Revenue Service has developed a list of twenty factors that fall under three categories for employers to use to determine if an individual working for them is an employee or an independent contractor:

IRS 20-Factor Test
Behavioral Control
1. Instruction: A company-employee relationship could exist if the company dictates where, when, and how the employee works.
2. Training: A training relationship indicates the company has control over the type of work done by the employee.
3. Business Integration: Workers are likely to be considered employees if the success of the business depends on the work they do.
4. Personal Services: Independent contractors are free to assign work to anyone. Likewise, a company-employee relationship may dictate a particular person to carry out a specific task.
5. Assistants: An independent contractor may hire, supervise, and pay their own assistants, while a company-employee relationship may indicate that the company has control over the hiring, supervising, and paying of the worker's assistants.
Financial Control
6. Payment Method: Usually, hourly, weekly, or monthly payments indicate a company-employee relationship. Independent contractors are usually paid by commission or upon project completion.
7. Business or Travel Expenses: Employers who pay business or travel expenses for their employees are usually part of a company-employee relationship.
8. Tools and Materials: A company-employee relationship usually exists if the company provides the worker with tools and materials.
9. Investment in Facilities: Independent contractors usually invest in their own facilities, while employees for companies are usually provided facilities.
10. Profit or Loss: Workers who realize profits or losses are usually independent contractors.
Type of Relationship
11. Continuing of Relationships: An ongoing relationship between a company and a worker could indicate an employment relationship.
12. Set Hours: The implementation of a set schedule indicates that a company-employee relationship exists.
13. Full-Time: While independent contractors choose to work when and for whom they choose, employees sometimes must devote their schedules to full-time work for employees.
14. On-Site Services: If the work must be done on company property, a company-employee relationship probably exists.
15. Sequence of Work: A company-employee relationship is indicated if the worker must perform work in order of company preference and is not able to choose the sequence themselves.
16. Reports: If a worker is required to give oral or written reports to a company, this may indicate a level of control the company has over an employee.
17. Multiple Companies: Workers who provide services for multiple companies at one time are usually considered independent contractors.
18. Availability to Public: Workers who make their work available to the general public are often considered to be independent contractors.
19. Right to Discharge: Employers who have the right to discharge employees indicate a company-employee relationship.
20. Right to Terminate: Independent contractors are usually under contract to work, so they cannot terminate their employment as easily as employees.

Portal-to-Portal Act (1947)

This amendment to the Fair Labor Standards Act (FLSA) deals with the *preliminary tasks*—activities prior to the start of principal workday activities—and *postliminary tasks*—activities following the completion of principal workday activities.

- Examples of postliminary tasks include on-call or standby time, meals and breaks, travel time, and training time. The act requires employers to pay employees who are covered under the Fair Labor Standards Act for time spent traveling to perform job-related tasks, if that travel is outside of the employees' regular work commute.

- Employers must also pay employees for any time they spend waiting to start work when requested to do so by their employer. Additionally, employees are to be paid for hours spent in job-related training that is outside of their normal workday.

Employers who fail to comply with this law may face consequences similar to those detailed above in the FLSA section.

Equal Pay Act (1963)

This law requires employers to pay equal wages to both men and women who perform equal jobs in the same establishment. The job titles need not be identical, but rather, the content of the jobs that must be equal in nature. Equivalent jobs are required to have equal skill, working conditions, effort, and responsibility defined as follows:

- Skill: The educational and professional background of the employee performing the job, combined with his or her ability and training

- Working conditions: The physical surroundings in which the work is performed, along with any associated hazards

- Effort: A measurement of the physical or mental exertion that an employee needs to have in order to perform his or her job

- Responsibility: The employee's degree of accountability in performing his or her job

The act does allow for pay differentials when based on other factors other than gender, such as seniority, merit, production quantities or quality, and geographic work differentials. If brought into question, the employer is faced with the burden to prove that these types of *affirmative defenses* do indeed apply.

If there is a need to correct a difference in pay, an employee cannot be penalized by having his or her pay reduced. Rather, the lower-paid employee's pay rate must be increased. Employers who fail to comply with this act may face up to $10,000 in fines and/or imprisonment up to six months.

Employee Retirement Income Security Act (1974)

The Employment Retirement Income Security Act (ERISA) establishes the minimum standards for benefit plans of private, for-profit employers. It states that in order to receive tax advantages, these plans must conform to the Internal Revenue Code's requirements.

This law also established the federal agency known as the Pension Benefit Guaranty Corporation (PBGC). In return for the plans or their sponsors paying premiums to the PBGC, it guarantees payment of vested benefits up to a maximum limit to employees covered by pension plans.

Vested benefits are simply benefits from a retirement account or from a pension plan belonging to an employee that they get to keep regardless of whether they remain employed at the company. Companies have different rules regarding the number of years at which benefits vest; many are five years. Therefore, if an employee resigns after the vesting period of five years, then they can retain the benefits.

Minimum eligibility requirements were also established by ERISA. In order to participate in a plan, an employee must be at least twenty-one years of age and have completed one year of service with the company. However, company plans may be more generous concerning these minimum eligibility requirements.

ERISA established minimum vesting schedules for graded and cliff vesting. *Graded vesting* is a set schedule where employees are vested at a percentage amount less than 100 percent each year, until they accrue enough years of service to be considered 100 percent vested. *Cliff vesting* refers to employees becoming 100 percent vested after a specific number of years of service. ERISA established that employees are always 100 percent vested in their own contributions towards their retirement plans. The vesting schedules differ based on the type of retirement plan an employer is offering.

Minimum reporting standards for benefit plans were set up by ERISA. The act requires benefit plan sponsors to prepare and distribute summary plan descriptions (SPDs) to participants at least once every five years. Participants must also receive a summary annual report (SAR) that contains financial information about the plan.

Employers who fail to comply with this act may face both civil and criminal penalties. Some criminal penalties can cost companies as much as $500,000 and up to ten years in prison.

Older Workers Benefit Protection Act (1990)
The Older Workers Benefit Protection Act (OWBPA) was passed as an amendment to the Age Discrimination in Employment Act (ADEA) of 1967. Under this act, it is illegal for employers to discriminate based on an employee's age in the provision of benefits, such as pension programs, retirement plans, or life insurance. The goal is for companies to offer equal benefits to all employees, regardless of age. However, when it can be justified by substantial cost considerations, an employer can reduce benefits to older workers.

The OWBPA also prevents older workers from waiving rights when it comes to the topic of severance agreements. An older worker is to be given twenty-one days for the purpose of consulting with an attorney and considering a severance agreement, which turns into forty-five days for group terminations. An older worker then has seven days after signing such an agreement in which they can revoke the agreement if they change their mind.

The releases associated with these agreements must reference ADEA age discrimination claims. This limits an employer's lawsuit exposure should an employee decide to challenge the criteria that was used to make decisions about which employees were retained and which employees were let go. Employers who fail to comply with this act may face both civil and criminal penalties.

Retirement Equity Act (1984)
This amendment to the Employee Retirement Income Security Act (ERISA) was passed to address concerns around the needs of divorced spouses, surviving spouses, and employees who left the workforce for some period of time to raise a family. Automatic survivor benefits were now required of

qualified pension plans in the event of a plan participant's death, and the waiver of these benefits could only occur with the consent of both the plan participant and the participant's spouse.

Additionally, pension plans are now required to make benefit payments in accordance with a domestic relations court order to the former spouse of a plan participant. Under this act, plans were no longer allowed to consider maternity or paternity leave as a break in service for the purposes of plan participation or vesting. Employers who fail to comply with this act may face both civil and criminal penalties.

Pension Protection Act (2006)

This amendment to the Employee Retirement Income Security Act (ERISA) was passed to strengthen the pension system by increasing the minimum funding requirements for pension plans, thereby eliminating existing loopholes that previously allowed missed payments for underfunded plans.

Additionally, the Pension Protection Act allows employees to be automatically enrolled in their employer's retirement plan at a default contribution rate after receiving notification. Employees are initially enrolled in default investments, typically according to the age group that the fall within, and there are provisions in place for their contributions to increase on a periodic basis.

If employees choose, they can elect to save at a different contribution rate, select different investments, or opt out of the retirement plan altogether. The automatic enrollment of employees into retirement plans allows employers to increase participation in their plans and employees to take advantage of pre-tax contributions. Employers who fail to comply with this act may face both civil and criminal penalties.

Consolidated Omnibus Budget Reconciliation Act (1986)

The Consolidated Omnibus Budget Reconciliation Act (COBRA) is an amendment to (ERISA) that allows for the continuation of healthcare coverage in the event that such coverage would end due to certain situations, such as the termination of employment, a divorce, or the death of an employee. The act covers employers with twenty or more employees.

Under this law, employees can pay to continue group medical insurance coverage for a period of up to eighteen to thirty-six months, if they elect to do so in a timely manner and pay the full costs of coverage. They can also be charged a 2 percent administrative fee. Employers who fail to comply with this act may face both civil and criminal penalties.

Health Insurance Portability and Accountability Act (1996)

The Health Insurance Portability and Accountability Act (HIPPA) is an amendment (ERISA). It was passed to improve the continuity and portability of healthcare coverage. This act addresses pre-existing medical conditions or those for which an employee or a member of their immediate family received medical advice or treatment during the six-month period prior to their enrollment date into the employer's healthcare plan, such as a serious illness, injury, or pregnancy.

If an employee had creditable healthcare coverage—a group health plan, Medicare, or a military-sponsored healthcare plan—for a period of twelve months, with no lapse in coverage of sixty-three days or more, then an employer cannot refuse them coverage in a new group health plan due to a pre-existing medical condition and cannot charge them a higher rate for coverage. However, if an employee did not previously have creditable healthcare coverage, then an employer can exclude coverage for the treatment of a preexisting medical condition for a period of twelve months—with the exception of pregnancy—or for a period of up to eighteen months for late enrollees in the plan.

Additionally, this act only permits covered entities to use or disclose protected health information for treatment, payment, and healthcare operations. If protected health information is to be released for any other reason, written authorization is required from the patient.

Medical records related to the request for work-related accommodations under the Americans with Disabilities Act (ADA) and leaves of absences under the Family Medical Leave Act (FMLA) are not covered under this law. Employers must have a designated privacy officer who will oversee the organization's privacy policy, along with conducting all necessary training for employees. Employers who fail to comply with this act may face both civil and criminal penalties. Some criminal penalties can cost companies as much as $250,000 and up to ten years in prison.

Patient Protection and Affordable Care Act (2010)

This act—also known as Obamacare, after President Barack Obama—was phased in over a four-year period, making access to healthcare available to several million more Americans. If individuals do not have access to employer-sponsored healthcare coverage, Medicare, or Medicaid, they are now able to purchase healthcare from an insurance exchange and possibly receive a subsidy.

One of the goals of this act is to keep the overall cost of healthcare coverage down by having individuals take advantage of preventative care, such as blood pressure and cholesterol screenings, well-woman visits, and vision screening for all children. Additionally, under this act, children are now permitted to stay under the coverage of their parents' healthcare until the age of twenty-six, and individuals with preexisting medical conditions cannot be denied coverage.

Every American citizen is now required to have health insurance each year or face paying an income tax surcharge. An employer mandate is also being enforced, which is a requirement that all companies employing fifty or more full-time employees provide at least 95 percent of those employees and their dependents with affordable health insurance or be subject to a per-employee fee, based on several factors.

Mental Health Parity Act (1996)

The Mental Health Parity Act (MHPA) was put into place to ensure that large group health plans provide coverage for mental health care in the same manner that they provide coverage for physical health care, such as surgical and medical benefits. For example, this act prevents an employer's group health plan from placing a lower lifetime limit on mental health benefits than the plan's lifetime limit on surgical and medical benefits.

This act applies to employers with more than fifty employees, as long as compliance with the act will not increase the employer's cost by at least one percent. It is important to note that this act does not require large group health plans to include mental health coverage in the benefits that they offer. The law only applies to large group health plans that already include mental health benefits in their packages.

Family Medical Leave Act (1993)

The Family Medical Leave Act (FMLA) was passed to allow eligible employees to take up to twelve weeks of job-protected, unpaid leave during a twelve-month period for specific family and medical reasons. Employees are covered under this act if their employer has at least fifty employees—full or part-time—working within seventy-five miles of a given workplace and if they have worked for their employer for at least twelve months and for a total of 1,250 hours over the past year.

FMLA covers leave for the following reasons:

- The birth of a child, adoption, or foster-care placement

- The serious health condition of a spouse, child, or parent

- The serious health condition of the employee, one requiring inpatient care or continuing treatment by a healthcare provider

- Qualifying exigency leave, or leave to address the most common issues that arise when an employee's spouse, child, or parent is on active duty or call to active duty status—e.g., making financial and legal arrangements or arranging for alternative childcare

- Military caregiver leave or leave to care for a covered service member, such as the employee's spouse, child, parent, or his/her next of kin, with a serious injury or illness. Employees are to be granted up to twenty-six weeks of job-protected, unpaid leave during a twelve-month period to care for a covered service member.

Instead of taking all of their leave at once, employees can choose to take FMLA leave intermittently or in blocks of time for specific, qualifying reasons as approved by their employer. One reason for doing so would be for an employee to attend medical appointments for his/her ongoing treatment and testing for a serious health condition.

Spouses who work for the same employer must share the amount of FMLA time they take for the birth of a child, adoption, or foster care placement or for the serious health condition of a child or parent. The total amount of leave taken by both spouses must add up to twelve weeks for the reasons stated above or twenty-six weeks for the care of a covered service member.

Employers also have the right to require employees to take unpaid FMLA leave concurrent with and relevant paid leave, such as sick time or vacation time, to which the employees are entitled under their current policies. In addition, a week containing a holiday still counts as a full week of FMLA, whether or not the holiday is considered to be paid time.

Employers are required to maintain an employee's group health care coverage while they are out on FMLA leave when the employee was covered under such a plan prior to leave. Once an employee's FMLA leave has ended, they are to be reinstated to their original job or to an equivalent job with equivalent conditions of employment, pay, and benefits.

Employers who fail to comply with the FMLA act may face both civil and criminal penalties. Also, if the Department of Labor finds that an employer did not post FMLA rights and responsibilities notices in the workplace, then a penalty of $110 can be assessed for willful failure to post.

<u>Uniform Services Employment and Reemployment Rights Act (1994)</u>
This law was passed to protect the employment, reemployment, and retention rights of civilian employees who serve in uniformed services, veterans, and members of the Reserve. The act requires covered employees to provide their employers with at least thirty days' notice of their need for leave, if possible, and covers them for up to five years of unpaid leave.

Under the Fair Labor Standards Act, exempt employees must be paid their full salary while out on leave, less any compensation that they receive for serving in the military. Employees who are out on military leave are also expected to receive the same seniority-based benefits that they would have received had they not been out of work on leave, such as vacation time and 401(k) contributions.

Additionally, if an employee's military leave will be less than one month, an employer must continue healthcare coverage under the same terms as if the employee is still actively employed. After the first month of military leave, employers are not required to continue group healthcare coverage at their expense. Instead, employers can make healthcare coverage available at the employee's expense for a period of twenty-four months or the duration of their military service, whichever is less. Employers are also not allowed to count an employee's military leave as a break in service for pension plan purposes.

The act requires covered employees returning from leave to apply for reemployment within a specific timeframe following completion of their military service:

- If an employee has been out on leave less than thirty-one days, they must return to work on the first workday following completion of military service.

- If an employee has been out on leave between thirty-one and 180 days, they must apply for reemployment within fourteen days of completing military service.

- If an employee's leave has been in excess of 180 days, they must apply for reemployment within ninety days of completing military service.

When an employee returns from military leave, they are to be reinstated to a position that they would find themself in if they had not been out of work on leave, which may require some retraining efforts on the part of the employer. If after some period of time and retraining efforts, the employee is found not to be qualified for the new position, the employee can return to the position that they held prior to military leave.

Under this act, employers are also encouraged to make reasonable efforts to accommodate disabled veterans returning from military leave. Such individuals have up to two years after completing their military service to apply for reemployment.

Employers who fail to comply with USERRA may face both civil and criminal penalties, ultimately repaying any wronged employees for backpay and lost benefits.

Old Age, Survivor, and Disability Insurance (OASDI) Program
The Social Security Act (SSA) of 1935 designed this program to ensure a continuation of income for individuals who are retired, spouses and dependent children of employees who are deceased, and individuals who qualify for social security disability. This OASDI program is funded by contributions made by both employees and employers.

At a minimum, employees must work at least forty quarters or ten years to qualify for this program. A surviving spouse or dependent child's eligibility is determined by the length of time the spouse or parent has worked. The amount of benefits paid out to individuals who qualify is dependent upon the length of time the employee worked and the amount they paid into the program.

The majority of payments under this program are made in the category of Old-Age benefits. Individuals who qualify must be at least sixty-two years of age to receive partial benefits and between sixty-five and sixty-seven years of age to receive full benefits, depending on the year they were born. In most cases, a non-working spouse can expect to receive half of the amount of benefits of the working spouse.

Individuals who qualify for Social Security disability and receive benefits under this program must prove that they are unable to perform profitable work because they are totally disabled.

Federal-State Unemployment Insurance Program

Unemployment Insurance was created under the Social Security Act (SSA) of 1935 as a way to provide partial income replacement for a period of time to individuals who find themselves unemployed involuntarily. This benefit is funded primarily by employers—via a state unemployment tax—and administered by the individual states under national guidelines.

The number of weeks for which an employee can receive unemployment benefits can range from one to thirty-nine weeks, with twenty-six weeks being the most common duration. During some periods of high unemployment, the period of twenty-six weeks can be extended up to an additional thirteen weeks.

Eligibility in most states is contingent upon an employee having worked a minimum number of weeks, not being terminated for misconduct, not having left their job voluntarily, not finding themself unemployed due to a labor dispute, being available and actively seeking work, and not refusing suitable employment.

Medicare (1965)

This program is an amendment to the Social Security Act (SSA) of 1935 with the purpose of providing healthcare for individuals age sixty-five and older, which is not dependent on their income or ability to pay. Some individuals under the age of sixty-five who are disabled, as well as those individuals suffering from end-stage renal disease, are also eligible for coverage under Medicare. The program is funded by employees and employers paying a percentage of salaries.

Medicare has four distinct parts:

- *Medicare Part A* is hospital insurance, which is considered mandatory, and most individuals do not have to pay for this coverage.

- *Medicare Part B* is medical insurance and covers such healthcare expenses as physicians' services and outpatient care. Medicare Part B is optional, and most individuals pay a monthly fee to have this coverage.

- *Medicare Part C* is referred to as Medicare Advantage Plans, such as HMOs or PPOs that are offered by private companies and approved by Medicare. The Medicare Advantage Plans are available to individuals who are entitled to Medicare Part A and enrolled in Medicare Part B. These plans provide participants with hospital and medical coverage, as well as with additional coverage, such as dental, vision, and hearing, and, in some cases, prescription drug coverage. Medicare Advantage Plans can provide substantial cost savings for individuals who are eligible to enroll in them once a year, during an open enrollment period.

- *Medicare Part D* is prescription drug coverage and is considered optional. Individuals who choose Part D pay a monthly fee to have this coverage. Part D is available to individuals who are entitled to Medicare Part A and enrolled in Medicare Part B.

Compensation Policies/Programs

Pay Structures

Following the completion of job evaluations and the collection of data from salary surveys, a company works to establish an overall pay structure. A *pay structure* provides the overall framework for an organization to use to deliver its total rewards strategy. When creating a pay structure, companies establish pay grades by grouping jobs together that are found to have the same relative internal worth. Jobs within the same pay grade will pay the same rate or within the same pay range. When employers are setting pay ranges, they determine the minimum, midpoint, and maximum compensation for a pay grade and set some overlap between pay ranges.

Not every employee fits perfectly within the set pay ranges. For example, an employee who is paid a *red-circle rate* is paid at a rate above the range maximum. If this tends to be a common occurrence, it may mean that the organization's pay ranges lag the market and need to be re-examined. In contrast, an employee who is paid a *green-circle rate* is paid at a rate below the range minimum.

Broadbanding

This type of pay structure occurs when employers decide to combine multiple pay levels into one, which results in only a handful of salary grades with much wider ranges. This type of pay structure is easier to administer and eliminates the green-circle and red-circle rates as described in the section above. Broadbanding also leads to a flatter organizational structure, which encourages employees' horizontal movement through skill acquisition versus the traditional vertical movement through promotions to new pay grades. Therefore, employees may feel that there are fewer promotion opportunities in a broadbanding pay structure.

Wage Compression

This takes place when a new employee is paid at a higher wage than an individual who is currently employed in a similar position and with similar skills in an organization. Wage compression creates a pay inequity and should be avoided, if possible, as it can lead to existing employees becoming unmotivated.

Compa-ratio

A *compa-ratio* is computed by dividing the pay level of an employee by the midpoint of the salary range.

For example, in Company A, salaries in a certain position range from $12-$16 an hour, and an entry-level employee's salary is $12 an hour. The midpoint of the salary range is $14. The pay level of the employee ($12) is then divided by the midpoint of the salary range ($14), resulting in a compa-ratio of .86 or 86 percent.

Compa-ratios are used as indicators as to how wages match, lead, or lag the market. If a compa-ratio is below 100 percent, as with the example above, the employee is paid less than the midpoint of the salary range. This can be attributed to the fact that an employee is new to a job and/or an organization, is a low performer, or is working for a company that has adopted a lag behind the market pay strategy.

If a compa-ratio is above 100 percent, the employee is paid more than the midpoint of the salary range. This can be attributed to the fact that an employee is long-tenured, a high performer, or is working for a company that has adopted a lead ahead of the market pay strategy.

Base Pay

Base pay is fixed compensation that an employee receives in return for work that they have performed. An employee's base salary does not include any additional compensation, such as bonuses, and can be paid out in the form of an hourly wage or a salary, based on the nature of the job. Hourly wages are paid out per pay period, based on the number of hours an employee works; a salary is paid out the same amount of money each pay period, no matter how many hours an employee works.

Base pay is determined by a number of factors, such as the value of the job to the organization, an individual's knowledge, skills, and abilities, and the supply/demand of talent. An employee is often paid at a higher base pay if their job is perceived to have greater value as it has a greater impact and contribution towards an organization's strategic goals and objectives.

Additionally, an employee's base pay is often reflective of the essential duties and responsibilities associated with their position, along with the required knowledge, skills, educational background, and professional experience to perform in the role.

Finally, supply and demand of talent refers to the availability of individuals who are able to perform a specific role within the employer's geographic location. This determines how quickly the employer is able to fill an open position. For example, if an electric company is located within close proximity to a college with a reputable engineering program, then engineer talent will be readily available and will not need to be recruited at a premium base pay.

Differential and Performance-Based Pay (Merit Pay)
Even though it is not required by law under the Fair Labor Standards Act (FLSA), many employers elect to reward their employees in certain situations with compensation that is in addition to their base pay. Pay practices regarding these types of situations vary greatly among employers.

Differential pay programs are used to reward employees for performing work that is viewed as less than desirable. There are time-based and geographic differential pay programs.

- *Time-based differential pay* is allotted to employees based on when they work. For example, some employees receive additional pay, called *shift pay*, for working second or third shift or for being called in to work during an emergency, also known as *emergency shift pay*.

- *Premium pay* is sometimes paid to employees as a higher rate of overtime pay for working holidays or vacation days.

- Employees who work in a risky environment can be paid *hazard pay*.

- *Reporting pay* can be paid to employees who arrive at their place of employment and find that there is no available work for them to perform.

- *Geographic differential pay* is allotted to employees based on where they work. For example, sometimes employers have different pay structures for different locations and pay extra to attract workers to certain locales, such as remote, offshore oil rigs, and institute pay differentials for work in foreign countries.

Performance-based pay plans are used to motivate employees to perform their work at a higher level. Performance-based pay plans can be instituted at the individual, group, and organization-wide levels.

- Examples of *individual performance-based pay plans* are piece rates, commissions, and cash bonuses. These promote productivity (by 30 percent) but do not promote teamwork, and may be difficult to measure.

- In *group performance-based pay plans*, an entire group is rewarded for exceeding performance standards and each person in the group receives the same amount of incentive as a percentage of their pay. An example of a group performance-based pay plan is a gainsharing plan, where a portion of the gains an organization realizes from group effort is shared with the group. These promote teamwork but have a moderate impact on productivity (13 percent).

- *Organization-wide performance-based pay plans* are profit-sharing plans, performance-sharing plans, and stock ownership plans. These increase shareholder returns and company profits, but generate only a 6 percent increase in productivity.

Internal/External Equity
A company's total rewards system should be appropriate for its workforce and be both internally and externally equitable. *Internal equity* exists if employees are compensated fairly according to their performance on the job, as well as for the knowledge, skills, and abilities that are required for their positions and the responsibilities that are expected of them. A lack of internal equity can lead to employees' perceptions of unfairness, poor attitudes, and lack of commitment.

External equity exists if a company's rewards are equitable when compared to other organizations in similar industries, occupations, and geographic locations. Employers can measure external equity by referring to salary surveys and benchmarking competitors' compensation policies. A lack of external equity can make it difficult to recruit individuals who are truly qualified and in high-demand, and it can result in higher turnover.

Managing Payroll Information

New Hires
There are several tasks that need to be completed as part of the on-boarding process during a new employee's first day on the job. A new hire must complete an Employment Eligibility Verification form, better known as an I-9 form. This form verifies the eligibility of an employee to work legally in the United States. A W-4 form, or Employee Withholding Allowance form, must also be completed by a new hire to ensure that the correct amount of taxes will be withheld from their paycheck.

In addition, a new hire will need to be enrolled into any of the employee benefits programs that they elect to participate in, and the new hire will also need to be added to the company's workers' compensation plan per the law.

Adjustments

A pay rate adjustment occurs when there is a need to pay an employee more or less than their regular rate of pay. Adjustments can be made in the payroll system for employees at the end of the fiscal year or during an off-cycle, made at any time during the year. Pay rate adjustments can occur for the following reasons:

- Change in the number of hours an employee works
- Employee receives a merit or a promotion
- Employee accepts a transfer to another department that involves a different rate of pay
- Employee's job is reclassified

Terminations

Following an employee's termination, several pieces of data must be entered in the company's payroll system in a timely manner, in order to remain compliant with several laws. At a minimum, the employer will enter the termination date and the reason for the employee's termination in the payroll system.

The entry of this information will assist in the calculation of any outstanding salary and leave entitlements due to the employee, along with the cancellation of any active enrollment in benefits programs. Most payroll systems also allow an employer to select whether or not an employee is eligible for rehire and to add some additional notes, which can assist future recruiting staff.

Additionally, payroll systems provide employers with the ability to calculate and manage severance pay and unemployment benefits, when needed. Some payroll systems also include fields that provide the ability to track the various stages of the dispute, litigation, and appeals process if an employee disagrees with the employer about termination or the amount of severance.

Managing Outsourced Compensation and Benefits Components

Payroll Vendors

Some of the reasons that companies may elect to outsource their payroll function include the following:

- Freeing up staff time to allow resources to be more strategic in nature
- To reduce costs
- To improve compliance
- Possibly to avoid fines associated with incorrect/late payments or IRS filings
- To have the ability to offer direct deposit of payroll checks to employees

An employer can choose to outsource its entire payroll function or only one or more areas of its payroll function, such as W-2 form printing services. When outsourcing payroll, an employer should select a vendor with an excellent reputation for paying employees on time and providing a high level of customer service.

In an effort not to create additional work, it is important to determine if the vendor's systems are able to effectively integrate with the employer's systems—e.g., time tracking and self-service technologies used to update employees' personal data and payroll-related information. An employer should ensure that the vendor chosen will be able to provide the level of service that the company requires at an affordable cost.

COBRA Administration

When administering COBRA, the length of time that an employee is eligible for coverage is determined by the type of qualifying event. For example, eighteen months is the period of eligibility for an employee's reduction in hours or an employee's termination, while twenty-nine months is the period of eligibility for the disablement of an employee. Additionally, thirty-six months is the period of eligibility for a divorce/legal separation or death of an employed spouse, as well as for a dependent child who loses eligibility status under the plan rules. Employees and their family members have sixty days to elect COBRA coverage from the time that a qualifying event has taken place.

Covered employers are required to provide an initial COBRA notice within ninety days of the date an employee/spouse is covered under the plan. Employers are also required to provide a notice of unavailability of continuation of coverage within fourteen days of the date of the qualifying event, if the employee/spouse is not covered. Employees must be notified of their coverage ending before the maximum continuous period allowed.

Employee Recognition Vendors

Due to a lack of staff resources, time, or in-house expertise, companies may choose to outsource their employee rewards program to a trusted recognition vendor. Since a vendor can, ultimately, determine the success or failure of a company's rewards program, there are a number of items that an employer should evaluate when entering into this type of relationship.

An exceptional recognition vendor will take the time to learn about a company's culture, business goals, employee rewards needs, and program budget. The recognition vendor should have an offering of high quality awards and be able to accommodate rush orders and unique or custom awards, if needed.

Additionally, world-class customer service is the key to employees receiving timely reward fulfillment and recognition for their efforts and achievements. An employer should be assured that the company will receive correct invoices and accurate reporting from the vendor. The ultimate goal for both the employer and the recognition vendor is to ensure that employees feel valued and remain loyal.

Conducting Needs Assessments

Benchmarking

Employers use salary surveys to assist them when working to establish the pay structures for their organizations. These surveys collect information from multiple employers regarding salary and benefits, such as employees' starting salaries, merit increases, bonus amounts, and work hours. In order to be comparable, salary surveys are conducted by focusing on a specific geographic region or industry.

Employers can make use of free government salary surveys and inexpensive industry-specific salary surveys, such as those for civil engineering and construction. Employer associations, like the Society for Human Resource Management (SHRM), also conduct salary surveys and provide the results to their members at no charge. Additionally, companies can elect to outsource a salary survey to a survey vendor, which can be quite pricey.

It is important to note that salary survey data contains time-sensitive data that can become outdated rather quickly. Salary data may also need to be aged and/or leveled. *Aging* is the process of adjusting salary data to keep pace with market movement. *Leveling* can be used if a job included on the salary survey is similar—but not identical—to a position within the organization. The data for that job can be weighted or leveled to create a better match.

<u>Employee Surveys</u>

Employee surveys are an additional tool that can be used by companies to gather input on needs or preferences regarding compensation and benefits programs, as well as employees' satisfaction with the existing offerings. Some examples of the types of questions that employees may be asked include the following:

- Whether employees feel that they are compensated fairly compared to the local market
- If they feel that the company offers a competitive benefits package that meets their needs
- If they feel they are recognized for their performance when they go above expectations
- If performance incentives are clearly linked to strategic objectives.

In order to gather the most candid feedback, employees are usually allowed to remain anonymous when responding to these surveys. Management is expected to provide feedback to the participants upon conclusion of the survey and to address any outstanding concerns in a timely manner.

<u>Trend Analysis</u>

In order for a company's compensation and benefits offerings to remain meaningful, it is important for employers to track current and upcoming trends in these areas. In the field of health and welfare, additional employers will promote consumer-directed healthcare by introducing high-deductible health plans. A new cost savings innovation to assist employees will involve a way to visit medical professionals virtually—via video chat on the computer or telemedicine.

Additionally, employers will continue to stress the importance of employees using health saving accounts (HSAs) or health reimbursement arrangements (HRAs) to assist in funding their out-of-pocket healthcare expenses. Employees will also be encouraged to become informed consumers by researching the necessity of procedures, along with the most affordable facilities in which to have their procedures performed.

In the field of compensation, employers will move away from granting across-the-board increases for the entire employee population. Rather, a move will be made towards gaining a greater return on investment by rewarding top performers through the creation of customized rewards packages. Employers will also continue to provide greater transparency to employees regarding the communication of their companies' pay philosophies.

Managing Benefit Programs

Employee benefits fall into two categories: discretionary and non-discretionary.

<u>Non-Discretionary Benefits</u>

Non-discretionary benefits are those benefits that employers are mandated to provide based on certain statutes. These benefits include social security, Medicare, workers' compensation, unemployment insurance, unpaid family medical leave (based on FMLA), and continuation of healthcare coverage (based on COBRA).

<u>Discretionary Benefits</u>
Discretionary benefits are not mandated by law. Employers choose to provide these benefits in order to attract, motivate, and retain their workforce. Discretionary benefits fall into three main categories: health and wellness, deferred compensation, and work-life equity.

- *Health and wellness benefits* include all aspects of healthcare coverage that employers offer, such as major medical plans, dental and vision plans, prescription drug coverage, addiction and substance abuse programs, employee assistance programs (EAPs), wellness programs, and disability/life insurance.

- *Deferred compensation* includes the various types of retirement plans that employers offer, where income is realized at a later date as compensation for work that is performed at the present time.

- *Discretionary benefits* that fall under the category of work-life equity help employees to manage their work schedules with their personal commitments, paid time off for holidays, short-term illness, vacation, jury duty, and bereavement, along with flexible work schedules and telecommuting options. Some employers provide additional discretionary benefits that fall into this category, such as on-site childcare, tuition reimbursement, and relocation assistance.

<u>Health and Welfare</u>
Employers are moving towards consumer-directed healthcare in an effort to keep costs manageable. This simply means making employees responsible for how they spend their healthcare dollars, with the goal of smarter choices.

A direct outcome of this has been the evolution of high-deductible health plans. These plans do not pay for medical services until employees have first paid a very steep out-of-pocket amount, which can be close to a $2,500 deductible for an individual plan and a $5,000 deductible for a family plan. In an effort to help employees offset their costs, high-deductible health plans are often coupled with either a health savings account (HSA) or a health reimbursement arrangement.

- A *health savings account (HSA)* allows employees to pay for approved healthcare expenses pre-tax up to the contribution limits that are set by the IRS. Employers may also make contributions to these accounts, and any remaining balances roll over to the next calendar year, are portable, and can be used into retirement.

- A *health reimbursement arrangement (HRA)* is an employer-funded medical plan that reimburses employees only for eligible healthcare expenses. Each employee receives an employer-paid contribution that is treated as a benefit, not as compensation. Employees can roll over any unpaid funds into the next calendar year, but the funds are not portable.

<u>Managed Care Plans</u>
Managed care plans are healthcare plans that seek to ensure that the treatments an individual receives are medically necessary and performed in a cost-effective manner. There are several different types of managed care plans:

Health Maintenance Organization
A health maintenance organization (HMO) is structured to emphasize preventative care and cost containment. Under this plan, physicians are paid on a per-head basis, rather than for actual treatment. Employees covered under an HMO must seek treatment by physicians who are under the HMO contract.

Preferred Provider Organization
A preferred provider organization (PPO) is formed by an employer who negotiates discounted fees with networks of healthcare providers. In return, the employer guarantees a certain volume of patients. Individuals enrolled in a PPO can elect to receive treatment outside of the network, but they will pay higher copayments or deductibles for doing so.

Point-of-Service Organization
A point-of-service organization (POS) is a combination of a PPO & HMO that provides direct access to specialists.

Exclusive Provider Organization
An exclusive provider organization (EPO) is a plan in which the participants must use the providers who are in the network of coverage or no payment will be made.

Flexible Benefit Plans
Flexible benefit plans—under section 125 of the Internal Revenue Code—allow employers and employees to save taxes on the money they pay toward their group-sponsored health and dental plans, as well as on out-of-pocket medical expenses.

Flexible Spending Accounts
Flexible spending accounts (FSAs) allow employees to use pretax dollars to pay for approved, out-of-pocket healthcare expenses that are not covered by insurance and dependent-care expenses. This increases employees' take-home pay while decreasing employer payroll taxes, since Social Security (FICA) payroll taxes are lowered.

Each employee determines the amount of pay to have deposited into their FSA account each month during the year. Unpaid funds cannot be rolled over into the next calendar year, so the money is commonly referred to as "use it or lose it." However, if the employee decides to leave their company prior to the end of the year before contributing the full dollar amount of a claim that was previously paid by the company, they cannot be held responsible for the remaining balance of the claim.

Full Cafeteria Plans
Full cafeteria plans—under section 125—allow employees to choose from a menu of eligible, qualified healthcare benefits and typically pay for them with pre-allocated benefit credits. Some plans permit employees to cash out any unused benefit credits or to buy additional benefits through pretax salary reductions. Full cafeteria plans allow employees to choose the benefits that are most important to them and their families.

Dental and Vision Insurance
Dental and vision insurance are additional health and wellness benefits frequently provided by employers. Dental and vision plans often stress preventive care, and it is common practice to have employees share in paying a portion of plan premiums.

Life Insurance
Life insurance is another health and wellness benefit typically provided by employers. In the event of an employee's death, the surviving family members will normally receive anywhere from one to two times the employee's annual salary as payment. Some companies allow their employees to purchase life insurance in addition to what they provide.

Disability Insurance
Disability insurance is provided by employers as a health and wellness benefit.

- *Short-term disability insurance* pays an employee a percentage of their salary—typically 50 percent to 70 percent—after a brief waiting period. This is in the event that they are unable to work for a short period of time—normally between ten and twenty-six weeks—following a non-work related injury or illness.

- *Long-term disability insurance* takes over when an employee is still unable to return to work after being out on short-term disability. Long-term disability insurance pays an employee a percentage of their salary—typically 50 to 60 percent—until he or she can return to work or for the number of years listed in the company's policy.

Wellness
Corporate wellness programs are gaining in popularity and are used to maintain and improve employees' health before serious problems arise, in an effort to offset the rising costs of healthcare. Often companies kick off these programs by having their employees participate in voluntary health risk assessments and biometric screenings, testing for such things as blood pressure, body mass index, and cholesterol/blood glucose levels.

Based on employees' individual scores, they can be referred to participate in various wellness workshops—e.g., cardiovascular disease prevention, diabetes prevention, healthy aging, nutritional counseling, or understanding back pain—and/or personalized coaching in order to bring about healthy changes. Employee participation in a wellness program is often tied to an incentive, such as a specific dollar amount taken off of their healthcare premiums, in order to create a change in behavior. Employers directly benefit from employee participation in wellness programs through decreased absenteeism, improved productivity, and decreased spending on healthcare and workers' compensation.

Retirement
In *defined benefit plans*, employers agree to provide employees with a retirement benefit amount based on a formula. There are different approaches to this formula:

Flat-Dollar Approach
Plans using a flat-dollar approach pay a set dollar amount for each year of service under the plan. This is usually seen in plans covering hourly employees under a collective bargaining agreement.

Career Average
Plans utilizing a career average have two methods of computing their formula. In the first method, an employee earns a percentage of pay for each year they are a plan participant. In the second method, an employee's yearly earnings are totaled and then averaged over the number of years they are in the plan. At retirement, the benefit equals a percentage of the career average pay multiplied by the employee's years of service.

Final Pay Approach
Plans using a final pay approach base their benefits on the average earnings during a specified number of years—usually towards the end of an individual's employment.

Cash Balance Plans

Cash balance plans are a specific type of defined benefit plan. These plans express the promised benefit in terms of a hypothetical account balance. They are easily communicated to plan participants, and the accrued benefit is portable. Each year, a participant's account is credited with two types of credits:

- Pay credit: equates to a percentage of their compensation
- Interest credit: a fixed or variable rate linked to an index, such as U.S. Treasury bills

Defined Benefit Plans

Some advantages of defined benefit plans are that the benefit is known to the employee, and the employer bears the burden of the financial risk. However, the cost is unknown. These plans tend to create higher rewards for longer-tenured employees.

Defined Contribution Plans

In defined contribution plans, employees and/or employers pay a specific amount into the plans for each participant. Employer contributions are often based upon a percentage of salary or a percentage of profits. Performance of the funds in these plans ultimately determines employees' benefits.

Examples of defined contribution plans are 401(k) plans, where the yearly amount employees can put into the plan is set by the IRS and adjusted annually for inflation. 403(b) plans are similar in nature and set aside for employees of certain tax-exempt organizations, such as K – 12 public schools, colleges and universities, hospitals, libraries, churches, and philanthropic organizations. Additionally, profit-sharing plans are yet another example of this type of plan.

Some advantages of defined contribution plans are that they can provide valuable benefits to employees with less service and the cost is known. However, the benefit is unknown, and the employee bears the burden of the financial risk.

Here's a breakdown:

Characteristics Of Defined Benefit And Defined Contribution Plans Advantages		
	Defined Benefit Plan	**Defined Contribution Plan**
Employer Contributions and/or Matching Contributions	Employer funded. Federal rules set amounts that employers must contribute to plans in an effort to ensure that plans have enough money to pay benefits when due. There are penalties for failing to meet these requirements.	There is no requirement that the employer contribute, except in SIMPLE and safe harbor 401(k)s, money purchase plans, SIMPLE IRAs, and SEPs. The employer may have to contribute in certain automatic enrollment 401(k) plans. The employer may choose to match a portion of the employee's contributions or to contribute without employee contributions. In some plans, employer contributions may be in the form of employer stock.
Employee Contributions	Generally, employees do not contribute to these plans.	Many plans require the employee to contribute in order for an account to be established.
Managing the Investment	Plan officials manage the investment and the employer is responsible for ensuring that the amount it has put in the plan plus investment earnings will be enough to pay the promised benefit.	The employee often is responsible for managing the investment of his or her account, choosing from investment options offered by the plan. In some plans, plan officials are responsible for investing all the plan's assets.
Amount of Benefits Paid Upon Retirement	A promised benefit is based on a formula in the plan, often using a combination of the employee's age, years worked for the employer, and/or salary.	The benefit depends on contributions made by the employee and/or the employer, performance of the account's investments, and fees charged to the account.
Type of Retirement Benefit Payments	Traditionally, these plans pay the retiree monthly annuity payments that continue for life. Plans may offer other payment options.	The retiree may transfer the account balance into an individual retirement account (IRA) from which the retiree withdraws money, or may receive it as a lump sum payment. Some plans also offer monthly payments through an annuity.
Guarantee of Benefits	The Federal Government, through the Pension Benefit Guaranty Corporation (PBGC), guarantees some amount of benefits.	No Federal guarantee of benefits.
Leaving the Company Before Retirement Age	If an employee leaves after vesting in a benefit but before the plan's retirement age, the benefit generally stays with the plan until the employee files a claim for it at retirement. Some defined benefit plans offer early retirement options.	The employee may transfer the account balance to an individual retirement account (IRA) or, in some cases, another employer plan, where it can continue to grow based on investment earnings. The employee also may take the balance out of the plan, but will owe taxes and possibly penalties, thus reducing retirement income. Plans may cash out small accounts.

Stock Purchase

Employee stock plans are another tool that companies can use to incentivize employees by making them think and behave as owners in the company. A stock option plan affords employees the opportunity to purchase a fixed number of shares of the company's stock at a fixed, or exercise price, during a certain period of time. Employees hope to buy the shares of the company's stock when those shares are trading at a price higher than the exercise price, which will lead to a profit.

An *employee stock ownership plan* (ESOP) is an example of a qualified defined contribution retirement plan that is a stock bonus program. ESOPs give employees significant stock ownership in their companies and allow them to benefit from any associated profitability and growth, which can motivate them to be more focused on the performance of their organizations. Although ESOPs can provide valuable benefits, the employees bear the burden of the financial risk.

<u>Employee Assistance Programs (EAPs)</u>
These are employer-sponsored benefit programs that are used to provide help for employees who are experiencing difficulties in the areas of anxiety, depression, marital or family relationship problems, legal issues, and financial concerns. These programs assist employees with identifying their problems with short-term interventions. For instance, employees may be referred to an expert for assistance with complex matters. Employees' use of EAPs is voluntary and confidential, and employers typically provide this service by contracting with a counseling agency.

Training in Compensation and Benefits Programs

Communication and training on a company's compensation and benefits programs, policies, and processes is essential to ensure that employees have realistic expectations about benefits and pay decisions, understand the link between performance and rewards, and are informed about potential career paths. Companies should also share information with employees when a competitive market analysis is performed and how the study was completed.

In addition to more formal, organization-wide communications that may take place only a few times a year, ongoing, informal communications should be encouraged between managers and employees. In an effort to make these communications more personal, companies are distributing total reward statements to their employees to demonstrate that their pay is just one piece of the picture.

A *total reward statement* breaks down the rest of an employee's comprehensive benefits package to show them everything that goes into their total compensation, along with the company's contributions towards each of the items. The goal is to show employees an overall picture of the value and associated cost of their total compensation package.

Another component of the overall strategy is to communicate a *rewards program* that will drive employee behaviors that are needed to accomplish the business strategy. For example, creative problem solving may be the employee behavior directly related to customer loyalty—a strategic business goal—which may result in the creation of an employee training and development program in that area.

<u>Self-Service Technologies</u>
Self-service technologies allow employees, via an online system, to complete personal data updates— e.g., contact information, direct deposit information, federal and state withholding information—as well as their annual benefits selections, during an open enrollment period. Throughout the year, employees are also able to make any necessary, allowable benefits changes and check their benefits balances, as well as submit questions they may have regarding their benefits to human resources and, possibly, to benefits providers. Additionally, some self-service applications allow employees and managers to complete the performance management process and access their pay statements and end-of-the-year tax documentation.

Employee self-service programs are user-friendly, available twenty-four hours a day, seven days a week, and are accessible either from the office or from employees' homes. These programs greatly reduce the number of inquiries made to the human resources department, since employees can typically answer a vast majority of their own questions. Additionally, there is a significant reduction in paper printing and postage as well as in transaction processing costs. Transactions are also posted faster in these systems and with a higher degree of accuracy.

Budgeting and Accounting Practices

Since the costs of providing employee benefits continues to rise, employers should take part in strategic planning to ensure they are providing affordable benefits that are desired by employees. This, in turn, will result in the creation of controlled budgets.

Based on the withholdings that an employee has selected on their W-4 form, federal income tax is withheld from an employee's gross wage income. State income tax is then deducted from an employee's gross pay. Employers are also responsible for withholding FICA—Federal Insurance Contributions Act—or Social Security taxes from an employee's pay. FICA is broken down into two taxes: Medicare and OASDI—Old Age, Survivor, and Disability Insurance.

Then, employee deductions for participation in a company-sponsored healthcare program are computed. Other potential deductions from an employee's pay could include city and county taxes, pretax employee contributions, and contributions to a 401(k), 403(b), HSA account, or FSA account. Employers can make payments on behalf of their employees, which may include matching 401(k) or 403(b) contributions, workers' compensation premiums, Federal Unemployment Tax (FUTA), State Unemployment Tax (SUTA), and the employer portion of Social Security taxes.

When considering accounting practices as they relate to employee benefits, dollars spent by employers on company-sponsored healthcare programs are excluded from their employees' gross income. Therefore, wellness program incentives, such as reductions in employee healthcare premiums and employer contributions to employees' health savings accounts (HSAs) and health reimbursement accounts (HRAs), are non-taxable, as these types of incentives and accounts are being used for medical care and treatment.

A gift card used to incentivize an employee is considered taxable income. However, a tangible achievement award given to an employee in a meaningful presentation to recognize their years of service is non-taxable. Additionally, an employee's business use of a company vehicle, as well as employee discounts on employer goods and services, are also considered non-taxable income.

Job Evaluation Methods

After a job analysis is performed, which results in job descriptions and job specifications, a job evaluation is conducted to determine the relative worth of each job position by creating a hierarchy. This ultimately leads to the establishment of a pay structure.

- Job analysis: the process used to determine the requirements and importance of duties for a particular job

- Job descriptions: a list of general duties and responsibilities for a particular job

- Job specifications: a statement of the essential parts of a particular class of jobs. This includes a summary of the duties to be performed, and responsibilities and qualifications necessary to do the job.

- Job evaluation: the ways to determine the value or worth of a job in relation to other jobs in a company

There are two main job evaluation methods: non-quantitative and quantitative.

Non-Quantitative Job Evaluation Methods
Non-quantitative job evaluation methods are also known as *whole-job methods*. The three specific examples are job ranking, paired comparison, and job classification.

Job Ranking
Job ranking involves a job-to-job comparison by developing a hierarchy of jobs from the lowest to the highest, based on each job's overall importance to the organization. This is a quick, inexpensive way for small organizations to compare one job to another.

Paired Comparison
Paired comparison is a process of comparing each job to every other job for the purpose of ranking all jobs on a scale from high to low. This is also an effective, low-cost job evaluation method for small companies.

Job Classification
Job classification involves grouping jobs into a predetermined number of grades, each of which has a class description to use for job comparisons. Benchmark jobs that fall into each class can be defined as reference points. An example of job classification put into practice is the Federal Government's use of the General Schedule classification system.

Quantitative Job Evaluation Methods
Quantitative job evaluation methods use a scaling system and provide a score that indicates how valuable one job is when compared to another job. The two specific examples are the point factor method and the factor comparison method.

Point Factor Method
The point factor method is less complex and most commonly used. This method uses specific, compensable factors, such as skill, responsibility, effort, working conditions, and the supervision of others, in order to evaluate the relative worth of each job. Each job receives a total point value, and then, the relative worth of all jobs within an organization can be compared.

Factor Comparison Method
The factor comparison method is more complex and rarely used. This method involves a ranking of each job by each selected compensable factor and then identifies dollar values for each level of each factor to develop a pay rate for an evaluated job. It is best to use this method when wages are not frequently changing and the organization uses a flat rate of pay for each job. This method can sometimes be used as part of a labor contract.

External Labor Markets and/or Economic Factors

When developing a total rewards strategy, companies should take into consideration certain *environmental factors*, such as political/social unrest and employee demographics, and the effect these items will have on turnover, unemployment rates, and the ability to attract and retain employees.

Companies should also consider *competitive factors*, such as industry consolidation and off-shoring—certain parts of a business's operations being sent overseas—and the effect these items will have on the cost of labor. Additionally, companies should also consider items in both the legal environment, such as laws, accounting, and tax regulations, and in the labor market, such as the availability of skilled and technically qualified employees, when developing a total rewards strategy.

Non-Cash Compensation

Non-monetary compensation is the category of employee benefits that do not carry tangible value. This includes flexible working schedules, company parties, a nice office, rewarding work, and a supportive work environment.

Equity Programs

Equity Compensation
Equity compensation is another form of non-cash compensation; it is used to attract and retain employees to work for a startup company. Employees who decide to work for a startup company often do so to gain real world experience, make a difference in their line of work, and/or to have increased flexibility and a more laid-back office environment. In return, those employees are typically paid a salary that is less than the market. The balance of that salary is given in equity compensation, which is a way for the employees to have an ownership interest in the company. The company gives the employees stock options, allowing them to purchase shares of the company's stock at preset prices. Employees gain control of the option according to a set-vesting schedule, which encourages them to work for the company for many years.

Non-Cash Rewards
Managers are frequently being asked to do more with less, including stretching their compensation budgets. This is where non-cash rewards can be factored in with cash compensation to motivate the workforce effectively. Non-cash rewards include such items as personalized thank-you notes for a job well done, company merchandise, and gift cards. Some organizations have factored non-cash rewards into their formal recognition programs, making them more meaningful.

For example, there are peer-to-peer recognition programs in place, where one employee can send a personalized thank-you eCard to another employee for a job well done. In that same system, managers can acknowledge an employee for his or her extra effort on a project by assigning a number of recognition points, along with sending an eCard. Once an employee accumulates a bank of recognition points, they can cash in the points to receive either a gift card or an item from the company store.

Fiduciary Responsibilities

ERISA legislation contains a section dedicated to *fiduciary standards*—rules surrounding how plan fiduciaries, individuals who have a legal duty to act in another party's interest, should be conducting the operation of the benefit plan. According to ERISA, an employer must follow what is known as the *prudent person rule*, which means that the employer cannot take more risks than a reasonably-knowledgeable, prudent investor would take under similar circumstances.

Additionally, the benefit plan assets must be kept separate from other company assets. This rule was established to prevent employers from misusing funds set aside for providing benefits. Finally, the employer must follow minimum funding standards that apply to retirement benefit plans.

Practice Questions

1. The federal minimum wage is currently set at $7.25/hour. However, in the state of Maryland, where Rachel's ice cream parlor resides, the minimum wage is currently set somewhat higher at $8.25/hour. Which statement below accurately reflects the rate of pay at which Rachel's new employees starting out at the minimum wage would receive?

    a. The new employees will receive $7.25/hour. When the federal minimum wage is set lower than a state's minimum wage, an employer can go with the lower rate of pay as its standard.

    b. The new employees will receive $8.25/hour. When a state's minimum wage is higher than the federal minimum wage, an employer must use the higher state minimum wage as its standard.

    c. The new employees will receive $7.75/hour, which is an average of the federal minimum wage and the state's minimum wage.

    d. Rachel's ice cream parlor does not have enough employees to fall under the guidelines of the Fair Labor Standards Act (FLSA), which governs minimum wage.

2. Which of the following individuals would qualify for non-exempt status under the Fair Labor Standards Act (FLSA)?

    a. An employee whose position does not require specialized education

    b. An individual who supervises the work of two or more staff members

    c. An employee who must use independent judgment in their daily work

    d. An employee who earns more than $455 per week

3. Which of the following is NOT one of the three categories that the IRS's twenty factors fall under for determining if an individual working at a company is an employee or an independent contractor?

    a. Financial control

    b. Reporting accountability

    c. Behavioral control

    d. Type of relationship

4. Which of the following items is NOT a covered provision under the Fair Labor Standards Act (FLSA)?

    a. Overtime pay

    b. Employee classification

    c. Child labor

    d. Hazard pay

5. Which piece of legislation requires employers to pay employees for preliminary and postliminary tasks, such as job-related travel time that is outside of an employee's regular work commute and time spent in job-related training?

    a. Equal Pay Act

    b. Portal-to-Portal Act

    c. Fair Labor Standards Act (FLSA)

    d. Davis Bacon Act

6. Which of the following statements is true regarding differential pay?
   a. Differential pay is required by the Fair Labor Standards Act (FLSA).
   b. Differential pay programs are used to reward employees for performing work that is viewed as less than desirable.
   c. Pay practices regarding differential pay are standardized among employers.
   d. Differential pay programs are used to motivate employees to perform their work at a higher level.

7. A pension plan that meets the minimum standards set by the Employee Retirement Income Security Act (ERISA) must do which one of the following?
   a. Allow new hires to participate beginning in their first month of employment
   b. Provide plan participants with a copy of the summary plan description once every ten years
   c. Include schedules for graded and cliff vesting
   d. Allow the employer to keep pension plan assets together with other company assets

8. What is the compa-ratio for a salary range of $10 – $22 and an entry-level employee salary of $12.50?
   a. The compa-ratio is 70 percent.
   b. The compa-ratio is 78 percent.
   c. The compa-ratio is 1.04 percent.
   d. The compa-ratio is .96 percent.

9. Based on the compa-ratio determined for the question above, which of the following can be deduced about the employee and/or the company's pay strategy?
   a. The employee is new to the job and/or the organization, is a low performer, or is working for a company that has adopted a lag behind the market pay strategy.
   b. The employee is new to the job and/or the organization, is a high performer, or is working for a company that has adopted a lag behind the market pay strategy.
   c. The employee is long-tenured, a high performer, or is working for a company that has adopted a lead ahead of the market pay strategy.
   d. The employee is long-tenured, a low performer, or is working for a company that has adopted a lead ahead of the market pay strategy.

10. An employee has passed away on the job. For what length of time is his surviving wife eligible for continuation of healthcare coverage under the Consolidated Omnibus Budget Reconciliation Act (COBRA)?
   a. Three months
   b. Eighteen months
   c. Thirty-six months
   d. Twenty-nine months

11. Considering they have met all of the necessary requirements, which of the following individuals is eligible to take unpaid, protected leave from work under the Family Medical Leave Act (FMLA)?
   a. An employee who is non-weight bearing, recovering from ankle surgery, and who will have multiple follow-up appointments with his surgeon and numerous physical therapy visits to attend.
   b. An employee who is out of the office for three days sick with the flu.
   c. An employee who wants to take care of her Aunt who is suffering from end-stage lung cancer.
   d. An employee who wishes to travel to China to support her sister who is in the process of adopting a child in that country.

12. Which of the following benefits is considered to be discretionary?
    a. Unpaid family medical leave
    b. Life insurance
    c. Continuation of healthcare coverage
    d. Worker's compensation

13. Which of the following is considered to be indirect compensation?
    a. Bonus
    b. Incentive pay
    c. Pension plan
    d. Hourly wage

14. Which of the following is used to describe the knowledge, skills, abilities, education, and experience that are essential to performing a specific job?
    a. Job analysis
    b. Job description
    c. Job specification
    d. Job evaluation

15. Which of the following is a quantitative method of job evaluation?
    a. Job ranking
    b. Paired comparison
    c. Factor comparison method
    d. Job classification

16. Once a salary survey is completed, what is the term used for weighting the data for jobs included on the survey that are similar, but not identical, to positions with the organization? This process is done to create a more accurate match.
    a. Aging
    b. Benchmarking
    c. Leveling
    d. Wage compression

17. Which of the following is a direct result of broadbanding?
    a. Green-circle rates
    b. Taller organizational structures
    c. Red-circle rates
    d. Flatter organizational structures

18. Which of the following types of compensation is given to employees when they work during holidays or vacation days?
    a. Reporting pay
    b. Shift pay
    c. Premium pay
    d. Emergency shift pay

19. Under the Uniform Services Employment and Reemployment Rights Act (USERRA), which of the following actions are employers prohibited from taking?

a. Halting an employee's vacation accrual while they are out on military leave

b. Continuing health care coverage at their expense for an employee who is out on military leave for six months

c. Continuing to pay an exempt employee who is out on military their full salary, minus their earning for serving in the military

d. Making reasonable efforts to accommodate a disabled veteran returning from military leave

20. Which of the following is an example of a defined benefit plan?

a. Cash balance plan

b. 401(k) plan

c. 403(b) plan

d. Section 125 plan

Answer Explanations

1. B: The new employees at Rachel's ice cream parlor will receive $8.25/hr. When a state's minimum wage is set at a higher rate than the federal minimum wage, such as Maryland's minimum wage, an employer must use the higher state minimum wage as its standard when paying employees.

2. A: Employees who qualify for non-exempt status under the Fair Labor Standards Act (FLSA) are those who earn a salary of less than $23,600 per year or $455 per week, do not supervise others, and whose positions do not require specialized education or the use of independent judgment.

3. B: The three categories that the IRS's twenty factors fall under for determining if an individual working at a company is an employee or an independent contractor are Choice *A*, financial control, Choice *C*, behavioral control, and Choice *D*, type of relationship. Reporting ability is not one of the categories.

4. D: Hazard pay is not a covered provision. The Fair Labor Standards Act (FLSA) establishes guidelines around Choice *A*, overtime pay, Choice *B*, employee classification (exempt and non-exempt status), minimum wage, on-call pay, record keeping, and Choice *C*, child labor.

5. B: The Portal-to-Portal Act deals with the preliminary and postliminary tasks of employees. The act requires employers to pay employees who are covered under the FLSA for time spent traveling to perform job-related tasks, if that travel is outside of the employees' regular work commute. Additionally, employees are to be paid for hours spent in job-related training that is outside of their normal workday.

6. B: Differential pay programs are used to reward employees for performing work that is viewed as less than desirable, and these programs vary greatly among employers. Differential pay is not required by the FLSA.

7. C: The plan must include minimum vesting schedules for graded and cliff vesting. In order for a pension plan to meet the minimum standards set by ERISA, employees must be at least twenty-one years of age and have completed one year of service with the company in order to participate in the plan. Plan participants must be provided with a copy of the summary plan description at least once every five years. Additionally, the pension plan assets must be kept separate from other company assets.

8. B: The compa-ratio is computed by finding the mid-point of the salary range, which is $16 in this example. Then, the pay level of the employee ($12.50) is divided by the midpoint of the salary range ($16) to receive a compa-ratio of .78 or 78 percent.

9. A: Since the compa-ratio in question eight is 78 percent and, thus, below 100 percent, the employee is paid less than the midpoint of the salary range. This can be attributed to the fact that the employee is new to the job and/or the organization, is a low performer, or is working for a company that has adopted a lag behind the market pay strategy.

10. C: Thirty-six months is the period of eligibility under COBRA for a divorce/legal separation or death of an employed spouse, as well as for a dependent child who loses eligibility status under the plan rules. Eighteen months is the period of eligibility under COBRA for an employee's reduction in hours or an employee's termination. Twenty-nine months is the period of eligibility under COBRA for the disablement of an employee.

11. A: FMLA only covers unpaid, protected leave for the following reasons: the birth of a child, adoption or foster-care placement; the serious health condition of a spouse, child, or parent; the serious health condition of the employee—one requiring inpatient care or continuing treatment by a healthcare provider, qualifying exigency leave, or leave to address the most common issues that arise when an employee's spouse, child, or parent is on active duty or call to active duty status—e.g., making financial and legal arrangements and arranging for alternative childcare; and military caregiver leave or leave to care for a covered service member—employee's spouse, child, parent, or next of kin—with a serious injury or illness. Employees are to be granted up to twenty-six weeks of job-protected, unpaid leave during a twelve-month period to care for a covered service member.

12. B: Life insurance is a discretionary or voluntary benefit that is provided by employers. Choice A, unpaid family leave (based on FMLA), Choice C, continuation of healthcare coverage (based on COBRA), and Choice D, worker's compensation, are all non-discretionary benefits, since employers are mandated to provide them based on certain statutes.

13. C: Pension plan. Indirect compensation, most commonly referred to as employee benefits, includes such elements as healthcare coverage, retirement/pension plans, paid time off from work, and short-term and long-term disability.

14. C: Job specification is the knowledge, skills, abilities, education, and experience that are essential to performing a specific job. Choice A, job analysis, is the process used to identify the particular job requirements and duties and their relative importance. Choice B, job description, is a general written statement for a specific position based on a job analysis. Choice D, job evaluation, determines the relative worth of each job position by creating a hierarchy.

15. C: Factor comparison method. Quantitative job evaluation methods use a scaling system and provide a score that indicates how valuable one job is when compared to another job. The two specific examples noted are the point factor method and the factor comparison method. Choice A, job ranking, is when an organization defines the value of a specific job compared to other jobs in the organization. Choice B, paired comparison, is when an individual and their position is compared to another individual and their position. Choice D, job classification, is a system designed to evaluate the duties and authority levels of a job.

16. C: Leveling can be used if a job included on a salary survey is similar, but not identical, to a position within the organization. The data for that job can be weighted or leveled to create a better match. Choice B, benchmarking, is used to evaluate something by using a comparison. Choice D, wage compression, is when a new employee is paid at a higher wage than an individual who is currently employed in a similar position and with similar skills.

17. D: Broadbanding leads to flatter organization structures. Broadbanding occurs when employers decide to combine multiple pay levels into one, which results in only a handful of salary grades with much wider ranges. This type of pay structure is easier to administer and eliminates green and red circle rates. Broadbanding also leads to a flatter organizational structure, which encourages employees' horizontal movement through skill acquisition versus the traditional vertical movement through promotions to new pay grades.

18. C: Premium pay can be given to compensate employees as a higher rate of overtime pay for working on holidays or vacation days. Some employees receive shift pay, Choice *B*, for working second or third shifts or for being called into work during an emergency, also known as emergency shift pay, Choice *D*. Reporting pay, Choice *A*, can be paid to employees who arrive at their place of employment and find that there is no available work for them to perform.

19. A: Under USERRA, employees who are out on military leave are expected to receive the same seniority-based benefits that they would have received had they not been out of work on leave, such as vacation time and 401(k) contributions. After the first month of military leave, employers are not required to continue group healthcare coverage at their expense. An employer is expected to continue to pay exempt employees who are out on military leave their full salary, less any compensation that they receive for serving in the military. Additionally, employers are encouraged to make reasonable efforts to accommodate disabled veterans returning from military leave.

20. A: In defined benefit plans, employers agree to provide employees with a retirement benefit amount based on a formula. Cash balance plans are a specific type of defined benefit plan. Advantages of defined benefit plans are that the benefit is known to the employee, and the employer bears the burden of the financial risk. However, the cost is unknown. These plans tend to create higher rewards for longer tenured employees.

Employee and Labor Relations

Introduction

Employee relations, as the term suggests, refers to how the people who work for a company interact, both with one another and with other external parties. The term can refer to guidelines and rules that govern these interactions, but it can also focus on the methods and strategies used to determine the rules that shape the desired relationships.

Obviously this is an important consideration for any company. People are the driving force, the fuel, and the face of the organization. Anyone who has worked in a job that requires interacting with other employees or with customers probably has an interesting story about how quickly things can break down when these relationships are not well managed. When these breakdowns occur regularly, working conditions become strained, workers are inefficient, and outside observers are left with a negative impression of the organization. This negative impression cannot only affect a business, it also can sway talented people from joining the organization.

However, perhaps even more importantly, having good employee relations does not just make good business sense—it is the law. There is legislation at the local, state, and federal levels governing workplace environments and employee interactions. Therefore, an employer who does not keep track of the state of their workplace could well be in serious legal trouble.

Federal Laws and Regulations

Sherman Antitrust Act

The Sherman Antitrust Act (1890) is a piece of legislation intended to protect free trade. In simple terms, under the act, individuals or organizations cannot enter into any contract that unreasonably prevents others from engaging in similar commerce. Likewise, individuals and organizations cannot form monopolies. In other words, an organization cannot be the only company offering a service or product. There must be *some* competition possible. If a monopoly is suspected, the act gives district courts and/or government attorneys the authority to begin an investigation. It is important to note that the Sherman Antitrust Act does not apply if there is an existing law stating that an organization cannot be defined as a monopoly.

Clayton Act

The Clayton Act (1914) provides additional detail clarifying the Sherman Antitrust Act. The Clayton Act provides examples of potentially illegal or monopoly-forming activities, including mergers, exclusive dealings, and price discrimination. In addition, the act states that labor unions and agricultural organizations do not fall under the authority of the Sherman Antitrust Act. Finally, this legislation states that labor disputes are not subject to a court injunction, except in cases involving a threat of property damage.

Railway Labor Act

The Railway Labor Act (1926) puts limits on strikes by railroad and airline unions, if those strikes are found to cause major problems to the nation's transportation system and its ability to engage in trade. According to the act, railroad and airline employees can strike over a major contract dispute ("major" disputes are considered those involving pay, working conditions, or changes to the collective bargaining agreement), but only after engaging in a detailed process. All parties must first attempt mediation, arbitration, or another method of dispute negotiation through a National Mediation Board (NMB). If arbitration fails, and the NMB believes that a work stoppage may cause significant trade or transportation problems for the nation, they must alert the president. At this point, strikes are prohibited for a thirty-day cooling-off period. If, after that time, the president does not create a Presidential Emergency Board (PEB) to investigate the situation, employees may legally strike. If the president does choose to create a PEB, employees must observe another thirty-day cooling-off period while the board investigates and produces the report. After the report is completed, strikes continue to be prohibited for a third thirty-day period. The PEB report is non-binding. Therefore, if there has been no agreement, employees may legally strike after the third thirty-day cooling-off period.

Norris-LaGuardia Act

The Norris-LaGuardia Act (1932) is designed to protect workers' rights to form and join a union, as well as their right to strike. The act also protects all non-violent union activities from court injunctions. Lastly, the act protects employees from having to sign what are known as "yellow-dog" contracts, which are contracts that prevent employees from joining unions.

National Labor Relations Act (Wagner Act)

Passed in 1935, the National Labor Relations Act (NLRA) grants specific rights to workers who already belong to, or wish to join, a union. In addition to reinforcing the rights covered by the Norris-LaGuardia Act, this piece of legislation also grants employees the right to participate in collective bargaining activities, even if they are not a member of the union in question. There are some restrictions, however, such as the NLRA does not affect the special restrictions of the Railway Labor Act. In addition, the NLRA does not affect certain individuals who may make decisions on behalf of an employer, such as managers, supervisors, independent contractors, and immediate family.

The NLRA also defines what constitutes a legal and an illegal strike. A strike is considered legal when employees are seeking a better work environment, benefits, or compensation, or when an employer is using an unfair labor practice. A strike is considered illegal when employees have signed a contract with a no-strike clause, employees are striking to defend a union's unfair labor practice, or there is a significant concern that the striking employees are expected to cause property damage or bodily harm.

The NLRA also dictates what can be considered unfair labor practices, such as an employer doing one or more of the following: stopping workers from joining or participating in a union, taking control of a union or showing favoritism to any particular union, discriminating against union participants, discriminating against a worker who has filed charges with the National Labor Relations Board (NLRB), and refusing to bargain with the union representing its employees.

In addition, the NLRA created the National Labor Relations Board (NLRB) to encourage union growth. This board is primarily responsible for investigating potential unfair labor practices. The NLRB focuses on protecting employees from unfair treatment by employers or unions. The NLRB has the authority to take various actions to combat unfair labor practices, including the following: forcing employers to rehire employees, forcing employers to negotiate with a union, disbanding employer-controlled unions, forcing unions to refund excessive membership fees, forcing unions to negotiate with an employer, and forcing unions to reinstate members.

Labor Management Relations Act (Taft-Hartley Act)

Passed in 1947, the Labor Management Relations Act (LMRA) focuses on union activities that qualify as unfair labor practices. For example, unions cannot force employees to join. Employees also have the right to choose their union representative. Unions must bargain with the employer or its representative. Unions also cannot interfere with the negotiation and enforcement of an employer's contract. Unions cannot discriminate against non-union participants, or those who publicly oppose the union. Unions cannot encourage a secondary boycott (an attempt to encourage non-union members to cease business with an organization) or a hot cargo agreement (an attempt to force an employer to stop doing business with another company or individual). Unions also cannot charge unreasonable membership fees.

The LMRA also established the Federal Mediation and Conciliation Service. This piece of legislation granted power to the United States president to obtain an injunction ending a strike or lockout for an eighty-day "cooling off" period if the continuation of the strike could "imperil the health or safety of the nation."

<u>Labor Management Reporting and Disclosure Act (Landrum-Griffith Act)</u>
Passed in 1959, the goal of the Labor Management Reporting and Disclosure Act (LMRDA) was to protect employees from corrupt unions. This piece of legislation allowed for a closed shop exception for construction trades. The LMRDA also provided for a Bill of Rights for union members, which gave members the right to secret ballot elections for union offices, protection from excessive dues, freedom of speech in union matters, and the right to sue the union.

<u>WARN Act</u>
The Worker Adjustment and Retraining Notification (WARN) Act of 1988 requires that a minimum of sixty days' notice be given in advance of plant closings and mass layoffs. The notice must be given to local government, state dislocated worker units, and workers or their representatives. This piece of legislation applies to employers with one hundred or more full-time employees, or employers who have a total of full-time and part-time employees working 4,000 hours per week (not counting overtime) at all of their employment sites combined. A plant closing is the temporary or permanent shutdown of an entire site or one or more facilities or operating units within a single site that results in an employment loss during any thirty-day period of fifty or more full-time employees. A mass layoff is a reduction in force (not a plant closing) during any thirty-day period that results in an employment loss at a single site for either fifty or more full-time employees, if they make up at least 33 percent of the workforce at the employment site, or five hundred or more full-time employees. Employment loss is the involuntary termination of employment (other than for cause), layoff for more than six months, or at least a 50 percent reduction in hours for each month of a six-month period.

The WARN Act provides for three situations in which the sixty-day notice is not required, but the burden is on the employer to show that the reasons are legitimate and not an attempt to thwart the intent of the act. First, the "faltering company" exception applies only to plant closures in situations where the company is actively seeking additional funding and has a reasonable expectation that it will be forthcoming in an amount sufficient to preclude the layoff or closure, and that giving the notice would negatively impact the ability of the company to obtain the funding. The "unforeseeable business circumstance" exception applies to plant closings and mass layoffs, and occurs when circumstances take a sudden and unexpected negative change that could not have reasonably been predicted. Finally, the "natural disaster" exception applies to both plant closings and mass layoffs occurring as the result of a natural disaster such as a tornado, earthquake, or hurricane.

<u>Glass Ceiling Act</u>
The Civil Rights Act of 1991 was enacted to address workplace discrimination, specifically, the practice of preventing employees from reaching higher-level positions of management based solely on race, color, religion, sex, or national origin. The Glass Ceiling Act is part of Title II of this Act, and established a commission to study how businesses filled management positions, and whether there were significant

barriers to protected groups (such as women and minorities) that were preventing them from reaching those positions.

The commission did indeed find significant barriers in a number of organizations and divided the barriers into three categories. Governmental barriers occur when companies do not enforce existing equal opportunity regulations, thus preventing protected individuals from advancing to management positions. Internal structure barriers occur when company cultures (through official policies or unofficial but normal practices) prevent protected individuals from advancing to management positions. Societal barriers occur when protected individuals cannot receive the necessary education for management positions, or when pre-existing prejudice toward the protected group prevents expected advancements. (Note: societal barriers can refer to the larger society beyond that of the company in question).

Organizational Climate

Organizational Climate and Culture
How employees think and feel about a company is critical to an employer. If members of an organization have negative or even indifferent associations with it, it can be extremely difficult to motivate them to do their best work, or to prevent them from seeking work elsewhere. The overall "mood" of an organization is known as its climate, and organizational climate cannot be directly controlled. However, climate is closely affected by work environment, company standards, interactions, and a general sense of "how things are done around here." All these factors add up to what is called organizational culture. So, if an employer wants to improve the company's climate, they need to make changes to the company culture.

Encouraging Communication and Involvement
Encouraging communication and involvement are often a step in the right direction toward changing company culture. And much like climate and culture, communication and involvement are closely related, but not necessarily identical. For example, if John's boss gives him increased responsibility over an aspect of his work, then John has become more involved. However, if John still has no input from his boss on the decision process, or has no formal way to share his ideas with management, then the boss has not encouraged communication. Conversely, if John's boss starts sending regular memos detailing company activities and the strategies behind them, this is an increase in communication. However, if John and other employees have no way to act or contribute to this knowledge, then the boss has not encouraged involvement. To make meaningful changes to company culture, both communication and involvement should be addressed.

Involvement Strategies
There are numerous involvement strategies that companies can use. For example, the act of delegating authority allows an employee to make more decisions. By granting people more responsibility, an employer can encourage them to take a greater sense of ownership over a company's successes. An *employee survey* can be used to ask employees how they feel about the company. Surveys can be formal (written or online) or informal (simply asking around), and can address topics such as concerns, suggestions for improvement, and priorities. It should be noted that, even in an anonymous survey, employees may feel hesitant to share their true feelings if the workplace culture is viewed as unfriendly.

In addition to surveys, a *suggestion program*, via an idea box or an online submission form, allows employees to recommend ways to address company problems. Unlike a survey, a suggestion program is an ongoing part of company involvement. Employees can also work together in a formal capacity as part of a committee to address company concerns. Committees may be temporary or ongoing, and employees' service on a committee may also be for a specific term or a permanent appointment.

Moreover, an *employee-management committee* is a specific kind of committee where employees work alongside management to address company concerns. Sometimes known as employee participation groups, these committees also can be temporary or ongoing, depending on the needs of the organization. Finally, employees can also serve on a task force, which is similar to a committee but focused on a specific problem, and is usually temporary in nature. Employees on a task force work to determine the cause of a problem and work to develop a solution.

Communication and Strategies

There are also numerous communication strategies that companies can implement. For instance, a brown bag lunch program is an informal meeting, usually including employees and management, that is used to discuss company problems over a *brown bag* lunch. The lunch setting and company-provided meal can help create a relaxed setting for exchanging ideas. Department meetings, formal gatherings of employees and management in a given department that typically take place on a set day and time, allow everyone involved to share ideas and offer solutions to company challenges.

Town hall meetings, formal gatherings for the entire company that are commonly referred to as "all-hands meetings," tend to focus on sharing information "from the top down" concerning the overall organization, and thus are not usually designed to allow feedback from employees about smaller detail issues. An open-door policy is used to establish a relationship where employees feel comfortable speaking directly with management about problems and suggestions. In essence, an open-door policy enables a supervisor or manager to be a "human suggestion box." There are several potential roadblocks to a successful open-door policy. In certain situations, it can be difficult to create an environment where employees feel comfortable discussing problems in person with management. In addition, depending on the problem reported, it may not be possible to maintain confidentiality. However, in the right situation, an open-door policy can help companies identify problems quickly, almost in real-time, without having to wait for a formal meeting to address an ongoing issue.

Management by Walking Around (MBWA), as the name suggests, involves having managers and supervisors physically get out of their offices and interact with employees in person. MBWA allows management to check on employee progress, inquire about potential issues, and gain other feedback without relying on employees to "make the first move" through an open-door policy or online suggestion form. This strategy also helps prevent management from becoming isolated behind a desk and seeming distant and disinterested in employees' problems.

Communication Types

There are multiple means that a company can use to communicate with its employees. Each method has its own potential advantages and drawbacks. *Email* makes it easy to get information to a lot of people very quickly. However, this communication method can result in employees suffering from "information overload" from too many emails, making it more likely that important information is overlooked. Also, there is a danger that confidential information may be accidentally communicated to the wrong people.

The *intranet* (internal website and computer network) has the benefit of no risk of important information being accessed by someone outside the organization. Intranets can be very effective at communicating important ongoing information about the company, such as policies and procedures. In addition, companies often store necessary workplace documentation, such as HR-related forms, on an intranet, allowing employees to access that information when they need it. However, if outside parties need information on the intranet, they cannot access it. In addition, intranet communication is often "top-down" and does not allow for feedback from employees. It is also important to note that some intranet systems are not user-friendly, and employees can be discouraged from using them.

Newsletters can provide a variety of information, and have the potential to do so in an engaging, welcoming manner. However, newsletters can be labor-intensive. Since they are relatively infrequent (compared to the ease of sending an email), newsletters are not always useful for communicating urgent or immediate information. In addition, newsletters do not allow for formal two-way communication from employees (although this can be remedied by involving employees in the creation of the newsletter).

Finally, *word-of-mouth* communication can quickly spread information throughout a group of people. However, as in the children's game "Telephone," information can become muddled, misinterpreted, and downright unrecognizable as it is passed from person to person. A manager or supervisor has no control over misinterpretations and misunderstandings that can result from word-of-mouth communication.

Employee Relations Programs

Recognition Programs
These programs are used to promote a positive organizational culture by recognizing individual employees for the work they have completed. Recognition programs include personalized thank you notes for a job well done, company merchandise, and gift cards. For example, there are peer-to-peer recognition programs in place, where one employee can send a personalized thank you eCard to another employee for a job well done. In that same system, managers can acknowledge an employee for extra effort on a project by assigning a number of recognition points along with sending an eCard. Once an employee accumulates a certain number of recognition points, they can cash in the points to receive either a gift card or an item from the company store.

Special Events
Companies can use special events as a way to engage employees and promote a positive organizational culture. These events can involve managers serving lunch to employees during customer service appreciation week, organizing monthly employee events such as an ice cream social on a random Friday afternoon or an after-work happy hour, or planning an annual holiday party or company picnic for employees to enjoy with their co-workers and their families at a local amusement park. Additionally, these events can incorporate an element of community service, such as employees getting together to assist a local organization (an animal shelter or a food bank) during a "day of caring" event. Employee wellness can also be factored into these special events by scheduling yoga classes onsite for employees to participate in, or by providing monthly chair massages in a conference room at a reduced price for staff.

Diversity and Inclusion Programs
Companies are making more of a conscious effort to recognize, embrace, and value the talents, backgrounds, and ideas of employees through their recruitment, training, and career development efforts. To promote a positive organizational culture, it is important to embrace employees' unique qualities, seek their diverse opinions, and listen to and consider their ideas, instead of always accepting the status quo. Therefore, it is imperative for management to cultivate a workplace environment that encourages staff to share their thoughts and suggestions. Staff must work to identify unconscious biases and be aware of how these biases affect their actions and decision-making processes. Employees must

make an effort to reach out to team members with whom they have not previously connected, and to find opportunities for diversity and inclusion in their daily work activities.

Organizations are also working to increase the level of employee engagement by connecting colleagues across locations, generations, and functions through the formation of employee business resource groups. These also further promote diversity and inclusion efforts. Examples include groups for African-Americans, Asian-Americans, Latino-Americans, disability awareness, LGBT (lesbian, gay, bisexual, and transgender), former members of the military, multicultural, emerging professionals, and women.

Effectiveness of Employee Relations Programs

Employee Surveys
Employee surveys are a tool that management can use to determine how HR programs are being received by staff, to uncover problem areas in the organization, and to reveal employee preferences or needs. These surveys can be distributed as attitude surveys with the goal of measuring employees' job satisfaction or as opinion surveys with the goal of gathering data on specific issues. It is important that employees know they will be guaranteed anonymity in return for their participation in the survey so they will, in turn, be as honest as possible on how they view their jobs, supervisors, coworkers, organizational policies, etc. This type of employee input provides management with data on the "retention climate" in the company. Collecting this data is extremely important to an organization's retention measurement efforts. It is important for management to share the results of the survey with employees, even if the feedback is negative. By continuing to administer employee surveys annually or at set intervals, management is able to measure improvements in responses over time.

Exit Interviews
Individuals who are leaving a company are given an exit interview to uncover their reasons for parting ways with the organization. Exit interviews are typically conducted by a neutral party, such as an HR professional, rather than by the departing employee's direct supervisor. HR will typically summarize and analyze the data from exit interviews at regular intervals to share information with management regarding possible improvement opportunities.

Turnover Rates
Turnover rate is the percentage of employees who leave the workforce during a period of time, typically during a calendar or fiscal year. To calculate turnover rate, you simply take the number of employees who exited the company during the year, divide it by the average number of employees during the year, and then multiply that amount by 100. A high turnover rate can be a costly problem for a company and can have a negative effect on many aspects of organizational performance, such as productivity, safety, and financial performance.

Workplace Policies and Procedures

Policies, Procedures, and Rules
Policies are more general in nature and are guidelines that focus on organizational actions. They reflect a company's philosophy, standards, or objectives. An example of a policy is how employees receive vacation time according to their years of service with a company. Procedures and rules are more specific to situations. Procedures are customary methods of handling activities. They are detailed descriptions that answer the when, what, who, how, and where. An example of a procedure is the specific method that employees use to request and authorize their vacation time. Rules are the most specific guidelines that regulate and/or restrict individuals' behavior. They reflect management's decisions in regard to

actions that should be avoided or taken in situations. Employees being required to give at least a one-week notice when requesting vacation is an example of a rule.

Employee Handbooks

Employee handbooks are important tools to communicate information to staff concerning the company's culture, work hours, safety, harassment, attendance, benefits, pay, electronic communication policies, and discipline policies. It is important for companies to keep employee handbooks current, simple to read, and to make accommodations for any multilingual requests. Additionally, it is important to include a disclaimer that the employee handbook is not intended to be any type of contractual agreement between the company and the employee. By making the employee handbook accessible on the company's intranet site, this eliminates outdated paper copies from floating around the office, and employees can access important policies at any time. Companies typically also require employees to sign off on a form stating that they have received and read the latest version of the employee handbook.

Discipline Policy

Progressive Discipline

Progressive discipline is a system that, rather than defining a single "one size fits all" response to an employee infraction, attempts to address each incident as a unique situation and then develops consequences accordingly. Typically, factors like severity and frequency (in other words, "how bad" and "how often") are key in determining the appropriate response. Many organizations make use of a five-stage process. Coaching is the first stage, where the manager discusses the behavior problem with the employee. This stage is typically used for small or first-time infractions. Then the employee receives a first warning. This is also called the counseling stage and usually involves the employee receiving a verbal warning. Then the second warning follows, which is also called the formal warning stage. This stage progresses to the employee receiving a written warning. A disciplinary action follows. At this stage, the employee is suspended for his or her behavior. Finally, if the chain of progressive discipline has not corrected the behavior, the final step in the progressive discipline process is to terminate the individual's employment.

Termination Process

Termination

Termination is the final step in the progressive discipline process and when an employee is removed from their job. Terminations occur for behavioral issues, poor job performance, and policy violations. It is imperative that employees receive sufficient warning regarding the seriousness of their offenses prior to their termination.

Once the decision is made to end a staff member's employment, the actual termination takes place in a swift manner, typically during a face-to-face meeting. During the termination meeting, with the employee's manager and sometimes with a member of HR, the employee's building and systems access is deactivated, while the employee's co-workers are gathered together in a conference room. This allows the terminated employee a few minutes of privacy to gather personal belongings under the supervision of building security, HR, or the employee's manager. Then the terminated employee is escorted out of the building.

In some situations, terminated employees are given formal contracts known as separation agreements. The agreements state that the terminated employees agree not to sue the employer in exchange for some previously agreed-upon severance pay and/or other conditions.

Reductions in Force (RIFs)

RIFs are the planned elimination of a number of personnel to make an organization more competitive through reducing costs, using technology to replace labor, leveraging mergers and acquisitions, or by moving a company to a more economical location. Although RIFs do help companies to cut costs in the short-term, they often hurt productivity. For an organization to successfully implement a RIF, it should communicate with employees throughout the entire process; provide any downsized employee with outplacement services to assist them with resume writing, career counseling, interview preparation, and referral assistance; and strive to build the trust and commitment of the remaining employees to boost their morale.

Employees who are laid off are typically asked to sign a document known as a separation agreement and general release. This document, when signed, is a legally binding agreement that states the employee cannot sue or make any claims against the company in exchange for agreed-upon severance benefits. Severance pay is not required by law, but most companies will pay employees who are laid off a set number of weeks of salary continuation based on their years of service (typically one or two weeks' pay per year of service) to ease their financial burden and to preserve the organization's image. Some companies also include a continuation of health care benefits for a set period of time. An employee is given the agreement during their exit meeting and is allowed to take it home and review it with a lawyer. They ahve twenty-one days to sign and return the agreement for an individual separation and forty-five days to sign and return the agreement in cases of a group RIF. Once the agreement is signed, an employee still has seven days to revoke their signature.

Wrongful Discharge

A wrongful discharge occurs when an employee is terminated after they refuse to do something unsafe, unethical, or illegal, such as a pharmacist refusing to sign off on a prescription to be dispensed that does not have a date. This type of termination is wrongful because it violates public policy. Additionally, a charge of wrongful discharge can also occur when an employee is terminated after an employer promised them job security, thus violating an implied employment agreement.

Grievance Management

Grievance Procedures

A grievance is a complaint made by an employee that is formally stated in writing. A formal grievance procedure allows management to become aware of employee concerns and to respond to employee dissatisfaction appropriately and effectively through formal channels of communication. Additionally, if a unionized employee is being questioned by management in a situation where a disciplinary action may result, they have the right to union representation during that conversation, which is also known as Weingarten rights (after a famous court case). If that right is violated and the unionized employee is let go, they can be reinstated with back pay.

Every contract will lay out a slightly different process to address potential contract grievances. However, many will follow a similar pattern. The goal is always to address and remedy the situation before escalating to the need for arbitration. Typically, employees first discuss the grievance with the union steward and the supervisor. Next, the union steward discusses the grievance with the supervisor's manager and/or the HR manager. The next step is for a committee of union officers to discuss the grievance with the appropriate managers in the company. Then, the national union representative discusses the grievance with designated company executives. If, after this process, the grievance is still not settled, then it goes to arbitration. Grievance arbitration is a process in which a third party is used to settle disputes that arise from conflicting interpretations of a labor contract. Decisions that are reached through this process are enforceable and cannot go to court to be changed.

Employee Complaints

Settling Discrimination Charges

Unfortunately, discrimination does exist in some organizations, and sometimes official charges are brought forth. In these cases (and even in cases where the organization is confident that no wrongdoing has taken place), an organization has a decision to make. It can follow the process through the Equal Employment Opportunity Commission (EEOC) and be investigated by a Fair Employment Practices Agency (FEPA) at the local or state level, or the organization may choose to settle the charges rather than face an investigation. Employee charges of discrimination must be filed with the EEOC within 180 days of the alleged incident. The EEOC has a formal complaint process, and if probable cause is found, then the EEOC will attempt conciliation, and the employer is required to provide remedies to settle. The complaint charge is either settled, or the process may move to litigation with either the EEOC or a private court. If the EEOC is not able to determine probable cause, the employee can request a right-to-sue letter after the end of the 180-day period and must file suit in court within ninety days. Finally, if the EEOC does not find probable cause, the employer and employee are both notified, the employee can request a right-to-sue letter, and the EEOC's involvement with the case ends. The employee can then sue the employer in court.

There are a number of factors that can influence a company's decision to settle discrimination charges. There is the financial cost of an investigation. Lawyers and court fees can be an incredible financial strain on a company's finances, not to mention the possibility of additional obligations if the court rules against the company. There are also the challenges of the investigation itself to consider. If charges are brought to the EEOC or FEPA, a company may be required to devote considerable time and resources to cooperating with the investigation. Thus, an organization may decide that a one-time financial penalty is preferable to an extended period of disruption to its processes. A company also faces damage to its reputation. A long, drawn-out trial and investigation, potentially widely covered on social and traditional media, can do irreparable harm to the company's image. Even in cases where the company is eventually found to be free of blame in the case, the general public, as well as current and potential customers, may still associate the organization with the charges of discrimination. Therefore, a company may find it is better to accept the financial expense to avoid the potential long-term damage to its reputation. Finally, there are systemic problems to think about. If the company is aware of deeper issues of discrimination among its employees, it may choose to settle charges to avoid having the investigation uncover an ongoing pattern that it may be hard-pressed to address.

Front Pay

If a company is found guilty of workplace discrimination, it is usually required to allow the individual in question to return to their contested position within the organization. However, in some instances, the court may instead rule that the company should require front pay. Front pay is money awarded to an individual in a workplace discrimination case, and is generally equal to lost earnings. Front pay is usually required when the position in question (or a similar or equivalent position) is not available, the employer has not made any effort to address an ongoing issue of discrimination throughout the company, or the employee would be forced to endure a hostile work environment if they were to return to the original position.

Mediation Process

Mediation often serves as a precursor to the more official step of arbitration. In general terms, arbitration is sometimes thought of as a form of mediation, but legally there are important differences. Most notably, a mediator doesn't serve as a final "judge" of the dispute, but rather attempts to work with both parties to help them reach a resolution without having to take additional legal steps.

The mediation process usually begins with both parties agreeing to use a mutually acceptable mediator. The mediator sets the ground rules for the process and defines details such as what the dispute is about, who is involved, when and where the negotiations will take place, and the negotiation procedure. When the actual meeting takes place, the mediator reiterates the ground rules for the process. Both sides present their case. The mediator attempts to help both parties reach a compromise or find other solutions. If both sides agree to a compromise, a written document will be signed to ensure that both sides will follow through on the agreed-upon actions. If both sides do not agree, they may choose to pursue arbitration or litigation (court action).

Constructive Confrontation

Constructive confrontation is a type of mediation used in some extremely complicated or contentious disputes, particularly ones where neither party is able to agree to a compromise. Constructive confrontation can sometimes break these stalemates by temporarily skipping the main issue in dispute, and instead, focusing first on secondary issues. Sometimes, by first resolving these smaller details, a mediator can affect parties' willingness to compromise on bigger issues.

Arbitration

Arbitration is a way to settle disputes without taking the issue to court. In a general sense, arbitration is a form of mediation. However, arbitration typically refers to a more formal process that takes place after an initial mediation attempt has failed. In arbitration, a neutral third party (known as an arbitrator) makes a decision based on the facts presented. There are different kinds of arbitration, decisions, and arbitrators.

In *compulsory arbitration*, the disputing parties are required by law to go through the arbitration process. This could be the result of a court order, but it could also arise from a contract that dictates that arbitration take place in certain situations.

In *voluntary arbitration*, the disputing parties choose to undergo the arbitration process, usually because they cannot come to an agreement, but do not want to go through a potentially expensive and time-consuming lawsuit.

In a *binding decision*, the disputing parties are required by law to follow the decision reached as a result of the arbitration process. This means that the losing party must follow the actions laid out by the decision (such as payments or reinstatement to a disputed position). In addition, a binding decision marks the end of the legal process. No party may pursue further legal action after the decision has been reached.

As the name suggests, *non-binding decisions* carry no legal weight. Either party may choose to follow or not follow the terms of the decision. In addition, a dissatisfied party may choose to follow additional legal action after the decision of the arbiter is reached.

A *permanent arbitrator* is someone who routinely judges arbitration cases for a company or other organization. An arbitrator may be trained and certified by a professional organization, but they also may simply be a person who the disputing parties trust to provide an unbiased opinion on the dispute.

An *ad-hoc arbitrator* may also be a certified professional or a mutually trusted third party. But unlike permanent arbitrators, ad-hoc arbitrators do not have a regular arbitration relationship with either party. Instead, they are chosen as a one-time solution to address only the unique dispute in question.

An *arbitrator panel* functions just like an ad-hoc arbitrator, but it is comprised of multiple arbitrators (usually three). They are sometimes called arbitral tribunals or tripartite arbitration panels.

Collective Bargaining Activities

Unions
In its broadest sense, a union (also known as a labor union) is simply a formally organized group of employees who work together to accomplish goals. These goals usually involve working conditions, pay, and other aspects of a common trade, but can vary widely depending on the union and the particular situation.

Types
A *local union* refers to either a union for a small organization or a union for a smaller geographic area. In many cases, the local union serves as a branch of the larger national union for a particular trade. A *national union* is often comprised of smaller, local unions. These groups represent a wide geographic area. A national union could represent employees of a single organization or employees of multiple organizations that happen to be working in the same trade. A *federation* is made up of different national unions representing different industries that nevertheless share some commonalities and have common goals. Finally, an international union represents workers in multiple countries.

Organizing Process
Unions must go through a specific process to be officially organized and recognized as a legitimate representative for a group of workers. Employees must demonstrate an interest in participating in the union and must sign authorization cards indicating their interest in the union. At least 30 percent of eligible employees are required to sign authorization cards by the NLRB before they can order an election. The union must inform the employer of the employees' desire to unionize. If at this point the employer refuses, the union may take action through the NLRB. The NLRB then holds an election where employees vote on whether to be represented by the union. Employees are eligible to vote in the election if they were on the company's payroll during the pay period directly prior to the calling of the election and during the pay period immediately preceding the election date. Any employees who were striking and then were permanently replaced are allowed to vote in an election that is conducted within twelve months following the end of the strike.

Picketing
Picketing is an act of protest where a group of people (picketers) gather in front of a business to raise awareness of an issue or to discourage people from entering a building to work or do business. The NLRB outlines what kinds of picketing activities unions may legally participate in. Employees may engage in informational picketing, where they picket to announce to the public that they are not represented by any one authority and thus plan to organize. Employees may also engage in organizational picketing, where they picket to convince employees to join or support their union. Finally, employees may engage in recognitional picketing, where they picket to encourage the employer to recognize their union as the employees' representative.

While in disputes with an employer, unions may engage in common situs picketing. This is where employees picket at a location used by the targeted employer as well as other organizations. This is legal as long as the picketers make clear which employer is being protested, so that other organizations are not adversely affected by the picketing. Unions may also use consumer picketing, where employees picket to discourage the public from doing business with the employer in question. Finally, unions can take advantage of double breasting picketing, where employees picket at a location where the employer's workers are not unionized. This is only legal in certain situations.

Decertification

If a company's employees feel that their union is not doing a good enough job to represent them, they can go through the process of decertification, which strips the union of its official status as the employees' representatives. To decertify the union, 30 percent of employees must first sign a petition. Then, the employees can file the petition with the NLRB. The petition cannot be filed less than twelve months after the union was officially certified. If the NLRB approves the petition, then it holds a decertification election among the company employees. The union is decertified if a majority of the voting employees vote in favor of the decertification (a tie vote also means the union is decertified).

Deauthorization

Deauthorization is a process of removing a union's security clause and its authority to negotiate. A security clause is basically a condition in a contract that requires employees to join a union. The deauthorization process is identical to that of decertification. First, 30 percent of employees must sign a petition in favor of deauthorization. Then, the employees file the petition with the NLRB. If the NLRB approves the petition, then it holds a decertification election among the company employees. Deauthorization is approved if a majority of the employees who are eligible to vote vote in favor of deauthorization. In this instance, a situation where employees who are eligible and do not exercise their right to vote equates to a vote against deauthorization.

Collective Bargaining

Collective bargaining is the act of negotiation between an employer and its employees, where a union represents the employees' interests. The NLRA specifically addresses the collective bargaining process and lays out legal definitions for negotiating in good faith, both on the part of the employer and the union. Some examples of negotiating in bad faith include employers making contract proposals directly to employees without working through the union that represents them, employers urging employees to engage in activities that would weaken the union's negotiating power (for example, encouraging employees to decertify the union), and employers making unfavorable changes to workplace terms and conditions (such as pay, hours, and special pay) during the process of collective bargaining. Additional examples of negotiating in bad faith include unions refusing to disclose critical information during the collective bargaining process, unions refusing to reasonably cooperate in the logistics of the negotiation process (for example, time and location), and unions engaging in an unfair labor practice, as defined by the Labor Management Relations Act.

The NLRB also helps define and limit the subjects that can be discussed during a collective bargaining negotiation. Illegal subjects cannot be discussed during negotiations and generally involve actions that fall outside the realm of contract negotiations. Examples could include hot cargo agreements, security clauses, or any activity on the part of the employer or union that is against the law. Mandatory subjects must be discussed during negotiations. Mandatory subjects typically involve the basics of employees' working conditions and terms, covering areas such as hours, benefits, pay, and worker safety concerns. Voluntary subjects are topics that parties are permitted to discuss but may choose not to. Voluntary subjects include all issues not covered under the categories of illegal or mandatory subjects.

The goal of collective bargaining is to develop a mutually agreed-upon collective bargaining agreement (CBA). The CBA should address basic terms and conditions including hours, benefits, pay, and workplace safety; the contract grievance process, which is a clear statement of the procedures to be followed in case of a dispute as well as the actions the organization can take if employees do not follow the terms of the contract; and a zipper clause stating that the CBA has been agreed to and is final. The zipper clause also dictates that any issues not covered in the current contract cannot be discussed until it expires.

There are several strategies that are commonly employed by unions during a collective bargaining negotiation. Single-unit bargaining occurs when union representatives meet with one employer at a time, concerned only with that particular agreement, and not attempting to use the process as a springboard or advantage in separate negotiations. Coordinated bargaining takes place when several unions within an organization meet with the employer to negotiate beneficial results for all the different groups they represent (also called multi-unit bargaining). Multi-employer bargaining occurs when a union with employees in multiple companies meets with all of those companies as a single negotiation. Finally, parallel bargaining occurs when a union successfully negotiates an agreement with a company, then uses the result of that negotiation as an example while dealing with a different company (also called leapfrogging or whipsawing).

Organization or union representatives typically use one of two approaches when engaging in a collective bargaining process. Distributive bargaining takes place when a group negotiates with the goal of achieving specific objectives (also called positional bargaining). Principled bargaining occurs when a group negotiates while remaining mindful of the key issues to each side of the process. The negotiation then becomes a process of searching for solutions to those issues from both sides, in hopes that an agreement can be reached in which both sides find a mutual benefit.

Employment Rights

Employment-at-Will
Employment-at-will means there is a shared understanding the employee may quit at any time and for any reason, and that the employer has the same power to end the employment agreement at any time and for any reason. Employment-at-will arrangements do not, however, supersede existing employment law, public policies, or even organizational policies regarding the rights of employees. In addition, contracts may provide additional conditions that must be met before an employer or employee can terminate an agreement.

Contracts
A contract is an agreement between parties that can be enforced by law. In the context of employee relations, a contract often helps prevent an employer from unjustly terminating an employee, but it can also serve to protect an employer from legal action if it can be shown that the employee did not meet the requirements of the contract. Contracts can be divided into two categories: expressed and implied.

Expressed Contract
An expressed contract is what most people think of when they use the term "contract." It's an official agreement, usually in written form, that states the terms of the agreement. In a legal situation, the events that occur can be compared with the terms in the contract to determine if a termination was justified or not.

Implied Contract
The concept of an implied contract can be a bit more complicated. While it can still refer to a written document, it more often refers to a verbal agreement or a shared understanding. An example is the implied contract that people enter into when going to the emergency room. There is no written (or expressed) contract that the hospital will provide care in exchange for payment. However, it is generally

accepted and understood that patients are expected to pay for their treatment. In an employment context, this shared understanding could come from a precedent (the way something is consistently done within a company) or from an existing company policy.

Good Faith and Fair Dealing

When two people enter into a contract, they are both expected to carry out their actions in such a way that the contract can be completed as agreed upon, or as someone would reasonably interpret the terms of that agreement. Thus, an employee or employer is expected to not twist the words of the contract in a way that is clearly not how it was meant to be interpreted. Likewise, an employee who exaggerates claims of their abilities is not acting in good faith, and an employer who makes promises of benefits that are later withheld for insubstantial reasons are not dealing fairly.

Promissory Estoppel

Promissory estoppel relates specifically to promises made by an employer. Simply put, promissory estoppel protects employees in situations where an employer promises an outcome or a reward for a job-related action, and that reward is never given.

For example, John's boss promises a bonus for everyone who meets sales figures for the next three months. Unfortunately, the economy takes a downturn during those three months, and when the time comes, the company can't afford to pay the bonuses. Since the boss had the intention of fulfilling the promise, this is not an issue of good faith and fair dealing. However, John may still claim promissory estoppel, since the promise was ultimately not fulfilled.

Respondeat Superior

Respondeat superior translates as "let the master answer." The basic idea behind this legal concept is that the employer can be held responsible for an employee's wrongful actions, if they take place while the employee is on the job. However, certain conditions are needed for respondeat superior to apply. Most notably, the offense in question must be related to the employee's normal job routine or expected work behavior. The most common example is that of a truck driver or bus driver who causes an accident while on the job. Generally speaking, the company of the employee will be at least partly responsible under the terms of respondeat superior. This concept applies even if the employer is unaware of the action in question.

Defamation

Defamation refers to an employer making untrue statements about an employee that damages that individual's reputation. Defamation is a term that extends beyond the realm of employee relations, but in this context, it refers to statements that can prevent a person from finding work at another organization in the future. As stated above, defamation could include outright lies about a person's abilities, or simply center on providing personal information about an employee, such as their political views or sexual orientation.

Constructive Discharge

Constructive discharge is when the employer makes working conditions unbearable to the point where an employee is forced to quit. For instance, Mary's boss wants to fire her, but he really has no good reason for doing so. Instead, he decides to make her *want* to quit by creating a hostile work environment. Perhaps he is rude to her and encourages others to be rude to her as well. Perhaps she is disciplined or cited for minor infractions routinely overlooked when committed by other employees. Maybe he creates unrealistic performance expectations or gives her bad employee reviews, regardless of the quality of her work. With constructive discharge, every situation is unique. None of these individual examples listed would probably be enough to qualify as a hostile work environment, but when combined together, Mary may have legitimate concerns.

The law is complex, and state legislation on the subject varies, but if Mary can prove that she was treated unfairly and, in effect, had no choice but to quit, the situation may be found to be a constructive discharge. In this case, the situation is regarded as being similar to that of wrongful termination, and the employer can be held legally responsible.

Negligent Hiring/Retention

Negligent hiring occurs when an employer hires an employee, and the employer either knew or should have known that the employee posed a risk to other employees or to customers. For example, a temp agency that helps a company employ an individual as a controller at a financial institution, and that person is under investigation for embezzlement, can be found liable if the agency fails to inform the new employer or fails to do the necessary background checks. This is especially an issue if the new employee is later charged with embezzling from the new employer. Employers can prevent negligent hiring claims by conducting criminal background checks, verifying employment histories and college degrees, checking on past employment gaps, and reaching out to the references of potential employees. In some industries, employers can also perform drug screenings and require physicals, along with performing credit checks and checking driving records for specific jobs.

Negligent retention occurs when an employer either knew or should have known that an employee is unqualified to remain in their position at the company but was allowed to stay in the role, and the employee caused a violation of rights or an injury to another party during or after work hours. An example of negligent retention is a supervisor who chooses to "look the other way" when one of their employees is found drinking on the job. Perhaps later that employee offers to drive a co-worker to an offsite meeting, and they are involved in a motor vehicle accident with injury sustained by the innocent co-worker due to the employee's elevated blood alcohol level. Employers can prevent claims of negligent retention by making a point to acknowledge problems with employees in a timely manner, reference company policies, and document issues in employees' evaluations. In some cases, employers may also need to provide employees with additional training. If the problems are repeated, it is important for employers to initiate a progressive discipline process, documenting the disciplinary actions as they occur.

Workplace Behavior

While there are many potential behavioral issues a company may have to face, the two most common are absenteeism and insubordination. Absenteeism (taking a disproportional amount of time off from work) can create problems for management and other employees, since they will be unable to rely on the employee to complete the tasks they were hired to do. Insubordination (ignoring instructions or showing a lack of respect to management) leads to the same set of problems. Both of these issues can make it extremely difficult for a department or an entire organization to succeed.

Sometimes behavioral issues result when employees do not have a clear picture of regulations and expectations. Therefore, it is important to ensure the desired behaviors are specifically defined to avoid any confusion. To address absenteeism, employers should clearly state the amount of sick time available (and how it is earned), what qualifies as a legitimate reason to take sick leave, how to process sick time requests, and the consequences if the guidelines are not followed. Likewise, a basic code of conduct addressing appropriate and inappropriate professional behavior can help prevent unintended insubordination or other performance issues. A process should be outlined that details how performance problems will be handled, up to and including termination.

Important Terms

Back pay: A mediation remedy that involves paying one of the parties the equivalent of the pay that would have been received if they had continued working.

Charge: In the context of equal employment opportunity, a formal discrimination claim filed with a Fair Employment Practice Agency (FEPA) or with the Equal Opportunity Employment Commission (EEOC). There is potentially some overlap between the involvement of a FEPA and the EEOC. For example, if the alleged discrimination is a violation of federal and state law, a FEPA may file a charge with the EEOC (or vice-versa) while the investigation is still ongoing.

Complainant: A complainant is the alleged victim of discrimination and is also referred to as the charging party.

Compressed workweek: This is a flexible scheduling practice that allows employees to work longer shifts in order to earn corresponding time off. Some examples include four ten-hour days followed by one day off, three twelve-hour days followed by two days off, and nine nine-hour days followed by one day off.

Employee communication strategy: A method used by a company to encourage increased communication and interaction between employees, between management, or between different levels of an organization. Different strategies will be more effective for companies of different sizes and cultures, and for different kinds of information involved.

Employee involvement strategy: Much like an employee communication strategy, this is a method used by a company to encourage increased employee participation in the organization's processes, operations, and decision-making. This is often achieved through a company or department-wide program, but can also refer to an individual action taken to address a specific employee or a small group of employees.

Fair Employment Practices Agency (FEPA): This agency has the authority to enforce state and/or local anti-discrimination laws. If an employee believes they are being illegally discriminated against in the workplace, they can file a charge with the appropriate FEPA. FEPA can also work with the Equal Employment Opportunity Commission (EEOC) if the discrimination may be a violation of state or federal law.

Featherbedding: The act of forcing an employer to keep employees in paid positions even when they are no longer necessary. For example, this may occur if a position is made obsolete by a new technology, technique, or process. Featherbedding is specifically mentioned in the Labor Management Relations Act (LMRA) as an unfair labor practice.

Flextime: An alternative scheduling system that allows employees to set their own work schedules as long as they work a set number of hours per week. In addition, flextime often requires employees to work during some required time periods. For example, if Mary is required to work forty hours a week and to be present Monday through Friday from 9 a.m. to 3 p.m., she could choose to work from 7 a.m. to 3:30 p.m. or from 9 a.m. to 5:30 p.m. on any given day. Even with flextime, employers often require a set schedule so fellow employees know when they can expect their co-workers to be present.

Front pay: A mediation remedy involving paying one of the parties the equivalent of the pay that would have been received had the party continued working at the organization. Front pay differs from back pay in that it is typically used in situations where returning to the contested position is not a practical option.

Hot cargo agreement: In the context of labor disputes, this is an agreement between a union and an employer forbidding an organization to conduct business affairs with a particular person or company. Hot cargo agreements are specifically mentioned in the Labor Management Relations Act (LMRA) as an unfair labor practice. Hot cargo agreements were often used to try and prevent employers from working with companies whose employees were not unionized.

Jurisdictional strike: This type of strike has the intent of forcing an employer to show preference to union workers when distributing work. Jurisdictional strikes are specifically mentioned in the Labor Management Relations Act (LMRA) as an unfair labor practice.

Part-time scheduling: This is a scheduling system that allows employees to work shorter hours per day or fewer hours per week. Part-time employees often have reduced or no benefits, depending on company policy and the number of hours worked.

Remedy: The method a company or organization uses to address workplace discrimination. Also called "relief," this could be in the form of a monetary award or a particular action the company takes to solve the issue brought forth in a charge.

Respondent: The party accused of unlawful workplace discrimination, sometimes referred to as the charged party.

Secondary boycott: This type of boycott occurs when a union encourages non-members not to do business with a specific organization or individual. Secondary boycotts are specifically mentioned in the Labor Management Relations Act (LMRA) as an unfair labor practice.

Sit-down strike: This type of strike occurs when employees protest against a company by refusing to work, but still remaining onsite. The National Labor Relations Board (NLRB) specifically prohibits sit-down strikes.

Wildcat strike: This type of strike occurs when employees strike despite having entered into a contract with a no-strike clause. Wildcat strikes are specifically mentioned in the National Labor Relations Act (LMRA) as an unfair labor practice.

Work slowdown: This occurs when employees protest against a company by intentionally working more slowly, rather than ceasing work altogether. The National Labor Relations Board (NLRB) specifically prohibits work slowdowns.

Practice Questions

1. Which of the following statements is true about the Landrum-Griffith Act?
    a. This act outlawed yellow-dog contracts.
    b. This act established the Federal Mediation and Conciliation Service.
    c. This act created the NLRB to encourage union growth.
    d. This act created a Bill of Rights for union members.

2. Which of the following pieces of legislation dictates what are known as unfair labor practices?
    a. The Wagner Act
    b. The Norris-LaGuardia Act
    c. The Taft-Hartley Act
    d. The Railway Labor Act

3. Which of the following is prohibited by the Taft-Hartley Act?
    a. The formation of monopolies
    b. Forcing employees to join a union
    c. Refusing to allow for a closed shop exception for construction trades
    d. Union members' inability to sue their union

4. Under the WARN Act, which of the following employers are required to provide a minimum of sixty days' notice to their employees in advance of a plant closing or mass layoff?
    a. An employer shuts down a plant facility that employs fifty total employees, twenty-five of which are working part-time. The company employs over one hundred full-time employees.
    b. Thirty full-time employees are laid off by a company at a single site that employs 120 full-time individuals for a three-month period.
    c. A company lays off 250 full-time employees at a single site that employs 650 full-time individuals for more than a six-month period.
    d. An employer shuts down a plant facility that has already been partially idled for quite some time. Only forty employees remain working at the site. The company employs over one hundred full-time employees.

5. Which of the following pieces of legislation established a commission to study how women and minorities face significant barriers and are prevented from reaching management positions?
    a. Title II
    b. The Civil Rights Act of 1991
    c. Equal Pay Act
    d. The Glass Ceiling Act

6. Which of the following is a guideline that focuses on organizational actions?
    a. Policy
    b. Rule
    c. Procedure
    d. Standard Operating Procedure (SOP)

7. Which of the following is more specific to the situation and is used to regulate and/or restrict an individual's behavior?
    a. Policy
    b. Rule
    c. Procedure
    d. Standard Operating Procedure (SOP)

8. In an organization with a progressive discipline policy, an employee has received a verbal warning for a performance issue. The same employee is later found to be in violation of a different company policy. How should this infraction be handled?
    a. The employee should be immediately terminated.
    b. The employee should receive coaching from their manager.
    c. The employee should receive a second warning, followed by a formal written warning.
    d. The employee should receive another verbal warning, since this is for a different violation.

9. After a staff member violates a work rule that is a dischargeable offense, an HR professional should follow through with which of the following actions?
    a. Terminate the staff member on the spot.
    b. Coach the staff member immediately.
    c. Give the staff member a final written warning.
    d. Conduct an investigation after placing the staff member on administrative leave.

10. The best guidelines for employee handbooks include which of the following?
    a. A disclaimer that states the handbook is not intended to be any type of contractual agreement between the company and employee.
    b. Requiring employees to sign off on revised versions of the handbook.
    c. Inclusion of policies that prevents the employee from leaving the company.
    d. Distributing printed copies of the handbook to new staff members during new employee orientation.

11. On January 1, 2015, an employer had 1,000 employees, and on December 31, 2015, the same employer had 1,200 employees. During the year, the employer had 125 employees exit from the organization. What is the employer's turnover rate for 2015?
    a. 10.42%
    b. 11.36%
    c. 12.5%
    d. 62.5%

12. Which of the following communication strategies is used to establish a relationship where employees feel comfortable speaking directly with management about problems and suggestions?
    a. Town hall meetings
    b. Management by Walking Around (MBWA)
    c. Open-door policy
    d. Department meetings

13. Which of the following communication strategies is used to allow management to check on employee progress, inquire about potential issues, and gain other feedback without relying on employees to "make the first move"?
   a. Open-door policy
   b. Brown bag lunch program
   c. Town hall meetings
   d. Management by Walking Around (MBWA)

14. Which of the following involvement strategies allows staff to work together in a temporary fashion to focus on a specific problem?
   a. Task force
   b. Committee
   c. Employee participation group
   d. Employee-management committee

15. Which of the following communication types, while making it easy to distribute information to a large group of individuals very quickly, may also lead to "information overload"?
   a. Intranet
   b. Email
   c. Newsletter
   d. Word-of-mouth

16. Which of the following is an example of an employee recognition program?
   a. An end of year bonus
   b. A plaque given for fifteen years of service to the organization
   c. A thank you note and a gift card for a job well done
   d. A merit given during annual review time

17. Which of the following is an example of a wrongful discharge?
   a. An employee who shared company information with a competitor
   b. An employee who takes home office supplies to help with an in-home consulting business
   c. An employee who accepts a gift in excess of $50 from a single client
   d. An employee who took time off from work to serve on a jury

18. Which of the following is true regarding severance pay?
   a. Severance pay is not required by law.
   b. Receipt of severance pay guarantees a former employee will not file a lawsuit against the employer.
   c. Severance pay increases an employer's contributions to unemployment tax.
   d. Severance pay guarantees that an employee will receive other benefits such as the continuation of health care coverage or outplacement services.

19. An HR professional uncovers during an exit interview that an employee is leaving the organization because she was bullied by two of her co-workers. The employee chose not to file any type of complaint or talk with HR during the course of her employment. She simply wants to leave the company and move on. Now that the HR professional is aware of the bullying and has details of the employee's experiences, what should the next move be?

    a. Terminate the identified co-workers who were performing the bullying.

    b. Conduct a full investigation and take the matter seriously.

    c. Comply with the exiting employee's wishes and ignore the matter.

    d. Let the matter go, since the affected employee is exiting the organization.

20. A company is laying off 20 percent of its workforce. Which of the following must be afforded to the individuals whose positions are being eliminated and are presented with documents known as a separation agreement and general release?

    a. They must sign and return the agreement during the meeting where they are presented with it.

    b. They must be given severance pay in return for signing the agreement.

    c. They must be given a period of forty-five days to sign and return the agreement, with a seven-day revocation period.

    d. They must be given the advantage of having a lawyer review the agreement for which they will be reimbursed by the company.

21. An employee files a grievance. After the employee discusses the grievance with the union steward and the supervisor (who are both in agreement), what is typically the next step in the formal grievance process?

    a. A committee of union officers will discuss the grievance with the appropriate managers in the company.

    b. The national union representative will discuss the grievance with designated company executives.

    c. The grievance will go to arbitration.

    d. The union steward will discuss the grievance with the supervisor's manager and/or the HR manager.

22. An employee must file a complaint charge of discrimination with the Equal Employment Opportunity Commission (EEOC) within a period of how many days of the alleged incident?

    a. 180 days

    b. 90 days

    c. 120 days

    d. There is no time limit associated with filing a complaint charge of discrimination with the EEOC.

23. In which of the following elements of alternative dispute resolution are the parties required by law to follow the decision reached as a result of the arbitration process?

    a. Compulsory arbitration

    b. Binding decision

    c. Voluntary arbitration

    d. Constructive confrontation

24. Which of the following types of picketing is done by employees for the purpose of convincing other employees to join their union?
    a. Informational picketing
    b. Recognitional picketing
    c. Organizational picketing
    d. Common situs picketing

25. Which of the following types of picketing is done by employees for the purpose of letting the public know that they are not represented by any one authority and thus plan to organize?
    a. Recognitional picketing
    b. Organizational picketing
    c. Consumer picketing
    d. Informational picketing

26. What percent of eligible employees are required to sign authorization cards by the National Labor Relations Board before it will order an election where employees can vote on whether to be represented by a union?
    a. At least 30 percent
    b. At least 50 percent
    c. 51 percent
    d. A majority of the employees who are eligible to vote

27. If employees win the vote to decertify their union on August 31 in a given calendar year, what is the next earliest date that a new election can be held?
    a. After January 1 of the following year
    b. After one year has passed
    c. After thirty days
    d. After ninety days

28. If a manager is questioning a union employee and it may ultimately lead to a disciplinary action via the Weingarten rights, the employee is entitled to have which of the following present?
    a. A relative or close friend
    b. An attorney
    c. A representative from the union
    d. Another manager

29. Which of the following is considered to be an illegal subject that cannot be discussed during a collective bargaining negotiation?
    a. Voluntary subjects
    b. Worker safety conditions
    c. Working conditions and terms
    d. Security clauses

30. Which of the following types of strategies that are commonly employed by unions during a collective bargaining negotiation occurs when a union successfully negotiates an agreement with a company, then uses the result of that negotiation as an example while dealing with a different company?
    a. Parallel bargaining
    b. Coordinated bargaining
    c. Multi-employer bargaining
    d. Single-unit bargaining

31. Which of the following is an exception to the concept of employment-at-will?
    a. An employee who decides to willingly sever the employment relationship
    b. An employee who is terminated for whistleblowing or for reporting unlawful conduct by the employer
    c. An employer who lets an employee go who does not have an employment contract
    d. An employee who is fired for willful misconduct

32. A truck driver kills a family's small child in an accident, and it is later uncovered that the truck driver lied on his employment application, had a history of unsafe driving, and had his license revoked twice. The employer was ultimately held responsible by the family's attorney for which of the following?
    a. Negligent retention
    b. Constructive discharge
    c. Negligent hiring
    d. Defamation

33. Which of the following activities is considered to be a fair labor practice?
    a. Hot cargo agreement
    b. Jurisdictional strike
    c. Secondary boycott
    d. Sympathy strike

34. Which of the following employees would not be eligible to vote in an upcoming union election?
    a. An employee who is temporarily laid off
    b. An employee who is out sick with the flu
    c. An employee who is out on military leave right before the election
    d. A staff member who is out of the office on a medical leave of absence and who will not be returning to work

35. Under the Taft-Hartley Act, which of the following is illegal?
    a. Creating a company-sponsored labor union
    b. An employee deciding to contribute to a charity instead of paying union dues, due to their religious objection
    c. An employer filing an unfair labor practice charge against a union
    d. A union representing nonunion employees in the bargaining unit

Answer Explanations

1. D: The Landrum-Griffith Act created a Bill of Rights for union members. The Norris-LaGuardia Act outlawed yellow-dog contracts, Choice *A*. The Taft-Hartley Act established the Federal Mediation and Conciliation Service, Choice *B*. Finally, the Wagner Act created the NLRB to encourage union growth, Choice *C*.

2. A: The Wagner Act dictates what are known as unfair labor practices. The Norris-LaGuardia Act, Choice *B*, outlawed yellow-dog contracts. The Taft-Hartley Act, Choice *C*, established the Federal Mediation and Conciliation Service. The Railway Labor Act, Choice *D*, resolves labor disputes by substituting bargaining, arbitration, and mediation for strikes.

3. B: Forcing employees to join a union is prohibited by the Taft-Hartley Act. The Sherman Antitrust Act prevents individuals and organizations from forming monopolies, Choice *A*. The Landrum-Griffith Act allowed for a closed shop exception for construction trades and gave union members the right to sue their union, Choices *C* and *D*.

4. C: In Choice *C*, the employer has one hundred or more full-time employees. The mass layoff is expected to last for at least six months, and at least 33 percent of the workforce at the employment site is being laid off. Under the WARN Act, an employer is required to provide a minimum of sixty days' notice to their employees in advance of a mass layoff, if the employer has one hundred or more full-time employees (or a total of full-time and part-time employees working 4,000 hours per week, not counting overtime, at all of their employment sites combined) and the layoff will result in an employment loss at a single site for either fifty or more full-time employees, if they make up at least 33 percent of the workforce at the employment site, or 500 or more full-time employees, and the layoff is for more than six months. Under the WARN Act, an employer is required to provide a minimum of sixty days' notice to their employees in advance of a plant closing if the employer has one hundred or more full-time employees (or a total of full-time and part-time employees working 4,000 hours per week, not counting overtime, at all of their employment sites combined) and the plant closing will result in the temporary or permanent shutdown of an entire site or one or more facilities or operating units within a single site that results in an employment loss during any thirty-day period of fifty or more full-time employees.

5. D: The Glass Ceiling Act established a commission to study how women and minorities face significant barriers and are prevented from reaching management positions. This act was part of Title II of the Civil Rights Act of 1991, Choices *A* and *B*. Choice *C*, Equal Pay Act, is a law that seeks to abolish the wage disparity based on sex.

6. A: A policy is a guideline that focuses on organizational actions. A rule, Choice *B*, is more specific to the situation and is used to regulate and/or restrict an individual's behavior. A procedure, Choice *C*, is a detailed description that answers when, what, who, and where. Finally, a Standard Operating Procedure (SOP), Choice *D*, is a written set of instructions that documents how to perform a routine activity.

7. B: A rule is more specific to the situation and is used to regulate and/or restrict an individual's behavior. A policy, Choice *A*, is a guideline that focuses on organizational actions. A procedure, Choice *C*, is a detailed description that answers when, what, who, and where. Finally, a Standard Operating Procedure (SOP), Choice *D*, is a written set of instructions that documents how to perform a routine activity.

8. C: In a progressive discipline policy, a verbal warning is typically followed with a second warning that is paired with a formal written warning (even if the warning is for a different type of employee violation).

9. D: A staff member who violates a work rule that is a dischargeable offense does not need to go through all of the steps in the progressive discipline process before they are terminated. However, instead of terminating the staff member on the spot, it is best for an HR professional to place the staff member on administrative leave while conducting an investigation. This ensures that all parties are interviewed and all of the necessary facts are gathered to protect the company against any possible future claims of wrongful termination.

10. A: To guarantee that employment-at-will remains in effect, one of the best guidelines for employee handbooks is to include a disclaimer that states the handbook is not intended to be any type of contractual agreement between the company and employee.

11. B: The turnover rate is calculated by taking the number of employees that exited the company during the year, dividing it by the average number of employees during the year, and then multiplying that amount by 100. In this example, this equates to $\frac{125}{1100} \times 100$, which is 11.36%.

12. C: An open-door policy is used to establish a relationship where employees feel comfortable speaking directly with management about problems and suggestions. Town hall meetings, Choice A, formal gatherings for the entire company that are commonly referred to as "all-hands meetings," tend to focus on sharing information "from the top down" concerning the overall organization. These meetings are not usually designed to allow feedback from employees about smaller detail issues. Management by Walking Around (MBWA), Choice B, as the name suggests, involves having managers and supervisors physically get out of their offices and interact with employees in person. MBWA allows management to check on employee progress, inquire about potential issues, and gain other feedback without relying on employees to "make the first move." Finally, department meetings, Choice D, are formal gatherings of employees and management in a given department that typically take place on a set day and time, allow everyone involved to share ideas, and offer solutions to company challenges.

13. D: Management by Walking Around (MBWA), as the name suggests, involves having managers and supervisors physically get out of their offices and interact with employees in person. MBWA allows management to check on employee progress, inquire about potential issues, and gain other feedback without relying on employees to "make the first move." An open-door policy, Choice A, is used to establish a relationship where employees feel comfortable speaking directly with management about problems and suggestions. A brown bag lunch program, Choice B, is an informal meeting (usually including employees and management) that is used to discuss company problems over a "brown bag" lunch. The lunch setting and company-provided meal can help create a relaxed setting for exchanging ideas. Finally, town hall meetings, Choice C, tend to focus on sharing information "from the top down" concerning the overall organization. These meetings are not usually designed to allow feedback from employees about smaller detail issues.

14. A: A task force is an involvement strategy that allows staff to work together in a temporary fashion to focus on a specific problem. Employees can also work together in a formal capacity as part of a committee to address company concerns, Choice B. Committees may be temporary or ongoing, and employees' service on a committee may also be for a specific term or a permanent appointment. Moreover, an employee-management committee, Choice D, is a specific kind of committee where employees work alongside management to address company concerns. Sometimes known as employee participation groups, Choice C, these committees also can be temporary or ongoing, depending on the needs of the organization.

15. B: Email makes it easy to get information to a lot of people very quickly. However, this communication method can result in employees suffering from "information overload" from too many emails. The intranet, Choice A, has the benefit of no risk of important information being accessed by someone outside the organization. Intranets can be effective at communicating important ongoing information about the company, such as policies and procedures. Newsletters, Choice C, can provide a variety of information and have the potential to do so in an engaging and welcoming manner. However, newsletters can be labor-intensive. Finally, word-of-mouth, Choice D, can quickly spread information throughout a group of people. However, information can become muddled, misinterpreted, and unrecognizable as it is passed from person to person.

16. C: A thank you note and a gift card for a job well done is an example of an employee recognition program. An end of year bonus, Choice A, is an example of additional compensation an employee receives as a one-time payment that does not become part of their base pay. A plaque given for fifteen years of service to the organization, Choice B, is an example of a service award. Finally, a merit given during annual review time, Choice D, is an example of incentive pay given to employees for good performance.

17. D: Wrongful discharge can occur when an employee is terminated after they refuse to do something unsafe, unethical, or illegal, such as a pharmacist refusing to sign off on a prescription to be dispensed that does not have a date. This type of termination is wrongful because it violates public policy. Additionally, a charge of wrongful discharge can also occur when an employee is terminated after an employer promised them job security, thus violating an implied employment agreement. In this example, an employee should not be fired for taking time off work to serve on a jury, which falls under the category of violating public policy.

18. A: Severance pay is not required by law. Receipt of severance pay does not guarantee that a former employee will not file a lawsuit against the employer, Choice B. Severance pay does not increase an employer's contributions to unemployment tax, Choice C. Finally, severance pay does not guarantee that an employee will receive other benefits such as the continuation of health care coverage or outplacement services, Choice D.

19. B: Although the employee who was bullied is leaving the organization and did not file a complaint regarding the bullying during the course of her employment, the HR professional is still obligated to treat this matter seriously and should conduct a full investigation.

20. C: During a larger group RIF, the affected employees who are being laid off and given a document to sign, known as a separation agreement and general release, must be given forty-five days to sign and return the agreement, along with a seven-day revocation period. This allows them time to consider the terms of the agreement and to review the agreement with a lawyer, if they choose to do so.

21. D: The next step in the grievance process would involve the union steward discussing the grievance with the supervisor's manager and/or the HR manager. Then, a committee of union officers should discuss the grievance with the appropriate managers in the company. The national union representative would then discuss the grievance with designated company executives. If, after this process, the grievance is still not settled, it would then go to arbitration.

22. A: An employee must file a complaint charge of discrimination with the EEOC within a period of 180 days of the alleged incident.

23. B: In a binding decision, the disputing parties are required by law to follow the decision reached as a result of the arbitration process. In compulsory arbitration, Choice *A*, the disputing parties are required by law to go through the arbitration process. In voluntary arbitration, Choice *C*, the disputing parties choose to undergo the arbitration process. Finally, constructive confrontation, Choice *D*, is a type of mediation used in some extremely complicated or contentious disputes, particularly ones where neither party is able to agree to a compromise.

24. C: Organizational picketing is done by employees for the purpose of convincing other employees to join their union. Informational picketing, Choice *A*, is done by employees for the purpose of letting the public know that they are not represented by any one authority and thus plan to organize. Recognitional picketing, Choice *B*, is done by employees for the purpose of encouraging their employer to recognize their union as their representative. Finally, when in disputes with an employer, unions may engage in common situs picketing, Choice *D*. This is where employees picket at a location used by the targeted employer as well as other organizations.

25. D: Informational picketing is done by employees for the purpose of letting the public know that they are not represented by any one authority and thus plan to organize. Recognitional picketing, Choice *A*, is done by employees for the purpose of encouraging their employer to recognize their union as their representative. Organizational picketing, Choice *B*, is done by employees for the purpose of convincing other employees to join their union. Finally, consumer picketing, Choice *C*, takes place when employees picket to discourage the public from doing business with the employer in question.

26. A: At least 30 percent of eligible employees are required to sign authorization cards by the National Labor Relations Board before it will order an election where employees can vote on whether to be represented by a union.

27. B: If employees win the vote to decertify their union on August 31 in a given calendar year, after one year has passed is the next earliest date that a new election can be held.

28. C: Via the Weingarten rights, a union employee is entitled to have a union representative present if they are being questioned by a manager in a discussion that may ultimately lead to a disciplinary action.

29. D: Security clauses are considered to be an illegal subject that cannot be discussed during a collective bargaining negotiation. Voluntary subjects, worker safety conditions, and working conditions and terms are all legal subjects that can be discussed during a collective bargaining negotiation.

30. A: Parallel bargaining is a strategy that is used during a collective bargaining negotiation when a union successfully negotiates an agreement with a company, then uses the result of that negotiation as an example while dealing with a different company. Coordinated bargaining, Choice *B*, takes place when several unions within an organization meet with the employer to negotiate beneficial results for all the different groups they represent (also called multi-unit bargaining). Multi-employer bargaining, Choice *C*, occurs when a union with employees in multiple companies meets with all of those companies as a single negotiation. Finally, single-unit bargaining, Choice *D*, occurs when union representatives meet with one employer at a time, concerned only with that particular agreement, and not attempting to use the process as a springboard or advantage in separate negotiations.

31. B: An employee who is terminated for whistleblowing or for reporting unlawful conduct by the employer is an exception to the concept of employment-at-will, since these activities are protected under the law.

32. C: The employer was ultimately held responsible for negligent hiring. In this example, the employer should have known that the employee posed a risk to other employees or to customers. If the employer had completed a thorough background check, they would have checked the employee's past driving record (since it was relevant to his position).

33. D: A sympathy strike is considered to be a fair labor practice. Choice *A*, hot cargo agreements, Choice *B*, jurisdictional strikes, and Choice *C*, secondary boycotts, are all considered to be unfair labor practices.

34. D: An employee who is out of the office on a medical leave of absence and who will not be returning to work would not be eligible to vote in an upcoming union election. An employee who is temporarily laid off, an employee who is out sick with the flu, and an employee who is out on military leave right before the election would all be eligible to vote in an upcoming union election.

35. A: Under the Taft-Hartley Act, creating a company-sponsored labor union is illegal.

Risk Management

An organization engages in risk management when it identifies, targets, and strives to minimize unacceptable risks. While a variety of different risks may arise, an organization's principal risks are generally workplace health, safety, security, and privacy. Failure to protect from these risks can result in serious consequences and may lead to negative company publicity, low employee morale, and burdensome expenses. Organizations must prioritize risk management and comply with federal laws and regulations. By doing so, employers will increase productivity and build sustainable relationships between employees and management.

Federal Laws and Regulations

Workplace Federal Laws and Regulations
Workplace policies should strictly follow federal laws in order to legally secure a workplace that satisfies minimum health, safety, security, and privacy standards. Failure to meet federal standards can result in fines or the loss of a license. Federal laws and regulations function as minimum standards that all workplace policies must meet. Employers are allowed to pursue policies that go beyond what is legally required if they believe such policies will benefit the organization. Many employers strive to understand the delicate balance between meeting federal guidelines and maintaining high profit margins. Therefore, organizations often find innovative ways to meet federal standards while using efficient business strategies.

Five federal agencies and laws regarding workplace issues are the Occupational Safety and Health Administration (OSHA), the Drug-Free Work Place Act, the Americans with Disabilities Act, the Health Insurance Portability and Accountability Act, and the Sarbanes-Oxley Act.

The Occupational Safety and Health Act, passed in 1970, established the Occupational Safety and Health Administration (OSHA) of the federal government in 1971. This agency creates and enforces workplace safety standards. Employers who are engaged in commerce and have one or more employees must observe the regulations established by OSHA. Not only does OSHA set minimum standards, the agency ensures job training for workers in a language they can understand. Additionally, OSHA protects employees who work in substandard conditions and informs them of their rights. A critical provision of OSHA is the protection of employees who reach out to OSHA in an attempt to open an investigation of their working conditions. These employees are protected by OSHA from employer retaliation. OSHA regulations empower employees to help accomplish safety and security.

OSHA regulations focus on employer and employee rights and responsibilities. Employers must provide a safe workplace for employees. Employers are required to meet all OSHA safety standards and correct any violations. Employers are required to attempt to reduce hazards to workers, and must supply free protective equipment to workers. OSHA guidelines require employers to provide safety training and to prominently display OSHA posters that detail employee rights. Employers must keep accurate records of any injuries or illnesses that occur in the workplace and notify OSHA promptly of any injuries. Furthermore, employers may not retaliate if an employee uses their right to report an OSHA violation.

OSHA regulations provide specific rights to employees. Employees have the right to demand safety on the job and obtain information concerning work hazards. Every employee has the right to file a complaint with OSHA and request a workplace inspection without fear of employer retaliation. Employees have the right to meet privately with a licensed OSHA inspector. Additionally, OSHA regulations allow employees to refuse work that may be abnormally dangerous or life-threatening.

The Drug-Free Workplace Act of 1988 requires organizations to establish a drug-free workplace, provide a copy of this policy to their employees, and institute a drug awareness program. This law applies to federal contractors with contracts of $100,000 or more and all organizations that are federal grantees. These different penalties exist for employers who do not comply with the act, including contract suspension or contract termination. Although an employer may discuss alcohol and tobacco use in its policies, the Drug-Free Workplace Act does not address the use of these substances.

The Americans with Disabilities Act (ADA) is a federal law that prevents discrimination based on disability. This law requires employers to provide reasonable accommodations to employees with a disability. For example, an employer may accommodate a disabled employee by building a wheelchair accessible ramp to enter and exit the building. Additionally, the ADA stipulates that public entities be accessible for disabled persons. The ADA does include both mental and physical medical conditions, and temporary conditions may qualify as a disability. ADA protections apply to every aspect of job application procedures, employment, and promotions.

The Health Insurance Portability and Accountability Act of 1996 (HIPAA) addresses issues of healthcare access and portability as well as aspects of healthcare administration. HIPAA provisions allow workers that change jobs or become unemployed to transfer and continue their healthcare coverage. Additionally, HIPAA regulations establish standards for healthcare administration in order to reduce waste, fraud, and abuse. HIPAA laws strengthen privacy standards and provide benchmarks for medical records in areas such as electronic billing.

HIPAA is applicable to health insurance plans issued by companies, HMOs, Medicare, and Medicaid. Moreover, these regulations apply to healthcare providers who conduct transactions electronically and healthcare clearing houses that process certain information. HIPAA's Privacy Rule gives rights to the insured regarding the disclosure of medical information. Individuals may view health records and request an edit of inaccurate information. Additionally, individuals may file a complaint if rights are being denied or health information is not protected. Patient information with heightened protection is placed in the insurer's database, and may include conversations about patients between medical professionals and billing information. Lastly, HIPAA creates strict rules regarding how healthcare information is disseminated and specifies who is given access.

The Sarbanes-Oxley Act of 2002, or SOX, is federal legislation that is designed to establish higher levels of accountability and standards for U.S. public institution boards and senior management. The act was passed in reaction to major global corporate and accounting scandals such as WorldCom and Enron, companies caught engaging in dubious financial practices. Sarbanes-Oxley specifically targets senior executives responsible for accounting misconduct and record manipulation. The law protects shareholders from any activity that conceals or misleads investors about the firm's finances. The firm has a mandate to transparently and accurately report financial information either to shareholders or the Securities and Exchange Commission (SEC). Moreover, SOX imposes more stringent penalties for white-collar crime and requires detailed reporting to the SEC if a company's finances significantly alter.

Needs Analysis

A needs analysis is the process in which an organization gathers information about the principal needs and requests of its members. This analysis studies the expectations and requirements of subjects who are affected by workplace programs or regulations. Such individuals may include employers, teachers, administrators, donors, and family members of students. Needs analysis results may be used to clarify the objectives of an organization, or as a teaching tool in a classroom.

A needs analysis typically starts by gathering data. This process can be accomplished through a multitude of channels such as surveys, interviews, questionnaires, or polls. In a needs analysis, problems and inefficiencies are clearly identified. These issues are ultimately addressed by the organization through the implementation of improvements to maximize results. A needs analysis may serve as an efficient means of examining organizational procedures and techniques of training at minimal cost. Additionally, a needs analysis can be a helpful tool to develop occupational injury prevention programs within an organization.

If the needs analysis is conducted properly, the organization's next step is to implement the suggested changes in a way that promotes success. This endeavor requires the allocation of resources and personnel to the proposed plan. The proposed changes should meet the organization's productivity targets and fulfill the requirements of governmental agencies.

Occupational Injury and Illness Prevention Programs

Occupational Injury and Illness Prevention and Compensation Programs
Injuries and illnesses are a burden for both employers and employees. The loss of productivity due to workplace injuries and illnesses can be significant, and the loss of income for employees can affect an individual and economy as a whole. Therefore, organizations must establish programs that minimize or prevent these incidents. If a workplace injury or illness does occur, workers' compensation may provide fixed payments to the employee. Workers' compensation also covers dependents of those who are killed as a result of workplace accidents. Limits do exist for these compensation benefits, such as caps on what can be collected from employers.

OSHA, a federal agency that is designed to ensure safe working conditions for employees, established process safety management standards that deal with hazardous chemicals in the workplace. If an employee could potentially come into contact with the hazardous substance during the normal course of their jobs, these substances must be properly evaluated, classified, and labeled. This information is recorded in material safety data sheets (MSDS), which must be easily accessible to individuals who work with any hazardous materials. The MSDS should state what should be done if someone has inappropriate contact with the chemicals, such as an employee who splashes a dangerous chemical in their eye.

OSHA has developed standards for employee personal protective equipment (PPE) in hazardous working environments. These items may include safety glasses, hard hats, and safety shoes. Employees are provided these items at no cost and must be paid their rate of pay for the time required to put on and take off protective equipment.

OSHA has established guidelines to assist employers in the event of a pandemic disease outbreak by utilizing proper safety equipment and procedures. The guidelines are also meant to assist the company to continue operations with a reduced workforce.

Ergonomics, or the study and design of the work environment to address physical demands placed on employees, is yet another area addressed by OSHA. In the workplace, ergonomics deals with elements such as lighting, placement of controls, equipment layout, and fatigue. OSHA examines work-related injuries that result from repetitive stress and repetitive motion, such as carpal tunnel. These are also known as cumulative trauma disorders. These workplace injuries may be reduced by redesigning workstations and improving workplace environments.

Investigation Procedures of Workplace Safety

Strict enforcement of workplace safety and security is contingent on investigative agencies. If an employer is reported, OSHA will conduct an investigation into the workplace. Throughout an investigation, OSHA works in conjunction with employers and employees to ensure greater safety and security policies are implemented. OSHA agents look beyond the immediate causes of an incident and attempt to uncover the systemic causes of an incident. OSHA investigators attempt to discover why a particular problem exists if it is determined that the issue is not a result of individual carelessness.

Following an investigation, an OSHA compliance officer can issue citations depending on the severity of the violation. If an OSHA inspector observes a violation of imminent danger, the inspector will require the employer to correct the issue immediately, as the violation will lead to serious harm or death. Other violations may be labeled serious, which means that the violation will likely cause death or physical harm. Other-than-serious is the next level of violation. This means that the condition could impact employees' safety or health but probably would not cause death or serious harm. De minimus violations are not directly and immediately related to employees' safety or health and do not require fines or citations. Willful and repeated citations are issued to employers who are repeat offenders of hazardous workplace violations. Penalties for unaddressed or intentional safety violations are very costly.

Workplace Safety Risks

Minimizing injuries in the workplace is a primary concern for employers. Accidents and injuries triggered by safety risks diminish productivity and reduce savings because of costly workers' compensation payments. Furthermore, failure to adequately protect workers can result in employer penalties and fines. Two common workplace safety risks are tripping hazards and blood-borne pathogens.

Trip hazards cause a person's foot to hit an object that does not budge, plunging the person forward involuntarily. Tripping can occur in the workplace for many reasons such as obstructed views, poor lighting, excessive clutter, uneven walking surfaces, wrinkled carpeting, or unsecure wires. Tripping may result in injuries such as sprains, broken bones, or torn ligaments. Employers should maintain an orderly workplace and arrange for bright lighting to reduce the likelihood of tripping. Accordingly, employees should pay attention when walking, make wide turns when walking, and walk with feet pointed outward.

Bloodborne pathogens are infectious microorganisms in human blood that can cause disease in humans. Specifically, some of these pathogens are hepatitis B virus (HBV), hepatitis C virus (HCV), and human immunodeficiency virus (HIV). One potential cause of spreading bloodborne pathogens is through improper usage and/or disposal of needles. Occupations such as nursing, healthcare professionals, medical first responders, and housekeepers who work in medical environments are the most likely to encounter a needle with bloodborne pathogens. Due to growing concerns within the medical field, The Needlestick Safety and Prevention Act of 2000 revised OSHA's Bloodborne Pathogens Standard. This law provides requirements in selecting medical devices and establishes oversight through a sharps injury log, which details all sharps-related workplace injuries.

Additional workplace safety risks with OSHA regulations are occupational noise exposure, emergency exit procedures, control of hazardous materials, lockout/tagout procedures, machine guarding, and confined space environments.

Workers' compensation laws are designed to protect employees who are injured in the workplace. The primary purpose of workers' compensation is to provide injured employees with fixed monetary sums. Worker's compensation benefits cover medical expenses due to workplace injuries. Furthermore, workers' compensation benefits are extended to dependents of employees killed by an injury or illness that occurs in the workplace. In addition to employee protection, some worker's compensation laws protect employers by limiting the amount of money that can be distributed to employees. The program also has provisions that restrict co-worker liability in most workplace accidents. Most workers' compensation programs are structured at the state level by legislative bodies and agencies. However, worker's compensation exists at the federal level, where it is limited to federal employment and industries that considerably affect interstate commerce.

Return-to-Work Policies

Return-to-Work Procedures

A return-to-work program assists ill or injured employees to resume work as soon as they are able. An effective return-to-work policy should mediate the interests of company productivity levels and employees' health. Injured employees are generally less likely to return to the workplace the longer they are away from work. Return-to-work programs provide a safe and managed transition for employees to integrate themselves back into the workforce. These policies are usually incremental and do not require recovering individuals to function at maximum capacity. Employers may structure a return-to-work program by limiting the duration of time an employee has to recover. For example, a worker who suffered a broken leg on the job can be asked to perform administrative support while recovering. Such a strategy establishes general guidelines and standards, maintains a firm's competitiveness, and gives employees the time they need to recover.

Constant communication and interactive dialogue is essential in establishing effective and acceptable return-to-work procedures. Important aspects of the process include monitoring an employee's physical and psychological progress, setting timetables that are accommodating for both parties, and discussing the feasibility of a modified duty assignment. In this process, all parties should discuss the feasibility of modified duties and discuss a schedule that fulfills the interests of productivity and health.

One facet of a return-to-work policy is a modified duty assignment, sometimes dubbed "light work." This arrangement can be profitable to both employer and employee under the right circumstances. A modified duty assignment is a temporary arrangement that offers injured or sick employees the option to work through their condition at a reduced capacity. These assignments permit employees to earn income while recuperating. In addition, these employees have an opportunity to keep their physical and cognitive capacities fresh and refined. Depending on the severity of their condition, employees may be asked to continue their regular jobs in a diminished capacity or work in a completely different role. Modified duty can consist of reducing work hours or less physically demanding labor. An employee must pass a clearance test administered by a licensed physician to receive a modified duty assignment. However, a worker reserves the right to decline a modified duty assignment under certain circumstances.

A modified duty assignment is contingent upon appropriate and temporary accommodations. Because recovering employees are not at full strength, employers should be willing to offer reasonable accommodations. Accommodations may involve an easily accessible office or tasks consistent with an employee's temporarily limited capacities.

The Americans with Disabilities Act (ADA) of 1990 is a federal law that outlaws discrimination based on disability. This law applies to all employers with fifteen or more employees and requires employers to provide a reasonable accommodation to employees who have a disability. The ADA rests on the principal that qualified employees should not be barred access to employment or treated differently because they face physical impairments.

The ADA requires that a reasonable accommodation be provided to qualified employees whether they work full-time, part-time, or are within a probationary period. Identifying a reasonable accommodation is an interactive process. An applicant or employee may request a reasonable accommodation, and the employer and employee must identify individual barriers to the performance of the essential job functions. Both parties must work together to identify possible accommodation(s) that might be helpful in overcoming the barriers. The accommodation(s) are examined through an extensive process which determines whether the accommodation(s) are the employer's responsibility and will impose an undue hardship to the employer. Finally, appropriate accommodation(s) are chosen for the employee, if possible. An example of a reasonable accommodation is a wheelchair accessible ramp provided by an employer for a disabled employee to enter and leave the building.

An independent medical examination (IME) is an examination given to a patient by a licensed medical professional who has not previously dealt with that patient. A previous relationship between the medical professional and the patient cannot exist in order to provide an independent status. An IME is frequently conducted when assessing the extent of a work-related injury or illness. This independent opinion assists employers and insurers in determining the time and award package an injured employee should receive. If the medical professional determines that an employee's injury or illness is unrelated to a workplace incident or is not as severe as previously thought, the employer and insurer have the right to deny claims and refuse the payment of benefits.

Plans and Policies to Minimize Loss and Liability

Protecting employees, minimizing loss, and developing effective safety procedures are central goals for a successful organization. In order to meet these goals, firms must establish robust and creative policies, procedures, and standards. Among these policies should be organized responses to emergencies, workplace violence, and substance abuse.

Organizational Incident and Emergency Response Plans
All organizations must have procedures that secure an orderly response in the event of an emergency. Emergency response plans incorporate several elements of maintaining safety and order. These elements may include practiced evacuations, reserved resources to preserve organizational function, and a plan that seeks to minimize property damage. An organization with no emergency response plan is vulnerable to instability, disorder, and distrust. An effective emergency response plan not only protects lives and property but provides security that management has control over the situation. This knowledge provides an element of calm in an otherwise stressful emergency situation, which can be as important as the response protocol.

An emergency response is planned and practiced protocol used during an emergency. These strategies should be planned rationally and practiced frequently in order to mitigate the impact of a disaster. Workplace emergency responses should plan for a wide range of scenarios, such as machinery malfunctions or workplace violence. Once created, emergency response plans should be communicated to all staff, frequently tested by the organization, and kept up to date.

An evacuation is a coordinated and planned exit from a place that is considered to be dangerous. It is a principal component of general health and safety policies. Conditions that may prompt evacuation are fire, flood, or violence. The most effective way to orchestrate an orderly and calm evacuation is through practice of an evacuation plan. This routine practice familiarizes staff with expedient exit routes and ensures that exits remain visible and unobstructed.

Hazard communication is the notification of employees concerning the noxious health effects and physical dangers of hazardous chemicals in the workplace. Workers should be clearly notified of any physical hazards (corrosion or flammability) or health hazards (skin irritation and carcinogenicity) that they will come into contact with in the workplace. OSHA created the Hazard Communication Standard (HCS) to ensure that chemical information is accessible to all individuals who may interact with the substance. In addition to the HCS, all employers are required to implement a hazard communication program that encompasses training, access to material safety data sheets (MSDS), and labeling of hazardous chemical containers.

Workplace Violence Conditions
Workplace violence is any act of physical violence, intimidation, threat, or verbal abuse that occurs in the workplace. This behavior is disruptive both physically and psychologically. Employees may demonstrate violent behavior as a result of a history of violence, a troubled upbringing, issues of substance abuse, and psychological illness. These conditions may foster violent behavior from an employee but do not make violent behavior inevitable. Workplace violence not only interrupts immediate employees, but can cause an organization to lose clients, suppliers, and advertisers. Furthermore, a firm can suffer devastating economic consequences as a result of negative publicity from incidents of workplace violence. Workplace violence attacks the foundation of trust and safety that all workplaces need to operate successfully.

Although an employer cannot completely eliminate the possibility of workplace violence, several steps can be taken to avoid these incidents. One example is a mental health program, such as an Employee Assistance Program (EAP), which provides employees the option to improve their psychological wellbeing. Additionally, offering company parties and functions in alcohol-free locations may reduce the likeliness of workplace violence. Violence may also be introduced in the workplace from the public. In areas with high crime rates, statistics show a higher probability of violence for employers who operate at night. Finally, organizations should establish and enforce a zero tolerance policy for on-site weapons and acts of violence.

Employer/Employee Rights Related to Substance Abuse
Substance abuse is a dependence on an addictive substance such as illegal drugs. This dependency not only impacts the individual but also may affect families and communities. Programs specifically designed to combat substance abuse can be extraordinarily beneficial. Because substance abuse is not limited to adults, programs may be introduced that focus on children and adolescents as well. In addition to the physical dangers of substance abuse, subsequent behavioral patterns compound issues. If treatment is not sought, the likelihood of a life of crime and poverty greatly increases.

Effective substance abuse policies protect both employers and employees in the workplace. Privacy policies generally authorize employers to conduct random drug tests if the employee has given prior consent. The employee should be clearly notified when hired that these tests may be administered by the employer. Employee substance abuse is damaging to the workplace and often results in inappropriate conduct with co-workers, insubordination, and fatal injuries due to improper use of machinery.

Through the Americans with Disabilities Act, federal guidelines exist to protect both employers and employees in regards to substance abuse. Employers do have the right to ensure a drug-free workplace by prohibiting the use of illegal drugs and alcohol. Employers may test for illegal drug use, but must meet state requirements to do so. If an employee tests positive for current drug use through proper testing procedures, employers have the right to terminate that employee.

The ADA gives protection to employees who have successfully rehabilitated from past drug use but are no longer engaged in the illegal use of drugs. Employers cannot discriminate against any employee who has either completed a rehabilitation program or is undergoing rehabilitation. Reasonable accommodation efforts should be extended to those individuals who are rehabilitated or are undergoing current treatment.

Ergonomics refers to the ability of a person to fully utilize a product while maintaining maximum safety, efficiency, and comfort. Ergonomic risk factors in the workplace can lead to musculoskeletal disorders such as carpal tunnel, rotator cuff injuries, muscle strains, and lower back injuries. In order to reduce these risks, employers should evaluate workplace ergonomics and educate employees about potential issues. An ergonomic evaluation tests a product to determine its ease of use and potential safety risks. When employers identify and address ergonomic concerns in the workplace, they protect their workers and likely prevent serious injuries.

Security Plans and Policies Training

Workplace Security Risks
Obtaining a safe and secure working environment is not accomplished by simply strategizing. The staff of an organization must have adequate training to appropriately respond to diverse situations. Workplace security plans and policies address a variety of issues from a sudden crisis to an act of intentional harm. A clear understanding of security plans and policies can minimize unpredictability and panic and teach employees how to respond to a crisis.

Employees should understand security plans and how they address the physical security needs of the work environment. Workplace security plans and policies may include security measures such as control badges, keycard access systems, backup communication systems, locks on various rooms and closets, and concealed alarms. When developing workplace security plans, a team approach is vital to ensuring its success. Representatives are needed from human resources, legal counsel, security, and facilities to provide a comprehensive perspective of security needs. Once the security plans and policies are established, employees should be trained annually to review the plans and their importance.

Theft is the act of taking property without the consent of the owner. Theft can occur by deception or force, with or without the knowledge of the owner. Theft can be very costly to an organization, and management should take steps to prevent any opportunity for theft. Such measures may include hidden video cameras, a private security force, and incentives for employees who disrupt incidents of theft. Theft can be accomplished by employees, management, and customers. Therefore, prevention policies should apply to all levels of the organization.

Corporate espionage is a form of spying that occurs between competitive companies. The principal purpose of corporate espionage is to obtain industrial secrets and learn about a competitor's plans, future products, business strategies, or total profits. Knowing these secrets can give a competitor an unfair advantage when trying to increase market share. A company must hire trustworthy employees, particularly employees privy to classified information. A firm should employ strategies to test employee loyalty and offer incentives that encourage employees to report suspicious activity.

Sabotage is the act of purposely weakening or corrupting a country or a company. In the workplace, sabotage is the intentional thwarting of successful planning models to create dysfunctional conditions at odds with the organization's best interests. Those who commit sabotage are known as saboteurs, and they generally conceal their identity and intentions. Sabotage is debilitating to a company, and can cultivate an environment of distrust and hostility. Therefore, management must conduct frequent tests to ensure that all members and employees act in good faith.

Developing Business Continuity and Disaster Recovery Plans

In the event of a crisis, an organization may face multiple challenges such as mitigating casualties, protecting property, and testing disciplinary protocol. Aside from protecting human life, the most challenging priority during a crisis is maintaining business continuity. Business continuity maintains productivity during and after a potential disruption.

Business continuity plans identify potential threats and their associated impacts in order to maintain organizational productivity during an operational interruption. These plans establish procedures to handle disruptions and/or loss of business functions. There are four components to a business continuity plan: business impact analysis, recovery strategies, plan development, and testing and exercises. A business impact analysis (BIA) assesses the potential consequences of a disruption and collects information to develop recovery strategies. A BIA is a risk assessment tool, and information can be gathered by means of a questionnaire. The second step is to identify, document, and implement the most comprehensive of the proposed strategies. Recovery strategies frequently identify gaps in necessary resources. The third step, plan development, builds a business continuity team and crafts the business continuity plan. Finally, extensive training and testing are conducted to test strategies, personnel, and the business continuity plan.

Business continuity plans respond to a variety of crisis scenarios, such as a loss of administrative capacities, a hack into the operating system, and threat of workplace violence. These plans must be observed by all staff to ensure the plan's effectiveness. If an employee does not comply, disciplinary measures should be enforced by the organization.

A disaster recovery plan (DRP) is a set of procedures that prepares for a disaster so that destructive effects are reduced and essential data can be recovered. A DRP increases a firm's ability to recover from an unexpected, devastating incident. A DRP assists the organization in resuming normal business functions as quickly as possible. As information technology systems become more sophisticated and complex, solving critical organizational technology questions becomes more difficult. The ability of hackers and viruses to infiltrate these systems makes an effective organizational DRP more important than ever.

Secure data storage is a difficult but necessary policy to prevent corruption from malware and hackers. Data corruption is a widespread concern for firms of all sizes and locations. Organizations with sensitive and confidential data, such as government agencies, continue to take steps to strengthen their data security. Data backup requires copying and archiving current information to separate drives to restore information in the event of data corruption. Data storage and backup are essential to protect organizational plans, policies, and secrets in the event of a data breach.

Technological increases have created viable scenarios for employers to offer alternative work locations. If a corporation offers alternative work locations, these employees are allowed to work from home or another off-site location rather than a traditional office space. Communication between organizations and its remote employees generally takes place through the Internet and phone calls. Alternative work locations can be helpful in disaster recovery because organizational data is decentralized and more difficult to corrupt entirely.

A procedure is a recognized and established way of accomplishing a desired goal. Procedures provide a plan of action for organizations in a time of vulnerability or crisis. The business continuity plan, disaster recovery plan, and any additional organizational policies should be studied and practiced frequently by employees.

Business Continuity and Disaster Recovery Plan Training

A business continuity plan or disaster recovery plan is only as good as the organization's ability to implement the plan. If all levels of employees and management are not familiar with the plan they will not be able to execute it when the need arises. Employees and management must possess unwavering familiarity with the DRP. The best defense against disruption is training that allows the workforce to react according to the DRP, maximizing the allocation of resources and reducing panic.

The organization should devote sufficient time and resources to ensure proper training for its employees. This training should begin with an awareness of the plan and its components. Employees should understand the plan's framework and their role in the plan. If a staff member has a specific role in the plan, this staff member may require additional time and training.

Scenario training is the next essential step in ensuring a successful business continuity and/or disaster recovery plan. Employees and management respond to mock scenarios that provide them opportunities to utilize their training. These scenarios may also be used as an opportunity to test critical backup systems, applications, and facilities. During scenario training, all areas of response should be documented for further evaluation and review.

After scenario training is complete, the organization can review what aspects of the plan were successful and unsuccessful. This evaluation assists in determining potential changes to the plan and updating the plan as necessary. All areas of management should review the scenario training to determine the best possible course of action.

Electronic Media and Hardware Policies and Procedures

If a firm wishes to maintain competitiveness and maximize its capabilities, management should develop policies that streamline communication. These policies will allow for the freer flow of ideas and dialogue. Furthermore, the integration of electronic media will increase a firm's ability to reach out to consumers and market the company's products. Harnessing this technology can increase market share and make innovation easier.

Electronic mail, or email, is communication that occurs by exchanging digital messages. Email was developed in the early 1990s and came into widespread use by 1993. Email has become a common means of communication, particularly within a corporate environment. This mode of communication allows an individual to send messages to one or more recipients at once. Email has been enormously successful in streamlining the communication process while reducing the cost of using paper.

Many organizations currently integrate the use of social media into corporate strategies. Social media is online applications that allow users to share content. These sites have become so advantageous in marketing that companies hire employees to increase social media presence. Many firms presently require their employees to have social media skills, knowledge, and familiarity. Programs such as

Twitter, Facebook, and Instagram have proven to be tremendously successful marketing tools used by companies to reach a broader audience. In addition, social media has revolutionized advertising by placing a growing emphasis on Internet marketing instead of traditional television ads.

As technology has increased the use of the Internet, the necessity of a company website and the demand for website accessibility has grown. In order to promote equal access to websites, companies should attempt to accommodate those with cognitive, neurological, physical, visual, or auditory disabilities. In addition to disabled persons, elderly people who lack familiarity should be able to understand and navigate websites. Because the Internet is an integral resource for participating in commercial activity, gaining employment, accessing health care, and finding recreational activities, equal opportunity and access to website navigation is also crucial.

Data sharing is the practice of making information accessible through public or private networks. Individuals within the network have access to the information, while those not in the network require consent for access. Data sharing usually involves varying levels of access and is generally regulated by administrators in the system.

A password is a code that is required to access restricted information. A complex password provides more security to the user and better protects sensitive information. Typically, passwords consist of letters, numbers, and symbols. This unique combination affords better protection to the user. Password sharing should be limited to those individuals who may be trusted with confidential information.

Social engineering is the act of manipulating people for the purpose of revealing sensitive information. Typically, an attacker will employ deceptive tactics to convince the target to provide information such as bank numbers, passwords, and Social Security numbers. Social engineers take advantage of a target's natural tendencies of trust. Social engineers may gain access to information by infiltrating computer systems and installing malware. Organizations should educate employees on security and the identification of untrustworthy individuals. Employees should be able to assess suspicious situations and clearly recognize red flags.

Social media is a platform where people can freely express ideas, exchange information, market goods, and advertise. Social media establishes important individual connections and can even result in locating employment. While a helpful and useful tool in many circumstances, social media may also carry unintended consequences. For example, employers often use social media to obtain personal information about a potential or current employee. Questionable social media content can influence an employer's decision to hire an individual.

Monitoring software, also known as computer surveillance software, regulates the activity performed on a certain network. If this software detects anything that may threaten the safety and security of the network, it reports the activity to an administrator. This type of software may be employed in individual or corporate networks. Typically, monitoring software checks all information flow of network traffic on the Internet. Computer surveillance software is sophisticated enough to easily detect any abnormal or suspicious action in a multitude of network information.

In the field of computer security, biometrics refers to an authentication process that requires physiological proof to validate a user. Once the measure of the user's physiology is authenticated, they will be granted access to appropriate information. Biometric identification ranges from fingerprints, facial recognition, voice recognition, hand patterns, or eye patterns. The individual's biometric information is uploaded and stored in a security system that must recognize these physical characteristics to provide information access.

Internal and External Privacy Policies

<u>Internal Investigation, Monitoring, and Surveillance Techniques</u>
Companies should maintain maximum security while possessing the personal information of customers and employees. Each organization should utilize an apparatus that monitors and reports security breaches, notifying employees, customers, and various authorities. In addition, internal privacy policies must comply with current laws and regulations. These laws are intended to deter security breaches.

A company's internal privacy policy should address sensitive information such as addresses, telephone numbers, credit reports, medical reports, employee records, company technology, and data systems that collect personal information. An effective privacy policy explains the purposes of investigations and monitors the conduct of employees. Episodic privacy tests can be useful, particularly if management has reason to believe that employee misconduct has occurred. A company should communicate regularly with its employees about security issues and technology. Additionally, written policies must exist to protect employers from employee claims of privacy invasion. Employees should be notified of these policies and agree to all conditions. An effective privacy policy will identify and monitor employees suspected of violating protocol and procure the necessary information to review the employee's practices.

Identity theft occurs when a person wrongfully obtains and uses another individual's personal information, typically for financial gain. This form of fraud can be very damaging and is difficult to prevent. In order to commit identity theft, a perpetrator does not need a person's fingerprint. The criminal simply needs a Social Security number, credit card number, bank statements, or any piece of information that will allow access to personal documents. The expense of identity theft to the victim can be shocking, and in some cases may be in excess of $100,000. Identity theft primarily occurs in public places through methods such as "shoulder surfing." This technique involves watching over somebody's shoulder when they are using an ATM machine or rummaging through someone's garbage in search of confidential material that was not disposed of properly.

Data protection is the process of securing personal information from identity theft or other corruptive activities. Data protection involves storing important materials and can be done through a variety of means, such as file locking, disk mirroring, and database shadowing. The principal purpose of data protection is to maintain the integrity and proper storage of information. Two effective means of achieving maximum data protection while ensuring availability is to pursue data lifecycle management (DLM) and information lifecycle management (ILM), which may provide better data protection in the event of a virus or hack. A feasible data protection plan is also applicable to disaster recovery and business continuity.

Workplace monitoring is a policy that employers use in order to monitor a suspicious person and gather information. Employers may use a workplace monitoring program to discover activities that threaten the integrity and interests of the firm. Particular monitoring techniques involve wiretapping, reviewing Internet content usage, GPS tracking, checking employees' social media accounts, and interviewing other employees about suspicious activity. Management surveillance programs are easier to execute if employees are required to use company phones and computers. However, before such actions are taken by an employer, all employees should be given ample documentation of rules and regulations. This will ensure that any breach of protocol is intentional and deliberate on the part of the employee.

Financial Management Practices

Procurement policies are regulations that allow an organization to obtain and secure goods and services in an orderly and beneficial way to minimize cost and maximize savings. The size of a large corporation may be advantageous in securing discounts for goods and services. Small businesses typically do not have the size or economic influence to obtain such discounts. Procurement policies should address issues of credit and the ability of suppliers to deliver products and services in a timely manner.

An efficient credit card policy is based on considerations such as business size, inflow of revenue, general industry standards, current economic conditions, and organizational risk. Organizational credit card policies should allow for business expansion but minimize exposure to risk. Companies must closely examine the relationship between credit and sales to create an effective credit card policy. Greater availability to credit can boost sales, but losses can occur if customers default on their credit.

A clear and effective expense policy is a way for all organizations to reduce and manage costs. Business expenses are the second highest controllable cost in a company after employee salaries. Expense policies are established rules and regulations that describe how an organization manages costs. Management needs transparency, accountability, and the necessary tools to execute these policies. Expense policies may cover topics such as automated policy enforcement, expense categories, travel expenses, and expectations of employees and management to comply with the rules and regulations.

Practice Questions

1. Which of the following is a true statement regarding a modified duty assignment?
   a. A modified duty assignment is a temporary reassignment that seeks to accommodate employees who are recovering from illness or injury.
   b. A modified duty assignment is a permanent arrangement of work to accommodate employees who are injured.
   c. In order to make more money, a modified duty assignment is more work given to employees who ask for it.
   d. Injured employees must accept a modified duty assignment and be examined by a licensed physician to be cleared for the assignment.

2. Which of the following most accurately describes a procurement policy?
   a. A procurement policy is a strategy that employers use to find the most qualified employees.
   b. A procurement policy is an organization's strategy to obtain and secure goods and services in an orderly and beneficial way to minimize cost and maximize savings.
   c. A procurement policy is an analysis of an organization's inventory in order to determine what supplies are needed.
   d. A procurement policy is any action that an organization takes to find a new location.

3. What is a hazard communication program, and is it legally binding?
   a. A hazard communication program is a guideline that gives employers the option to inform employees when they are working with hazardous materials and is not legally binding.
   b. A hazard communication program is a mandate from OSHA that requires employers to inform employees when they are working with hazardous materials and the nature of each material and is legally binding.
   c. A hazard communication program is an evacuation procedure that is intended for emergencies and is legally binding.
   d. A hazard communication program is an educational training program that OSHA offers to employers regarding dangerous chemicals and is not legally binding.

4. What is the primary goal of a business continuity plan?
   a. A business continuity plan is a strategy that is implemented in a time of an organization's prosperity to sustain growth.
   b. A business continuity plan is a portion of the hiring process where employers ask job candidates how they specifically plan to contribute to the organization.
   c. A business continuity plan is the maintenance of productivity during and after a disruption.
   d. A business continuity plan is when an organization uses a disruption to fire workers in order to increase productivity.

5. In what ways can a social engineer impact an organization?

    a. A social engineer can impact an organization by implementing policies that promote a healthier and more enjoyable working environment.

    b. A social engineer can impact an organization if they are tasked with the responsibility of administering sanctions and punishments.

    c. A social engineer can impact an organization by implementing policies that promote equality and prohibit discriminatory behavior.

    d. A social engineer can impact an organization by manipulating members in order to extract sensitive or classified information.

6. What was the principal intent of the Sarbanes-Oxley Act of 2002 (SOX)?

    a. The SOX Act deregulated accounting standards for senior executives of accounting firms.

    b. The SOX Act established high levels of transparency and accountability for senior executives in accounting and recordkeeping.

    c. The SOX Act encouraged companies to increase transparency for shareholders by offering subsidies for compliance.

    d. The SOX Act decreased protections for shareholders that were defrauded by institutions.

7. Which is a true statement about the Americans with Disabilities Act (ADA)?

    a. The ADA is a federal law that prevents discrimination based on disability and requires employers to provide reasonable accommodations to disabled employees.

    b. The ADA applies only to full-time employees, but not part-time or temporary employees.

    c. The ADA exempts private employers and only applies to municipal, state, and federal organizations.

    d. The ADA was included in the Civil Rights Act of 1964.

8. What is a true statement about alternative work locations?

    a. No companies have experimented with alternative work locations, so their benefits cannot yet be evaluated.

    b. Alternative work locations are generally discouraged since it is difficult to trust employees to work outside of the office.

    c. Alternative work locations have been proven to reduce employee productivity.

    d. Because alternative work locations help decentralize operations, the organization is better protected from the destructive efforts of a single person.

9. Why should employers train employees to efficiently use social media?

    a. Employers generally do not like to train employees to use social media because it can be a distraction from their work.

    b. An employee with social media skills provides an organization with an advantage in the fields of marketing and advertising.

    c. Employees using social media are friendlier in the work environment.

    d. If employees can use social media, they are more likely to be up to date on current news.

10. Does OSHA offer any rights to employees, and if so, what do these rights entail?
    a. OSHA does not offer rights to employees, only safety protections.
    b. OSHA does grant rights to employees, and one example is the right to a pay increase if hazardous substances are introduced to the workplace.
    c. OSHA does grant rights to employees, such as the right to register complaints against their employer without fear of retaliation and the right to meet privately with an OSHA inspector.
    d. OSHA does grant rights to employees, but only after one year of employment.

11. What is a needs analysis?
    a. A needs analysis is a data-gathering activity where all members of an organization are surveyed about specific needs and requests. This information is assessed and then employed in ways to improve the functionality of the organization.
    b. A needs analysis is a data-gathering activity where only senior management is surveyed about their specific needs and requests. This information is assessed and then employed in ways to improve the functionality of the organization.
    c. A needs analysis is a data-gathering activity where all members of an organization are surveyed about specific needs and requests. However, the surveys must be completed in secret because employees can be fired for expressing critical views of management.
    d. A needs analysis is a data-gathering activity only performed at a company after a major safety or security incident.

12. A Material Safety Data Sheet (MSDS) contains which of the following elements:
    a. Lockout and tagout signs
    b. Directions regarding emergency exit procedures
    c. Information about confined space entry
    d. Information about how to handle contact with a hazardous chemical

Answer Explanations

1. A: A modified duty assignment is a temporary arrangement that offers injured or sick employees the option to work through their condition at a reduced capacity. These assignments are also dubbed "light work." Under many circumstances, modified duty is beneficial to both employers and employees, but employees do have the right to deny an employer's request if they are unable to perform the task.

2. B: Procurement policies are regulations that allow an organization to obtain and secure goods and services in an orderly and beneficial way to minimize cost and maximize savings. The size of an organization needs to be carefully considered when crafting a procurement policy, but the intent is to maximize productivity and minimize expenses. Typically, large organizations command greater bargaining power than smaller organizations.

3. B: A hazard communication program is a federal law mandated by OSHA that requires employers to inform employees when they are working with hazardous materials and the nature of such materials. It stipulates that dangerous health and noxious physical effects must be communicated to employees before they begin a specific job. The provision of OSHA that deals with hazard communication is the Hazard Communication Standard (HCS). In addition to the HCS, all organizations containing hazardous chemicals must provide hazardous material training to employees, access to material safety data sheets (MSDS), and proper labeling of containers. Hazard communication is legally binding.

4. C: Business continuity plans are tools used to identify potential threats and their associated impacts. These plans establish procedures to handle interruptions, disruptions, and/or loss of business functions. Business continuity plans respond to a variety of crisis scenarios, such as loss of administrative capacities, a hack into the operating system, and threat of workplace violence. These plans must be observed by all staff to ensure the plan's effectiveness. If an employee does not comply, disciplinary measures should be enforced by the organization.

5. D: A social engineer can impact an organization by manipulating members to extract sensitive or classified information. Typically, an attacker will employ deceptive tactics to convince the target to provide information such as bank numbers, passwords, and Social Security numbers. Organizations should educate employees on security and the identification of untrustworthy individuals. Employees should be able to assess suspicious situations and clearly recognize red flags.

6. B: The Sarbanes-Oxley Act (SOX) established high levels of transparency and accountability for senior executives in accounting and recordkeeping. Passed in the wake of global corporate accounting scandals, SOX provides greater protection to shareholders and investors by emphasizing transparency and accountability. The legislation mandates that senior executives report financial information to shareholders and the Securities and Exchange Committee (SEC). Furthermore, SOX imposes harsher penalties for white-collar crime and requires detailed reporting to the SEC whenever there is a significant fluctuation in a company's finances.

7. A: The Americans with Disabilities Act (ADA) is a federal law that prevents discrimination based on disability and requires employers to provide reasonable accommodations to disabled employees. Additionally, the ADA stipulates that public entities be accessible for disabled persons. The law applies to all types of work (part-time, full-time, or work during a temporary period) in organizations with fifteen or more employees. The ADA became a law in 1990.

8. D: Alternative work locations permit organizations to decentralize operations, thus minimizing the possibility for a person to cause significant destruction.

9. B: Employees who possess an aptitude for social media skills provide an additional asset to the company in the areas of marketing and advertising.

10. C: OSHA provides specific rights to workers. These rights include the right to register complaints against their employer without fear of retaliation and the right to meet privately with an OSHA inspector. Lastly, OSHA guidelines give workers the right to receive any information pertaining to health risks and hazards on the job.

11. A: A needs analysis is the process in which an organization gathers information about the principal needs and requests of its members. This analysis studies the expectations and requirements of subjects who are affected by workplace programs or regulations. Surveys and questionnaires are the primary means of procuring information about specific needs and requests. After the needs analysis is conducted, the information is assessed and incorporated into plans to improve the functionality of the organization.

12. D: A Material Safety Data Sheet (MSDS) identifies all hazardous substances in the workplace, and describes procedures for handling these substances. These sheets state what should be done if someone has inappropriate contact with a hazardous substance.

FREE Test Taking Tips DVD Offer

To help us better serve you, we have developed a Test Taking Tips DVD that we would like to give you for FREE. **This DVD covers world-class test taking tips that you can use to be even more successful when you are taking your test.**

All that we ask is that you email us your feedback about your study guide. Please let us know what you thought about it – whether that is good, bad or indifferent.

To get your **FREE Test Taking Tips DVD**, email freedvd@studyguideteam.com with "FREE DVD" in the subject line and the following information in the body of the email:

     a. The title of your study guide.

     b. Your product rating on a scale of 1-5, with 5 being the highest rating.

     c. Your feedback about the study guide. What did you think of it?

     d. Your full name and shipping address to send your free DVD.

If you have any questions or concerns, please don't hesitate to contact us at freedvd@studyguideteam.com.

Thanks again!

Made in the USA
San Bernardino, CA
27 April 2017